CHILDREN of the
OCCUPATION

D1713417

The Rutgers Series in Childhood Studies

The Rutgers Series in Childhood Studies is dedicated to increasing our understanding of children and childhoods, past and present, throughout the world. Children's voices and experiences are central. Authors come from a variety of fields, including anthropology, criminal justice, history, literature, psychology, religion, and sociology. The books in this series are intended for students, scholars, practitioners, and those who formulate policies that affect children's everyday lives and futures.

Edited by Myra Bluebond-Langner, Board of Governors Professor of Anthropology, Rutgers University and True Colours Chair in Palliative Care for Children and Young People, University College London, Institute of Child Health.

Advisory Board

Perri Klass, *New York University*

Jill Korbin, *Case Western Reserve University*

Bambi Schieffelin, *New York University*

Enid Schildkraut, *American Museum of Natural History and Museum for African Art*

CHILDREN of the
OCCUPATION
JAPAN'S UNTOLD STORY

WALTER HAMILTON

RUTGERS UNIVERSITY PRESS
NEW BRUNSWICK, NEW JERSEY, AND LONDON

Library of Congress Cataloging-in-Publication Data

Hamilton, Walter (Walter Stuart)
   Children of the occupation : Japan's untold story / Walter Hamilton.
      p. cm. — (The Rutgers series in childhood studies)
   Includes bibliographical references and index.
   ISBN 978-0-8135-1601-1 (hardcover : alk. paper) — ISBN 978-0-8135-1600-4
(pbk. : alk. paper) — ISBN 978-0-8135-1602-8 (e-book : alk. paper)
   1. Racially mixed children—Japan—History—20th century. 2. Racially mixed
children—Japan—Public opinion—History—20th century. 3. Racially mixed
children—Japan—Biography. 4. Japan—History—Allied occupation, 1945–1952—
Social aspects. 5. Public opinion—Japan—History—20th century. I. Title.
   DS889.16.H347 2012
   952.04'409253—dc23

A British Cataloging-in-Publication record for this book is available from the British Library.

First published in the United States 2013
by Rutgers University Press, New Brunswick, New Jersey

First published in Australia 2012
by NewSouth, an imprint of UNSW Press

Visit our website: http://rutgerspress.rutgers.edu

Manufactured in the United States of America

Contents

Preface

As I was about to depart Australia to take up my first posting as a correspondent in Japan, 33 years ago, a woman friend expressed the earnest hope that I would 'not go marrying some Chink' (by which she meant any Asian). The fact I eventually did marry a Japanese is one reason for my undertaking this book. Another derives from my experience of living for a dozen years in a country where I could only ever be an outsider, a *gaijin*: physically conspicuous but socially invisible. I was shown many courtesies as I went about my work for the Australian Broadcasting Corporation; being allowed to be ordinary was not one of them.

If I felt caught between two opposing ideas of where I belonged, how much more difficult it must be, I thought, for someone made to feel they did not belong *where they came from*? This is what struck me most when I encountered the mixed-race offspring of the post-war occupation. They were Japanese in every other respect – language, mentality and cultural orientation – except the way they looked. In their case, they were given no choice as to where they should be or which allegiance to hold. Worse still, their origins were perceived, rightly or wrongly, to be low and immoral. I found myself drawn to their story.

On the 60th anniversary of the Japanese surrender, I made a short documentary for ABC-TV's *Foreign Correspondent* program, retracing the lives of several individuals fathered by Australian members of the occupation forces. The freckle-faced, fair-haired children – so outstanding in films and photographs from the 1950s and 1960s – were now grey-haired, settled members of society. Their poignant reminiscences spurred my desire to learn more – to better understand not only Japanese attitudes to race mixing and the war but also why Australians of my own generation still spoke in terms of 'Chinks'.

Through document searches and personal contacts, I assembled a casebook on 150 men and women born mainly in the city of Kure, in Hiroshima prefecture, which served from 1946 to 1952 as headquarters for the British Commonwealth Occupation Force. I call the mixed-race children left in this part of western Japan the 'Kure Kids'. Their fathers were Australian, American, British, New Zealander or Indian. They stood out by their appearance and because so many were concentrated in one provincial area.

Unsurprisingly, when I began my research, many of the Kure Kids expressed reluctance to revisit unpleasant memories. In agreeing to be interviewed, they needed to find a way past lingering pain and resentment. It was a journey some declined to make, for their own sake or that of their families. Another challenge was tracking down those who had moved away to other parts of Japan or gone abroad. They had put a physical distance between themselves and the past; going back would entail a different kind of risk.

To satisfy both the historical and biographical aims of this book, I combine two styles of narrative. One tells the stories of selected individuals in their own words and through contemporary documents. The other chapters seek to position these lives within a richer context, by examining how attitudes to race mixing have evolved over the centuries and by tracing the impact of racial ideology on national policy and cultural identity in Australia, Japan and the United States.

Acknowledgments

Interviews and research were conducted in collaboration with my wife, Shizue Noguchi, whose patience, knowledge and language skills made this project possible. Special thanks go to Kuniko Ōmori, secretary-general of ISS Japan, for allowing access to the organisation's files related to the Kure Project. Earlier drafts of the manuscript greatly benefited from the comments of Deanne Whittleston, Hamish McDonald and John Tulloh. Dr Christine de Matos (University of Wollongong), Wakao Koike (Japan Foundation), Dr Duncan Williams (University of California, Berkeley, Center for Japanese Studies) and Dr Keiko Tamura (Australian National University) kindly provided forums in which I could develop my ideas. Dr Paul Spickard also lent generous support. Stephen Roche expertly brought the text up to scratch, and Phillipa McGuinness and Melita Rogowsky of UNSW Press were ideal editorial champions.

I wish to thank the following for agreeing to be interviewed or in other ways assisting this project: Johnny and Mamiko Akiyama; Teruko Blair; Peter Budworth; John Cameron; Barbara Chamberlain (née Evans); Takeshi Chida; Fumika Clifford (née Itō); Joan and Tony Dockerty; Glenda Gauci; Paul Glynn; Paul and Eiko Gray; Mitsuyoshi Hanaoka; Doug Helleur; Kumi Inoue; Mari Ishikuni; Yone Itō and Kenneth Wybrow; Jōichi Kawamura; Sachiko Kawana; Kiyotaka, Ritsuko and Ryo Kawasaki; Allan Kellehear; Kiyoe Koyama; John Menadue; Frank Mulhall; Ai and Mayumi Okamoto (née Kosugi); Kuniko Ōmori; Kazue Ozawa; John and Sharon Pate; Junko Shintani (née Fukuhara); Jōji Sugimaru; Keiko Tamura; George, Hatsue and Kōji Tsutsumi; Ted Weatherstone; and

Mitsuko Yoshida, Kazumi Purvis (née Yoshida), Mayumi Blanksby and Tamiko Blasse.

Abbreviations

ABC	Australian Broadcasting Corporation
ACC	Australian Council of Churches
Advertiser	*The Advertiser*, Adelaide
Age	*The Age*, Melbourne
Argus	*The Argus*, Melbourne
Asahi	*Asahi Shimbun*
ASIO	Australian Security Intelligence Organisation
AWM	Australian War Memorial, Canberra
BCFK	British Commonwealth Forces Korea
BCOF	British Commonwealth Occupation Force
Chu N	*Chugoku Nippo*
Chu S	*Chugoku Shimbun*
CPD	*Commonwealth Parliamentary Debates*
DoEA	Department of External Affairs
GHQ	General Headquarters
Herald	*The Herald*, Melbourne
HoR	House of Representatives
ISS	International Social Service
ISSAm	Archives of ISS America: Social Welfare History Archives, University of Minnesota Libraries
ISSJ	Records of ISS Japan: un-catalogued Japanese and English-language documents held in the Tokyo office
JCOSA	Joint Chiefs of Staff in Australia
Mainichi	*Mainichi Shimbun*
Mirror	*Daily Mirror*, Sydney

M Truth	*Melbourne Truth*
NAA	National Archives of Australia (Canberra, unless otherwise stated)
Nikkei	*Nihon Keizai Shimbun*
NLA	National Library of Australia, Canberra
NYT	*The New York Times*
PSS	*Pacific Stars and Stripes*
RAA	Recreation and Amusement Association
RAAF	Royal Australian Air Force
R & R	Rest and Recuperation
RSL	Returned & Services League of Australia
Sankei	*Sankei Shimbun*
SCAP	Supreme Commander for the Allied Powers
SMH	*The Sydney Morning Herald*
Sun	*The Sun*, Sydney
Sun-Herald	*The Sun-Herald*, Sydney
Sun-P	*The Sun-News Pictorial*, Melbourne
Telegraph	*The Daily Telegraph*, Sydney
Tokyo S	*Tokyo Shimbun*
VP Day	Victory in the Pacific Day
Yomiuri	*Yomiuri Shimbun*

Glossary

ainoko	half-caste
burakumin	former sub-caste minority
gaijin	foreigner
hāfu	mixed-race Japanese
harō-no-ko	child of 'hello'
Hokusai	Artist (1760–1849) famous for his 'Thirty-Six Views of Mt Fuji'
ie	household
Inland Sea	waterway separating three of Japan's main islands (also Seto Inland Sea)
kokusaiji	international child
kokusai-ka	internationalisation
konketsuji	mixed-blood child
koseki	household register
Manchukuo	the puppet-state in occupied China
Meiji period	reign of Emperor Meiji (1868–1912)
métis, mestizos	European-Native Indian mixed-blood
minzoku	ethnic group
modan gāru, moga	modern girl
mompe	women's labouring trousers
musume	daughter
nikkeijin	person of Japanese descent
Nisei	second-generation, foreign-born Japanese
onrī	mistress; de facto wife
panpan, pansuke	streetwalker; prostitute
shimbun	newspaper

tatami	straw-mat flooring
taxi dancer	female dance partner for hire
Tokugawa	ruling family in Edo Period (1600–1868)
Yoshiwara	Tokyo's former licensed brothel quarter
yukata	thin cotton gown

Japan and Korea

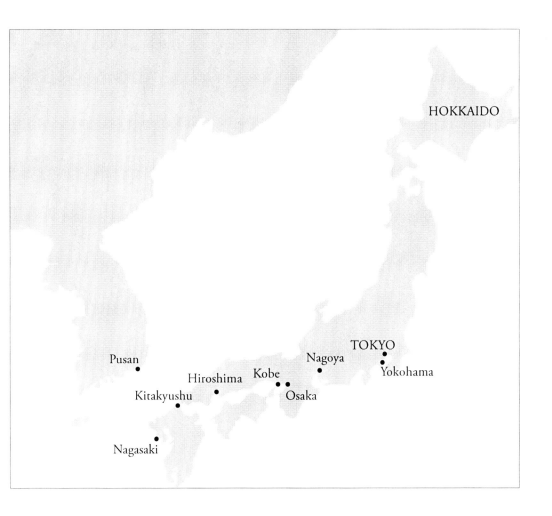

HOKKAIDO

TOKYO

Nagoya

Pusan

Hiroshima   Kobe

Yokohama

Kitakyushu

Osaka

Nagasaki

Kure and surrounds

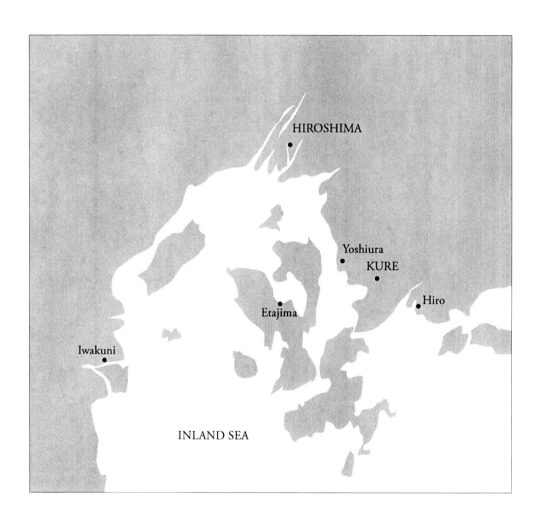

HIROSHIMA

Yoshiura

KURE

Hiro

Etajima

Iwakuni

INLAND SEA

CHILDREN of the
OCCUPATION

Introduction

The post-war occupation of Japan swept over the country like a tsunami, obliterating social boundaries, submerging moral landmarks, lifting up and carrying away lives to new and unexpected places. Once the tide receded, the familiar cultural topography re-emerged more or less intact, albeit with a new freedom installed. Only the detritus of jazzy music, coarse manners, foreign slang and unwanted babies needed clearing away. This, I would suggest, represents the majority view of that generation.

Few physical reminders of those shameful years remain to challenge the gaze of today's Japanese. Visitors to a new museum dedicated to the doomed battleship *Yamato*, in the city of Kure, need to look carefully to find any reference to the British Commonwealth Occupation Force (BCOF) formerly based there. Tokyo's cityscape has even less to declare about the past. Gone is the Dai-ichi Insurance Building, opposite the Imperial Palace, which served as headquarters for the imperious General Douglas MacArthur. Ichigaya Court, venue for the Tokyo War Crimes Tribunal, presided over by the Australian judge Sir William Webb, has also made way for developers.[1]

Instead of monuments, quizzical reminders linger in hidden corners. On the wall of a railway underpass in Tokyo's midtown Yurakuchō district – old haunt of the infamous *panpan* streetwalkers – a grimy shingle advertises a long-defunct VD clinic. At the exclusive Mitsui Club, beside the Australian Embassy, ungainly wooden bolsters fitted under the central staircase recall the outsized American officers once billeted there. At the Hotel New Grand in

Yokohama, which is more incongruous, General MacArthur sharing space in the picture gallery with Charlie Chaplin or the petrified chewing gum on a pillar in the lobby, left undisturbed through a million dustings? One has been reduced to mere celebrity; the other is no longer recognised for what it is.

The occupation was a daring social experiment at the end of a savage race war. It lasted twice as long as the Pacific conflict and brought a million Allied troops to Japan. Its most enduring legacy is not to be found in edifices, state institutions or cultural borrowings. It rests with the descendants of those who crossed the divide of race and culture and marked a true end of hostilities through marriage and childbirth. Their clans reach across oceans and continents, continuing to bind up old wounds.

One aspect of this historic encounter has remained largely unexplored: the links that connect Americans, Australians, Britons and others to Japanese blood relations never known, never met. I refer to the thousands of mixed-race children left behind after the occupation by fathers who never knew of their existence, refused to acknowledge them or were prevented by military dictate from marrying the mothers. The eminent American historian John Dower has called the children 'one of the sad, unspoken stories of the occupation'.[2] This book aims to give them a voice, an identity and a place in the lives of others.

So familiar is the idea of military conquest leading to the birth of supposedly unwanted children, they tend to be dismissed as a natural corollary of war. Their appearance in occupied Japan certainly came as no surprise; the Madame Butterfly tradition provided a ready-made model of Western men exploiting Japanese women. As if they were defined by their biological inevitability, the children received mostly superficial attention from Western politicians, scientists and writers, who acquiesced in facile assumptions about their fate. In the Australian author Hal Porter's over-ripe phrase, they were 'heirs of nothing except agony'.[3]

Japanese historical accounts have more to say on the subject without necessarily being better informed. Eiji Takemae's major study of the occupation (translated into English as *Inside GHQ*) claims most of the children were 'secreted away in poorly funded, ill-equipped private orphanages' and remained illegitimate unless acknowledged by their fathers.[4] Not so. Most were raised in the community, and a considerable number became 'legitimate' through adoption by a family member. Japanese fictional treatments of the issue evince a similar determination to link the children exclusively to prostitution, moral collapse and national humiliation. Unresolved feelings of shame and resentment over the war defeat have obscured a more complex reality.

The discrimination the children suffered in Japan was real enough; that is not in dispute. What has been missing from their story is a clearer understanding of what motivated society's prejudice, the forms it took and how the mixed-bloods responded to it. Leaving them trapped in the historical memory as 'heirs of nothing except agony' only serves to perpetuate the sort of image opponents of race mixing have exploited for centuries. Furthermore, it confines the issue to Japan, when their fate, to a large extent, depended on decisions taken elsewhere. Japan's racial intolerance was fully matched in the nations it fought against.

From its inception, the United States served as a hothouse for racial theories that underpinned slavery and then, after Abolition, were used to justify segregation. The word 'miscegenation', coined during the Civil War by two rabble-rousing New York journalists, lent a scientific-sounding gloss to an old fear. Black–white sexual intimacy had been unlawful in parts of America since the 17th century; the modern trend was towards even tighter control of interracial contact, by expanding anti-miscegenation statutes to include Asians. On the presumption that people of a different race or culture were unreliable citizens, the Roosevelt administration herded 110 000 Japanese Americans into internment camps during the

Second World War. Japanese migrants (apart from war brides) continued to be excluded from the country until 1952, and immigration quotas based on national origin remained in place until 1965. This statutory discrimination directly affected the mixed-race children born during the occupation.

Apologists for America's restrictive immigration laws often cited the White Australia policy as an example of what like-minded peoples were doing to defend their way of life. The first act of Australia's new federal parliament in 1901 was to make controls on the entry of non-whites uniform across the country. It was a nervy era of spy intrigues and invasion scares on both sides of the Pacific. Such was the enthusiasm for the visit to Sydney in August 1908 of 16 battleships of the US Navy – the 'Great White Fleet' – the welcoming crowds exceeded the turnout at the founding of the Commonwealth. A verse tribute in the *Sydney Morning Herald* imagined Australians and Americans ('the grand old Anglo-Saxon race') linking arms 'To check with stern unflinching mace/ The swarming hungry Orient'. More down-to-earth was the boast of a 'Mutt and Jeff' cartoon in the San Francisco *Examiner*: 'Does not yon sight make you want to punch a Jap in the nose?'[5]

A world war and a depression later, Americans were far less interested in punching foreign noses by the 1930s. Absent any idea of how to overcome their fears, Australians kept them in check by bowing to another imperial gesture. Fortress Singapore, standing guard over what British subjects called 'the Far East', was so far east of London the Admiralty calculated (in secret) it would take naval reinforcements 180 days to arrive in an emergency. The Japanese needed less than half that time.

The shocking unreality of the situation is illustrated by a little-known episode that occurred just weeks before the outbreak of the Pacific War. Confidential signals flew back and forth between Singapore and Australia on the subject of troops marrying local women and applying to take them home. The prospect so alarmed the

Secretary of the Department of the Interior, Joseph Carrodus – 'if any considerable number of such marriages were to eventuate it may possibly adversely affect British prestige in the East' – the Army was told to issue a 'discreet verbal warning' to servicemen.[6] Another official commented acidly on the visa application of one Eurasian wife: 'It is presumed that Australian soldiers who are unwisely led into marriage with a coloured woman would at least have the sense to choose those who are not too obviously dark and objectionable'.

The spurious risk of a few 'coloured' wives soon gave way to something truly objectionable: the fall of Singapore and Malaya in February 1942 delivered 130 000 Indian, British and Australian servicemen into captivity and brought the entire phantasmagoria of the Yellow Peril to Australia's doorstep. For Prime Minister John Curtin, the thought of invasion came with the added horror of blood incompatibility: he rallied the nation to defend the 'citadel' of the British race. Feted in Canberra after his narrow escape from the Philippines, General MacArthur waxed lyrical about 'that indescribable consanguinity of race' linking Australia and the United States. Around the same time, Admiral Ernest J King, US Chief of Naval Operations, laid before Franklin Roosevelt the vital case for maintaining Australia and New Zealand as 'white men's countries'.[7]

Racial pride is a virulent and recurring theme in Australian accounts of the war. Prisoner-of-war stories – a prolific and ever-expanding literature – often convey the impression that the physical hardships of captivity were easier to endure than the mental anguish of being lorded over by an inferior people. The idiom used by POWs is revealing. A whisky and soda was a 'half caste'. In a poem by another prisoner, his inferior and contaminated food was 'half-caste rice'. These men clung to their dignity by emphasising what neither captivity nor degradation could make them. After being liberated from an internment camp in Manila in 1945, the journalist Jack Percival published an indictment of his captors. The first complaint he brought against the Japanese military – before any mention of privations or brutalities – was their failure to prevent 'insults' to the civilian internees.[8]

An end to the self-described status of 'white coolie' required a swift restoration of the proper order of things. Lord Louis Mountbatten, Supreme Allied Commander South East Asia, issued an instruction that there be no shaking of hands or sitting at the same table with Japanese during surrender proceedings. Australian field commanders elaborated on this theme. At Wewak, in New Guinea, the diminutive General Hatazō Adachi was escorted the entire length of an airfield between lines of soldiers specially selected for their exceptional height. After attending a surrender ceremony in Borneo, one officer wrote: 'The yellow creatures were marched in again ... I felt almost guilty, sitting there quietly, knowing what atrocities his race had perpetrated – echoes of the darkest ages. I feel they are not humiliated enough'.[9]

Anglo-American wartime solidarity did not, however, rest on a shared commitment to the old imperial order. President Roosevelt might have held some peculiar views on race mixing (Japanese-European mixtures were 'thoroughly bad' in his opinion), but he was politician enough to recognise an irresistible trend. Looking ahead from the low foothills of 1942, he foresaw a world in which nations 'will more or less become melting pots'. His comment led the Australian representative on the Pacific War Council, Owen Dixon (later Chief Justice of the High Court), to remark: 'If we accept the President's thought in this matter, it would seem to be of little importance who wins the war'.[10]

For Dixon and the overwhelming majority of his compatriots, victory, when it came, equalled vindication for White Australia. They saw Japan as unchanging and unchangeable – best reassigned to the 'obscurity and isolation in which it had slumbered for 2,000 years', as one editorial writer suggested. The Australian Commander in Chief, General Sir Thomas Blamey, standing amid the ruins of downtown Tokyo in September 1945, restated his conviction that the enemy was 'sub-human'. The Melbourne *Argus* agreed: 'It is our solemn duty to hate those things that normal civilised persons regard as evil, and the Japanese race is the personification of those things'. The Americans' allegedly soft approach to the occupation was swiftly condemned. 'With all due deference to General MacArthur', declared the *Sydney Morning Herald*, 'the dropping of atomic bombs was much more effectual in enforcing the respect of the Japanese'.[11]

At a cocktail party in Tokyo, two years later, the Melbourne academic William Macmahon Ball, a member of the Allied Council for Japan, was telling General 'Pat' Casey, one of MacArthur's inner circle, why it was too early to resume trade with Japan, when the exasperated American cut him off. 'When, for Pete's sake', implored Casey, 'will you seven million Australians realise the importance of having 70 million allies in this country?' The comment merely confirmed for Ball that the occupation's reform agenda was being sacrificed to Big Power politics. In his opinion, Japan's leaders were as likely as ever 'to want to use war as an instrument of national policy'.[12]

Another influential Australian, the popular author Frank Clune, was visiting Japan at the time to gather material for a new book. *Ashes of Hiroshima* would set the tone for many a triumphal reckoning of history: 'The Japs were … exterminated and obliterated in New Guinea by a race of men who were superior to themselves in fighting ability, discipline, training, courage and intelligence'. He would waste no tears on a starving population, he told readers, if they were too 'stupid' to grow anything other than rice. Here was the 'uncrossable mental gulf' Clune was pleased to say separated Australians from 'Asiatics'.[13] Here also was the rest of the answer to General Casey's question.

Australia's colour bar, relaxed during the war to admit Asian merchant seamen and African-American troops on leave, was rigorously reinforced. Cinema newsreels showed Chinese and Malay seamen, who had had the effrontery to marry white women, being frogmarched along the Sydney docks and onto deportation ships. Most remaining ethnic Japanese, including residents of 50 years' standing, were expelled. In the summer of 1946, 2500 men, women and children put to sea from Melbourne crowded onto the decks and pressed into the dank holds of the *Koei Maru*. A local newspaper described, with unconcealed satisfaction, the miserable conditions aboard ship, under the headline 'Sons of Heaven Sent Home'.[14]

Rules for the admission of persons of mixed race were tightened, in the words of the policy document, 'to provide a desirable margin for error'.[15] Applicants for permanent residence needed to prove they were at least 75 per cent European in racial origin – up from 51 per cent – and predominantly European in 'appearance and upbringing'. A teenage girl of Japanese-French ancestry was denied entry in 1947 to attend school, even though she was travelling on a French passport and had family in Australia. The following year, a Portuguese national engaged to an Australian serviceman was also excluded because she was part Japanese.

A racially selective migration program, conceived as a strategic defence against Japan, attracted a million settlers in the decade to 1955. Former enemy nationals from Italy, Germany and Austria were granted access to the benefits of assisted migration, while almost all non-Europeans (who made up just 0.2 per cent of the Australian population in 1947) continued to be excluded. The Immigration Minister, Arthur Calwell, reminded parliament that the White Australia policy prevented the creation of 'an unfortunate class of half-breeds ... [who] would be ostracized by their brothers and lead miserable lives'.[16]

The BCOF troops sent to Japan were under instructions not to fraternise. The policy was presented as necessary to maintain military discipline and security – although this could hardly explain why Japanese Americans and African Americans were barred from BCOF recreational facilities. Servicemen who sought permission to marry a Japanese were, without exception, refused. Anyone defying the ban risked arrest and removal from the country. Once again, the chief motivation was political or racial, not military: civilians also were prevented from taking Japanese wives to Australia.

None of the nations involved in the occupation would allow automatic right of entry to deserted wives and children, unless husbands and fathers acknowledged them. The Australian government, however, went a step further. Anticipating that the children's plight was likely to arouse the sympathy of families in a position to help, the Immigration Department imposed conditions that made inter-country adoption from Japan almost impossible. Disingenuous welfare and legal arguments were used to dress up a decision based principally on race.

Confronted by rising public criticism of its stand, in the 1960s, the government agreed to allocate money for the children's education and welfare in Japan. This unprecedented concession greatly improved the lives of those assisted; it also represented the price the nation was willing to pay to keep the issue beyond its borders. In the words of a leading churchman of the day, the Reverend Alan Walker, 'there have been few more disgraceful incidents in the whole miserable history of Australia's racial immigration policy'.[17]

Before setting out, it is necessary to deal with some possible misconceptions. The expression 'racial purity' is an oxymoron. While this may be more apparent in the present era of multiculturalism and globalisation, scientists, politicians and others long believed they were describing something immutable and distinct when they spoke of 'race'. To better understand the arguments and motives of the past, it is necessary to employ this slippery term and its many brethren.

Konketsuji (mixed-blood child) and *ainoko* (literally 'the offspring of two things put together', equivalent to 'half-caste' or 'mongrel') are now considered discriminatory terms in Japan. *Hāfu* (from the English 'half') or *kokusaiji* (international child) are used instead. Once again, in retaining obsolete or pejorative words, I do so solely for the sake of historical accuracy. It is far from my intention to cause offence, and I beg the reader's indulgence.

Real names are employed throughout, either with the individual's permission or if already available on the public record. Once or twice, in handling sensitive information obtained in confidence or from unpublished sources, I employ pseudonyms. No essential detail has been changed. All personal names are rendered in the Western order of surname last. Diacritical marks are used for Japanese words, except with familiar place names (e.g. Tokyo) or if the person or entity does not retain them in English transliteration.

1

Karumi's story

Under a clear, autumn sky, a girl of eight wandered barefoot and alone in the hills above Kure. The harvest was over, and bundles of rice stalks were hung up to dry on bamboo frames erected beside the paddy fields: heavy heads of grain in gold and silver curtains.

Karumi Inoue delighted in watching the swallows that swooped and turned through the air, disappearing into the deep shadows of the surrounding forest and then darting back into the sunlight. Tirelessly, to and fro, they hunted above the silent parade of stubble.

> I was my own friend. I had no one else to play with, lots of times. So I was forever going up into the mountains: all stepped paddy fields. They'd harvested the rice – the ground was dry – but they'd left the scarecrows standing there still. You know, beautiful Japanese scarecrows! I used to find a long stick or bamboo, and I'd leap off the bank of one paddy onto another and onto the next, charging the scarecrows as if I was a samurai. Just charge: 'Pa, pa, pa, pa'. Kendo-like. It was great fun! Such a freeing experience, you know. And, of course, across the way, there'd be the farmers with their hoes up in the air, 'Aaaah', screaming at me. I'd take no notice and just run away.

Karumi's mother, Mitsuko, had also felt lonely as a child and envious of others with parents to nurture them. After hers divorced, she and her three siblings were raised by their grandmother.

In 1949, at the age of 15, Mitsuko was sent away to another city to work at a spinning factory. She returned to Kure two years later and, now unemployed, took up dressmaking.

> I remember her at the pedal sewing machine. She made me this dress. She allowed me to choose the fabric I wanted. And it was a white dress with a sort of wave design and whales floating, with water squirting out: blue on a white background, with just a pencil-line design. And I thought that was the most wonderful thing. I remember, after her finishing, saying, 'Can I put it on?' Tie it at the top. No zips, no buttons, just slip on, and tie at the waist. It was very cute.

Karumi's father came on the scene in the summer of 1953. According to a social worker's report, compiled a decade later, he was an Australian soldier. His mates called him 'George'. 'She met him only a few times. She did not know his exact name. She could not speak English, therefore, she could not let him know of her pregnancy.'[1]

Mitsuko was 19.

> My mother, what she did for me … Hand in hand, in summer, going up the street. She bought – this was very unusual, then, in Japan – but, somehow, she bought a block of ice cream, vanilla ice cream. And it was in a cardboard box. We used to have not a refrigerator but an icebox. Other Japanese people didn't have that. Anyway, we went up the street, and we bought this and a plate of strawberries and condensed milk. All right. My eyes! I may have been about two and a half. We got home and she emptied the whole ice cream into this big bowl. She topped it with strawberries and then poured condensed milk all over the top! We sat opposite each other. And we ate. This is just a fantastic memory I have of my mother. I knew my mother loved me then. Not because of what I was eating, but because we shared. We were sharing things.

Karumi was not the only mixed-race child in the house. Mitsuko's elder sister had formed a relationship with a young British soldier. They were together long enough for her to carry his photograph – and hope for more. Three months after the birth of Karumi's cousin, Jōji, the boy's father was posted to Cyprus and contact ceased.

The unwed mothers moved back in with their grandmother, amid reminders of what might have been: a sea chest, a greatcoat with golden buttons and a double bed. Other, more public, reminders were their offspring's physical features. Mitsuko took to dyeing her daughter's hair black, in a vain attempt to make her less conspicuous. Recalling the smelly, hated ritual, Karumi shifts between English and Japanese.

> I could look in the mirror. I knew I wasn't Japanese – even though, to foreigners, I look more Asian. But, to a Japanese, I wasn't. I mean, go to school, and there's a sea of black and a dot of brown. And that was me!
>
> I'd be walking down the street by myself, and men – I'm not talking about young kids, teenagers, but much older – would start charging. I'd turn around because I could hear their footsteps. Bang! Across the back of my head, they'd hit me. They'd see me, I guess, as having to do with *gembaku ga kita* [the dropping of the atomic bomb] … *Shiranai* [I don't know]. I was just a little kid. Other times, they'd walk past and go 'Puut'. Spit at you. People never stopped and thought – never once.

For four years, the sisters lived off odd jobs and a trickle of welfare money their grandmother received. It was never going to be enough.

Mitsuko was the first to marry and move out.

> My mother finds it very, very difficult to talk about the past, so I don't know if, you know, I came – might have come – under bad circumstances … Do you know what I mean? I don't know

whether she actually wanted this to happen to her. That's why it was so easy for her to give me up. You know, abandon me. I mean, I was abandoned – no two ways about it. She chose her life. She weighed up the pros and cons of it, then decided: 'It's my daughter's life or my life'. And she just said, 'No, my life'.

I can tell you what actually happened the last time I saw my mother. She came with this man – obviously it must be her husband – and visited me in the house where I was living with my great-grandmother. I must have been three [she was four], because my mother put me to her breast. And I went to sleep. I was startled when I woke up, by myself, alone in this cold bed. And I remember thinking, where's my mother? So I raced outside.

It's dark. And where the road meanders upwards, away from the house, just before the bend, there is a streetlight. That was the only light. It had an orangey tint to it. The sky was absolutely pitch black. And I remember screaming for my mother. And there were two figures standing just under that light. I saw them turn around, look at me, then turn back and walk. Disappear. And that was the last time I ever saw him, her husband.

Mitsuko's sister married the following year and went to her new family. The children remained behind with their great-grandmother – who was in her seventies, hard of hearing and showing signs of dementia.

Karumi sensed the old woman favoured Jōji because he was a boy. She resented it and made her gentle cousin pay: 'I was a big bully, you see. I think I used to overwhelm him sometimes, poor boy'. When they fought, she invariably won. Facing the world together, however, she was his chief protector.

I had no fear. You know what I mean? I remember high school boys quite often used to bully him. I'd run to protect him.

One day he got pushed into a stormwater canal and gashed his forehead. The moment I saw the blood I became just so angry. I had a very sharp mouth, thinking back to those days: me, smaller and younger, compared to high school boys. I got conked – smacked over the head – and I conked them back! They used to call us American. 'Don't eat our food. Rice is only for Japanese.' 'Go back to America.'

Teachers, on the other hand, were mostly kind and supportive. In primary school, Karumi found she could earn her classmates' respect on sports days by bringing home the relay, the fastest on the track. 'That was the only time I was ever acknowledged as anyone of any significance, I suppose. Other times, I was just nothing.'

She started wagging school and threatened to get out of hand. The child sought comfort in her own secrets, testing her powers of concealment. Social workers described her as 'wild and tomboyish', with above-average intelligence: 'She is susceptible to other's love and attention … and tests others often'.[2]

I trusted myself – but I found I couldn't trust others. One time, I was playing with kids in the neighbourhood, just up from my home. I happened to see this wallet: a lady's purse that obviously belonged to the mother of one of the kids. So, I just grabbed it. Looked at it. There was *hyaku-en* [a 100 yen note] and small change – and that's all. And so I took it, because I was hungry. I remember going for days without eating anything when I was living with my great-grandmother. But people never knew that. We didn't have food.

Anyway, when I saw this, I thought, 'Oh good, *hyaku-en*'. I figured, with that much money, I can eat for days. I went and bought *koppepan*. It's like a sweet bun [then worth about 5 yen]. But I was frugal, too. I bought one bun and put the change in my pocket. I threw the purse into some bushes; I didn't want to leave any evidence, you know. I didn't want to get caught. Stupid, innocent kid, thinking one can get away with that.

The woman called the police, and my mother got contacted. The policeman was a very kind man, so I confessed. I told him what I did with the wallet and what I bought with the money and gave him the change. But this woman, an opportunist, said there was a thousand yen. I was just … I kept on saying, '*Hyaku-en, hyaku-en dake* [One hundred yen, only a hundred yen]'. No, she said, '*Sen haitte ita* [There was a thousand in there]'. '*Iie, haitte nakatta* [No, there wasn't].' My mother somehow had to find a thousand yen to give to this woman. Then I was branded a thief. And I could never escape that; never escape from the fact that I was a thief.

What was worse, she had shamed her mother. She knew she must never expose Mitsuko to the eyes of society; their relationship had to remain hidden. 'I always respected that. I was *taught* to respect it.'

For the sake of her husband's family, Mitsuko had never told her daughter where she lived. Could the secret last?

I was so desperate to be with somebody. I just needed some motherly affection or love, some connection with somebody who cared for me. This day, I took a walk and began asking in the neighbourhood where my mother's place was. You know, mentioning the name. And a woman in her neighbourhood said: 'Just up there. See the hedge?' So I thought, 'OK'. But I never went to her house. I knew where she lived. I turned around and came home.

The neighbours told my mother there was '*gaijin ga …* [a foreigner]'. So, the next time she saw me, I was told: never, never, never.

In 1963, cousin Jōji was sent for adoption to a family in Hawaii.

Karumi suffered keenly from their separation. (The pain of missing her cousin, she says, lasted until the birth of her first child.)

Karumi's great-grandmother was so frail she could hardly take care of herself. The old wooden house was dirty and decrepit; meals were irregular and visitors rare. A reporter who came to investigate found the child 'extremely shy and terrified of being photographed'.[3] Mitsuko occasionally sent food and clothing, but Karumi and her aged guardian were often reduced to a primitive struggle for existence.

> I remember one time my great-grandmother came back with some fish. Little ones: *saba* [mackerel]. We each had a piece, and one was left over. She put that away. By this stage, we didn't have any icebox or anything. The weather was warm. She left the fish on a plate inside the cupboard, and obviously a fly got to it. This particular night I woke up because my great-grandmother was making some noise in the kitchen. The *shoji* [paper-panelled sliding door] was open. And the light from a full moon was coming through the window.
>
> I got up out of bed and asked, 'What are you eating, Grandma?' And she just kept on eating – just trying to push something back into her mouth. Anyway, I said, 'Give me some'. Because, I mean, she was hungry, I was hungry. But she wouldn't, she wouldn't share with me. So I took it away from her. I just wanted to know what it was. And I looked at it, and in the moonlight I could see something wriggling. Lots of them – it was glistening – maggots. Tiny ones. I screamed and threw the whole lot away. Just to get it away from me. Of course, she went really, really angry at me. But I remember screaming back at her, saying it was, you know, bad.

This went on for more than a year. After the old woman slipped and broke her hip, the main burden of nursing her fell on the ten-year-old. Even relatives who lived nearby were reluctant to lend a hand while a *konketsuji* (mixed-blood child) was in the house.

In the early hours of one morning, Karumi was called to her great-grandmother's bedside. 'I begged her not to go. I promised her: "I'll always be good girl from now on, if you stay with me. If you can't, can you just wait for me? I want to come with you".' Because I *knew* I had nowhere to go. She remembers being sent, before dawn, to notify the death to relatives: searching unfamiliar byways, with addresses written on a scrap of paper; and a terrifying moment, passing a cemetery, running from ghosts as fast as her legs would carry her.

Everything changed. Her uncle inherited the house and moved in with his family. Karumi overheard talk of an orphanage in Kure. When nothing came of that, she assumed such places were reserved for more-needy Japanese. Before long, the child was locked in an emotional and psychological struggle with her uncle's nasty wife.

Experience had taught her to expect blame for anything that went amiss. When sushi was ordered as a special treat, she refused to eat any – though her mouth watered at the sight – in case she was criticised for indulging herself. Another time, her uncle's son mis-behaved, and Karumi was ordered by the wife to take him outside. She resented being made the agent of the boy's unhappiness – and showed it. The woman sniped: 'You're the one who should really be put out!'

Karumi had always believed she was the reason her grandmother was divorced and living elsewhere. It came as a shock, therefore, when her rescuer appeared.

That December, my grandmother, who was remarried and living on one of the islands in the Inland Sea, came. 'Pack your clothes', she said, 'I'm taking you home with me'. It took her three months to convince her second husband, even though I'm *ainoko*, *gaijin* or foreign (I'm not a foreigner, you know what I mean) … She had to convince him that I was a good kid, that I wasn't a bad child, that I needed somebody. It took her three months. And, finally, my step-grandfather said, 'OK, bring her here'. And we were best friends.

I was nurtured for the first time in my life. I didn't have to ask for anything. If I needed a new dress … Because I just grew, thanks to the nutritious food she was giving me. She would give me treats, things I never had before. And I was ten before I first felt this warmth of what love is: a warm arm around me, kind words. I never, ever, ever, felt that.

She thrived under her grandmother's care, happy and settled. There was plenty of ground to make up: table manners and feminine graces to be taught. English lessons, too, on Sundays – because other preparations were in train.

Eighteen months earlier, Karumi had been invited to a tea party at the International Social Service (ISS) office in Kure. Wearing her best dress and carefully groomed for the occasion, she was introduced to some nice people who said they were from a country a long way away. Would she like to come and live with them? Oh, yes, said Karumi. She forgot all about the adoption plan, however, once her life took a turn for the better. Then the papers came through.

I said, 'Please, tell them to stop the process'. And my grandmother said, 'I think it's too late. It's already done. I've got notification here that you'll be leaving Kure city on *ju-ni gatsu nanoka* [7 December]'.

One thing that really affected me happened the weekend before I left Kure. As a farewell treat, my grandmother ordered a three-tiered ice cream cake, like a wedding cake. I was so excited. It cost a lot of money and, because we lived on an island, it had to come from the mainland. She knew I was a good kid. She couldn't see me as a half-caste; she saw me as her granddaughter.

I went to the shop with her and we walked in together. She went to the counter. And the lady, the vendor, greeted my grandmother with courtesy and everything. So, my grandmother said, 'I'm here to collect that ice cream cake'. And she said, 'Yes, it's here, just one moment'. Then this woman happened to notice me: 'Who are you?' or words to that effect. So, my grandmother says, '*Watashi no mago desu* [This is my grandchild]'.

With that, the vendor said: 'Oh, I'm sorry, I forgot about your order. I sold that ice cream cake to the last customer'. We left the shop. No ice cream cake. And it was there! The moment she found out I was her granddaughter … It's just so painful. I thought my grandmother doesn't need to be treated like that.

A few days later, Karumi embarked on the long journey from Japan to a new home abroad. She was bound for Australia. Her aunt and her mother, who was pregnant, came to see her off at Kure station.

My auntie said, 'Look at your mother's tummy. She's got another baby growing in there'. My mother told me: 'There are invisible threads that bind you – not only to Japan, but to your sister and brother'. And, of course, to her. She said, 'Invisible threads. Don't ever forget that'.

2

Butterfly and child

While visiting a Korean orphanage in 1903, the German doctor Erwin Baelz was struck by the weak physiques and subdued behaviour of the children – with the exception of one pretty individual 'with huge round eyes and brown hair'. She was altogether different from the rest, 'vigorous, lively, shrewd, interested in whatever goes on, and a little tyrant to the others'. The outstanding child was the offspring of a European father and a Japanese mother. He asked himself: 'Can race have so much influence as this?'[1]

Baelz was one of thousands of foreign scientists and technicians hired to assist with Japan's modernisation. He arrived in 1876, at the age of 27, and stayed for three decades. Baelz taught medicine, served as physician to the Imperial family, undertook pioneering anthropological research and married Hatsu (Hana) Arai, the daughter of an antiques dealer. An astute observer of the country's transformation, with a special interest in the human, biological encounter of East and West, he made a close study of children born of Japanese and European parents, including his own boy and girl.

When he first came to Japan, Baelz's views on race mixing were conventionally sceptical. He opposed an idea going about for Japanese to improve their racial stock by mixing with Europeans; such unions, he said, seemed to produce few offspring, and their eugenic effects could not be predicted (though 'hybrid' girls often were attractive). He did not completely condemn interracial marriage but suggested the 'Roman' races, with their similar skin and hair colour, would make a better match for Japanese than the 'Celtic-German' races.[2]

Marriage and fatherhood altered his opinion. His daughter, Uta, provided Baelz with compelling evidence of race mixing's more felicitous possibilities. The child had 'a marvellous way with her', he told his German relatives, and 'her unusually large and thoughtful eyes impressed every one as having a peculiar charm'. Her intelligence was 'amazing'.[3]

In 1898, when Uta was three, the family looked forward to celebrating *Hina Matsuri* (the Doll Festival) that March. The occasion was to be lent added importance by having the child dress in European clothes for the first time. In the midst of the happy preparations, Uta developed a fever. Baelz's heart sunk as he recognised the symptoms of peritonitis. The eminent physician could do nothing; by the following morning she was dead. 'It often astonished me to note the way in which almost fully grown girls in families of our acquaintance would positively fall in love with Uta', he wrote, conveying the dreadful news to Germany. 'When I expressed my surprise at this ... I always received the same answer: "She is not like other children".'

Grief did not drive Baelz back to his old opinion of race mixing – quite the reverse. By the time of his visit to the Korean orphanage, five years later, he was a noted proponent of Japanese-European interracial union.

With the benefit of hindsight, however, Uta's death can seem to us more tragically in tune with the temper of the times. Western 'scientific' racial theories had divided humanity into a rigid hierarchy of supposedly innate qualities, with the white man at the top. The United States, Australia, Canada and other nations were moving to close their borders to Asian immigrants and half-castes. Soon Japan would shift from emulating white civilisation to violently supplanting it in Asia. Dark days lay ahead. Racial fears and animosities, once unleashed, would twist and confine the destinies of nations and individuals right down to the present day. In referring to someone of mixed race, the comment 'She is not like other children' was more likely to accompany a sneer than express a heartfelt delight.

Beginnings

Japan's first close encounter with the West began with the arrival in 1543 of three shipwrecked Portuguese traders, who aroused interest mainly because of the unfamiliar firearms they carried with them. Six years later, the Jesuit missionary Francis Xavier introduced Christianity to 'the land of the gods'. One event changed the military balance inside a nation exhausted by a long civil war; the other upset the balance of secular authority.

Trading ships from Macao and Batavia (Jakarta) began making port each spring at Nagasaki and the nearby island of Hirado. The Portuguese (and, later, Dutch and English) crews stayed for four months, during which time it was not uncommon, for those who could afford it, to engage a concubine. Some men remained for decades and formed lasting relationships; their wives included well-born daughters of samurai and wealthy merchants. A few Portuguese women also married Japanese men. The Catholic padres who sanctified these unions won numerous converts to the faith.

Ordinary Japanese seemed mostly tolerant of the mixed-race children appearing in their midst, but the country's rulers grew alarmed at the spread of foreign blood linked to a foreign creed. When persecutions failed to deter the stalwart Christians and their converts, the ruling Tokugawa clan severed almost all contact with the outside world. An edict was proclaimed in 1636 for the deportation of the wives and children of Portuguese and Spanish. It was also applied to at least one Japanese couple with an adopted mixed-race child. Four galliots left Nagasaki for Macao carrying 287 people, who were warned not to return on pain of death. Three years later, the families of Dutch and other foreign nationals were exiled to Batavia.

The measures were said to be necessary to preserve the country's traditions and territorial integrity, although the overriding factor was political loyalty. As the Governor-General of Batavia, Anthonie van Diemen, told his superiors, 'the Japanese does not wish the mixing of blood, to prevent someone of that offspring from ruling over them in due time'.[4] Thus ended a century of engagement between Japanese and Westerners of all classes.

Only a handful of (safely non-Catholic) Dutch traders were allowed to remain – confined to a small, man-made island in Nagasaki harbour called Dejima. The 'red-haired people' and their dark-skinned servants (Javanese) were like exhibits in a human menagerie.[5] On their obligatory pilgrimages to Edo (old Tokyo), the Hollanders were required to dance and sing for the amusement of the nobility and promenade themselves before the curious eyes of court ladies, who remained discreetly hidden from view.

The inmates of Dejima were allowed out occasionally to visit the Nagasaki brothels, but a delivery service was always available between times. The 18th-century Swedish naturalist Carl Peter Thunberg, who spent two years on the island, described the arrangement:

> If anyone desires a companion in his retirement, he makes it known to a certain man who goes to the island every day for this purpose. This fellow, before the evening, procures a girl that is attended by a little servant maid generally known under the denomination of a *kamuro*, who fetches daily from town all her mistress's victuals and drink, dresses her victuals, makes tea &c, keeps everything clean and in order and runs on errands. One of these female companions cannot be kept less than three days, but she may be kept as long as one pleases, a year or even several years together.[6]

The Japanese authorities required any concubine who became

pregnant to leave Dejima before giving birth – although she could return with the child afterwards. Mixed-bloods were now officially treated as Japanese and forbidden to leave the country.

The number of children born to European fathers was small. We know, too, from the unusually detailed record of births and deaths kept by the authorities, that few survived to adulthood. Whether this was due to racial prejudice or the health hazards of being raised in a brothel is not clear. The philosopher-physician Shōeki Andō (1707–55) believed the offspring of a European and a Japanese could not live much beyond the age of ten – due to the incompatibility of metal (West) and wood (East). The father, he said, would need to spend many years in Japan, consuming grain animated by the same vital force (chi), for this incompatibility to be overcome.

Through contact with the exotic other, Japanese began to think more about themselves as a distinct people. But this was not race consciousness, in the modern sense, with its claims to intellectual and moral superiority. Leaving aside the details of Andō's fanciful theory, the point to note is that he sought to explain how healthy mixed-race children could exist, rather than suggest they should not be born at all. The conclusion he was headed for was: 'All human beings under Heaven are one'.[7]

Talented and well-connected mixed-bloods could attain success even in xenophobic Tokugawa society. A well-documented case is Ine Kusumoto, the daughter of Philipp Franz von Siebold, a German physician who opened the first school of Western medicine in the 1820s. Ine was barely three when von Siebold was expelled from the country on suspicion of spying. Japanese regulations prevented his concubine and daughter accompanying him, but he made sure they were financially secure. Ine was raised to revere her father's name and, under the tutelage of his former pupils, went on to become Japan's first female doctor.

She was famous – yet vulnerable: a woman without a father's protection, in a male-dominated profession, and Eurasian. She gave birth to a daughter, apparently as the result of being raped by one of her instructors, and never married. Her pleasure at being reunited with von Siebold in her thirties (after Japan relaxed its closed-door policy) gave way to anger, on discovering he had made his teenage maid pregnant. Late in life, Ine preferred not to admit she was the offspring of a foreigner.

Most un-Mongolian

A technologically backward Japan was powerless to resist pressure to reopen to foreign trade in the 19th century. Between 1857 and 1899, under treaties negotiated with the Western powers, it surrendered the right to set its own tariff and granted foreign residents immunity from local laws. There was little time, during the collapse of the Tokugawa shogunate, to readjust public opinion, long conditioned by the regime's policy of making the 'people hate the foreigner and the foreigner hate us'.[8] Few Japanese had ever seen an outsider and were susceptible to rumours of hairy Westerners drinking blood (it was wine) and carrying off young girls to impregnate.

But curiosity competed with anxiety; a craving for the new pushed aside prejudice. While some members of the first embassy to Washington in 1860 went full of anger and hatred, others were capable of admiring their hosts' generosity and openness. In mirrored rooms, ablaze with gaslight, the Japanese envoys were agog at seeing women in low-cut dresses mingling on equal terms with men. 'Women are white and beautiful, and they are handsomely dressed with gold and silver decorations', one reported. 'Although I am becoming accustomed to their appearance, I find their reddish hair unattractive, and their eyes look like those of dogs.'[9] Red hair and flashing eyes were clichés of Western otherness. More importantly, this individual was warming to the display of American wealth and power – and white skin.

For their part, Western admirers of the enterprising Japanese positioned them as high as possible on the racial stepladder. They were 'the most un-Mongolian people in Asia', with an 'Aryan capacity for progress'. ('Mongolian', or Chinese, was synonymous with a stubborn refusal to modernise – how things have changed.) The Irish scholar AH Keane, in his pioneering work *Ethnology* (1896), ranked the Japanese 'with the more advanced European nations, being highly intelligent, versatile, progressive, quick-witted, and brave'.[10]

Western anthropologists identified two types of Japanese – the squat, dark-skinned peasant and taller, fairer aristocrat – and posited a distant blending of Mongolian, Caucasian and Malay blood. The nation's vigorous re-emergence into world affairs was cited as an example of the Darwinian survival of the fittest among competing human strains. Japanese patriots turned necessity into a virtue by claiming that a capacity for absorbing and naturalising exotic influences was uniquely perfected in their race. At first sight, the 'mixed nation' theory would seem to be incompatible with a claim to ethnic uniqueness, but they were two sides of the same coin.[11] In Japanese responses to race mixing, we continually find intolerance coexisting with pragmatism.

On stepping ashore at the treaty ports, foreign traders, soldiers and adventurers found the customs officials who inspected their baggage were also ready to arrange their female companionship. By 1867, Yokohama had around 1000 prostitutes, including 200–300 who served as foreigners' concubines. The narrow scope of social contact between the races bred cynicism on both sides. Westerners called their temporary wives '*musume*', the Japanese word for 'daughter' but applied to any single young woman. The euphemism was ambiguous: Did it distinguish a *musume* from a licensed prostitute or mark all females as sexually available? Locals referred to prostitutes who served foreign customers as '*rashamen*' (sheep), harking back to an old belief that sailors kept the animals on board ship for unnatural purposes.

Soon after arriving with her parents from the United States, 15-year-old Clara Whitney recorded in her diary:

> Merchants – married men – keep native women in their houses as wives without marriage. Sailors are even worse still, and it is pitiful to see the poor little half-caste children running around uncared for, as the Japanese regard them as unclean and their fathers don't care. Then, the natives think all foreigners are like that.[12]

Gradually and begrudgingly, interracial unions were admitted into the anteroom of polite society: a transition mirrored in the life of young Clara. In the beginning, she recoiled from the thought of a member of the Anglo-Saxon race stooping to have 'intimate relations with a Mongolian'. At 17, she professed to be shocked to receive a love letter from a Japanese male friend: 'How could I ever like the ape?' When, eventually, she married a Japanese, the changeable Clara was already pregnant with the first of six handsome children.

Japan hitched its fortunes to an adventure that could only succeed, or so it seemed, by overcoming animosity between the races – including the possibility of race mixing. Once the centuries-old ban on Christianity was lifted in 1873, the Japanese authorities began registering international marriages. (They averaged about ten a year; most couples remained in de facto relationships.) Under the law, a woman who married a foreigner acquired his nationality, as did any children. If the father's identity was unknown or he renounced his claim to paternity, the child attained Japanese citizenship through being entered in the mother's family register (*koseki*). In either case, mixed-bloods were no longer forbidden to leave the country.

Remaking Japanese

The first interracial marriage to be registered was between a banker named Teisuke Minami and a 23-year-old gardener's daughter from London, Eliza Pittman. The groom counted himself among those progressive Japanese who wanted to improve their racial stock by producing 'mixed-seed offspring'.[13] The couple ended their turbulent relationship 11 years later without succeeding in this procreative mission.

The 'mixed-seed' idea, however, lived on. Journalist Yoshio Takahashi, writing in 1883, set out the case for encouraging interracial marriage:

> Granted the inferior physical and mental constitution of
> Japanese, compared to Europeans, it becomes inevitable that our
> descendants will surrender, exhausted, to their superior power and
> not be able to compete. Therefore, what policy should be adopted
> for the sake of this glorious imperial nation [literally, 'perfect
> golden jar']? What can we do? The only solution is to improve
> our racial quality by means of intermarriage [with the Caucasian
> race].[14]

Critics of Takahashi's plan included the philosopher Tetsujirō Inoue, who thought race mixing a 'very stupid' idea, because half-castes were 'no longer Japanese'. Inoue felt a healthier population would follow from expanding education for women and encouraging them to marry later. Hiroyuki Katō, president of Tokyo Imperial University, thought improved nutrition, clothing and housing would achieve the desired result. It was a matter of pride for Katō that Japanese should persevere as a distinct people: 'I would prefer we were defeated in the competition for survival with Westerners than become almost a Western race – [notwithstanding that] we share the same origin [with Westerners] and are brothers'. Notably, in putting forward their alternative solutions, both conceded Takahashi's original premise that Japanese were physically and mentally inferior.[15]

As the argument raged, an opinion was sought from the Western scientist most esteemed in Japan, Herbert Spencer. The Social Darwinist was staying at a country estate in Wiltshire when the letter arrived, so he decided to consult a local livestock breeder. The man – somewhat unfortunately, choosing sheep as an example – confirmed Spencer's belief that the result of 'inter-breeding of *those which are widely unlike* … is a bad one – there arises an incalculable mixture of traits, and what may be called a chaotic constitution'. The same was true of humans: 'The Eurasians in India, and the half-breeds in America, show this', he wrote back. 'By all means, therefore, peremptorily interdict marriages of Japanese with foreigners.'[16]

Spencer's reference to the Eurasians of colonial Asia settled the matter for most Japanese intellectuals – only too aware of their country's narrow escape from colonisation. In staking a claim for equality with the West, they had cause to disdain the illicit and demeaning aspects of race mixing. 'Blood is not the only tie between kindred spirits', wrote Inazō Nitobe, a leading campaigner for East–West reconciliation. He likened his malleable, self-renewing race to the contents of an old wine-bag, which improved with time: 'Her form may often seem Eurasian [by which he implied something inauthentic or expedient], but her spirit is a genuine heritage from her ancestors'.[17] Nitobe was no jingoist (he later married his American secretary); quite simply, he could not ignore that the dominant paradigm of race mixing in Asia was exploitative – and changing it would not be straightforward.

Enigma within an enigma

When foreign observers called the Japanese a 'paradox' or 'enigma', as they frequently did, they took care to draw a distinction between the sexes. The 16th-century Spanish merchant Bernardino de Avila Girón considered Japanese women 'of excellent character and as kind as their men folk are cruel'. The 19th-century English poet Sir Edwin Arnold rated them 'so amazingly superior to their men-folk, as almost to belong morally and socially to a higher race'.[18]

The Japanese female not only put her male compatriot to shame, she also made the emancipated Western woman seem ungainly and aggressive. Her feminine graces were thought to be pre-industrial and incapable of survival outside their native setting: inviolable in a racial, as distinct from a sexual, sense. Count Hermann Keyserling, a German admirer, saw something of the Noble Savage in her: 'She alone feels herself to be directly at one with her race; her intellect is rarely independent enough to suffocate her natural feeling'.[19] Childish, emotional and irrational, her attributes furnished that silken chamber of the Western imagination, Oriental Mystique.

This nostalgic impulse played a major part in alienating Western sympathies from Japanese claims to modernity. Japan's political leadership collaborated in this estrangement by formalising inequality of the sexes. A new civil code, introduced in 1898, provided wives with greater legal protection but severely restricted feamle advancement in society. Women were denied the vote (they were not even allowed to attend political meetings) and could aspire to no higher public office than a teacher in a government school. Their supreme mission in life was to bear and raise children.

Anglo-Saxons who regarded their own gallant treatment of women as a mark of racial superiority railed against the inequalities of Japanese family life and licensed prostitution. The British journalist Lancelot Lawton called them 'a blot upon the world' that made Japan an unworthy ally, undeserving of colonies, and its people unsuitable for assimilation. After a week in Yokohama, Henry Adams, of the distinguished American political family, wrote home: 'I have not yet seen a woman with any mechanism better than that of a five-dollar wax doll'. Clement Scott, an English theatre critic and travel writer, was equally unimpressed. *Musume* were 'all of them chips from the same block' (in Western aesthetics, uniformity was a mark of the savage). Georges Bousquet, a French legal adviser to the Meiji government, cautioned that 'one must remain barbarous, or cease to treat women as savages'.[20]

Depending on the observer's perspective, the kimono-clad female symbolised what was finest or worst about the country and the race. She was the enigma within an enigma. Her shifting identity found its ideal milieu in eroticism: where morality and sexuality contended, and pathos coexisted with cynicism. Its enduring power can be measured in many ways. At Harvard University library, during the Second World War, the books on Japan most often borrowed were not political, economic or military texts – but ones about women, geisha and prostitutes.

Pierre Loti's *Madame Chrysanthème* (1887), a contrarian response to the West's amour for all things Japanese, tells the story of a French naval officer (based on the author's own experience) who goes shopping for a temporary 'bride' during an enforced stay in Nagasaki. The novella is a study in ennui; there is no mixed-race child, no cruel abandonment. If it conveyed any message, it was that sexual relations neither affirmed the compatibility of distant races nor formed a basis for civilisations to reconcile their differences. The treaty port liaisons scandalising polite society amounted to nothing of significance – and thankfully so.

A decade later, the American John Luther Long created *Madame Butterfly* (1898). By making his heroine, Cho-Cho, a paragon of fidelity – the opposite of Loti's pouting courtesan – and introducing a mixed-race child, Long emphasised the importance of the institution of marriage for containing the sexual urge and preserving society from the tragic consequences of race mixing. In her despair at being abandoned by Lieutenant Pinkerton, Cho-Cho is saved from suicide at the last moment by the cries of her 'purple-eyed child'. In the stage play and opera adapted from *Madame Butterfly*, she *does* kill herself – further emphasising the destructive forces unleashed. A literary genre was born.

An early exponent was Onoto Watanna, the first novelist of Asian ancestry to be published in the United States. Her short story 'A Half Caste' (1899) opens with its 'Pinkerton' character returning to Japan in search of the daughter he left behind many years before. His quest is forgotten, however, after he becomes infatuated with a young geisha. She angrily rebuffs his advances and, in tortured English, tells him that she hates him – because he deceived her mother. Yes, *she* is their child:

> She suddenly loosened her hair, and it fell down around her in thick, shining brown curls.
> '*Thad lig* [that like] Japanese girl? – *thad?* – *thad?* – *thad? Thad?*'
> She pushed back the sleeves and showed him the white purity of her arms.
> Then she turned and left him, with the same still look of despair on his face and the pitiless sun beating on the golden fields.[21]

The melodramatic tale sets out a hopeless choice for the half-caste: die or disappear. She is both an agent of vengeance and a figure of pity, inheriting the conflicted identity of her concubine mother. As fate punishes the American for his past sin, we realise how close he has come to committing incest.

In the imagined figure of the Japanese concubine, writers and artists toyed with ideas of power and moral authority. Though seemingly in control, the white male proves no match for either the manipulative Chrysanthemum or the honourable Butterfly. The vulnerability of the mixed-race geisha is similarly inverted by the punishment she inflicts on her unwitting father-suitor. The concubine's shifting identity holds in abeyance an answer to the question: Who is exploiting whom? Her abandonment does not resolve the question because, the more it dwells on the pathos of female dependency and infant vulnerability, the more it provides the male viewpoint the satisfaction of forgiving the woman's promiscuity and the child's illegitimacy. A Japanese feminist has aptly said, about this kind of evasion: 'The compassion of the powerful is prerequisite to the self-sacrifice of the powerless'.[22] A similar hypocrisy lay behind the stereotype of the miserable mixed-blood.

The Madame Butterfly tradition distorted the Western imaginative response to Japan by assigning different moral valuations to women and men, substituting concubines for wives, disconnecting sex from procreation and representing interracial love as a temporary and dangerous aberration. It proved to be an irresistible formula, particularly when the country fell under military occupation.

3

War of purification

The answer to the question of why Japan went to war with the West usually includes a long list of political and economic factors. If we inquire as to what the Japanese *thought* they were about, one image, one idea, constantly recurs: purification. What did it mean?

After five years of fighting in China, and incurring 600 000 battlefield casualties, Japan was stuck in a quagmire. Nearer exhaustion than peak strength, it staked everything on a wider conflict in the Pacific. The attack on the American fleet at Pearl Harbor and the seizure of British and Dutch possessions in Southeast Asia were celebrated by the former socialist author, Ashihei Hino, in verse: 'What was before crusted with barbarian moss/ is now being cleansed/ now a bold enterprise has begun'.[1]

Intellectuals were forever reminding themselves of the virtue and justice of putting an end to the white man's domination of Asia. Japanese spirit – represented in films and novels by images of emaciated endurance – was going to scour away the West's twin corruptions of materialism and individualism. It was something in the blood, another dimension of purity: an imperial line stretching back to the gods – myth as history. Sei Itō (translator of *Ulysses* and *Lady Chatterley's Lover*) noted in his diary: 'We are the so-called "yellow race". We are fighting to determine the superiority of a race that has been discriminated against … Our war is a struggle for a predestined confidence'.[2]

Formalism penetrated every aspect of daily life. The young woman who described herself as being 'impressed with the beauty of correct regulations' captured the cultural disposition nicely. So did the girl of ten, sorting maggot-infested potatoes, who thought, 'If I can't do this, I'm not a Japanese'. So did the instructors, at the Army War College, who praised cadets for sticking to an opinion *regardless* of the facts. So, too, the engineers on the Thailand–Burma Railway, who sought to prove themselves worthy by imposing impossible work quotas on prisoners. One of their officers, sentenced to hang for war crimes, expressed this purity of purpose in verse: 'When the winning country judged me/ My faithfulness could not be understood'.[3]

Hawks or harpies?

Austerity campaigns suppressed public displays of luxury and sexuality. In solidarity with their fighting men, women donned an androgynous uniform of tunic and baggy trousers called *mompe*. A cartoon published in May 1942 showed a young woman scratching her scalp and imported ideas falling out like dandruff. The caption read, 'Purge the United States and Britain from your head'.[4]

Women took an increasingly active role in neighbourhood associations, distributing rations, building air-raid defences and sending off troops. Citizens were reminded that the youth who made it to the parade ground at eight in the morning relied on the 'true Nipponese mother' who got up at four. 'I was a black hen who gave birth to a hawk', went the war widow's song. Women and girls stepped in behind men, absent from the workplace, to a greater extent than German women, for instance. Three and a half million took up the reins in industry (including 470 000 'volunteer corps', some as young as 11, drafted to work in armaments factories), and millions more toiled in underground mines and on farms.[5] They felt proud to demonstrate their abilities; the gap between male and female wages narrowed.

The state, however, was never fully convinced women formed

a secure column on the home front. They were the subversive sex, prone to contrary impulses. In folk culture, the menstruating female was 'unclean'; what part, therefore, could she have in a victory of purification? War widows felt pressure to avoid the company of men, and the Army sent spies to check on the wives of absent soldiers. Female treachery was ferreted out: by the policeman who berated the 'unpatriotic' woman for scavenging food; by the air-raid warden, attending a house for showing a light, who complained, 'Hey! You've got rouge on your cheeks'. Michi Kawai, in her memoir *Sliding Doors*, quotes a teenage girl bemoaning the fact Mount Fuji now acted as a landmark, guiding in the American bombers: 'You are like a foolish woman who is proud of attracting friends and enemies alike by her beauty and allure. I hate to look at you'.[6] The most sacred of national symbols had turned coquette-betrayer.

Absenteeism among female war workers, off visiting men, was said to be 'extremely high'.[7] The journalist Kiyoshi Kiyosawa initially hailed this social 'revolution', but then grew apprehensive: 'It is enough for me to imagine the changes in ideas of chastity of young women'. Another way women defied authority was by trading on the black market to feed and clothe their families. Patriotic slogans hammered the theme that family and state were one and indivisible, but the risks and sacrifices taken by women more obviously served the practical needs of actual kin.

As disaster loomed, civilian–military solidarity began to falter. Soldiers trained never to surrender saw death in a different light: an escape from the consequences of defeat. Did this rob death of its honour? For every civilian under bombardment who thought, 'I must be ready for the next thing, I must survive', there was a straggler in uniform, lonely and defiant, who cried out, 'Have all the civilians deserted us?' Bitter, unresolved feelings clouded the nation's collective memory. The *konketsuji* – 'the invoice delivered later', as cynics called them – suffered, in part, because of the Japanese unwillingness to forgo a claim to righteousness and victim-hood.

Suddenly it was over. At noon on 15 August 1945, a gong sounded on the radio, and the assembled millions were told to stand for a broadcast by Emperor Hirohito. The national anthem died away, and an unfamiliar, quavering voice emerged through the static. Straining to listen, the writer and physician Shūichi Katō noted the cheerful reaction of a group of nurses at the hospital where he worked. War had 'ultimately failed to permeate into the world of these young women'.[8] He did not condemn their frivolousness, even though he realised the implications for what lay ahead.

Conditioned by years of all-or-nothing warfare, many Japanese expected the worst from defeat: an orgy of rape and murder by rampaging invaders. Thousands of women and children fled the cities, some carrying vials of poison. Newspapers printed instructions: 'When in danger of being raped, show the most dignified attitude. Don't yield. Cry for help'.[9] Confronted by an enemy who did not hesitate to obliterate whole cities in a flash, it was perfectly possible to believe the most outlandish rumours: that all males would be castrated or enslaved and only the females preserved to give birth to mixed-race children. Another country would be born …

Miles of ashes

The Liberator bombers descended until they were flying just 250 feet above the ground. On 28 August, a week before the signing of the surrender in Tokyo Bay, Allied war correspondents were getting their first glimpse of the ruined capital. An American reporter described the view:

> Reports of damage were not exaggerated; if anything, they constitute the most shocking understatement in the history of aerial warfare …
>
> There were blocks on which not a single building stood, where the construction and civilization wrought in the past

centuries had been obliterated, leaving reddish soil – and
nothing else.

Tokyo and Yokohama glittered today, but it was the glitter
of broken glass.[10]

Broken glass glittered in no fewer than 66 cities: 40 per cent of
urban Japan lay in ruins. Upwards of 330 000 people had died in
air raids, more than were killed on the battlefield by the Americans
alone. Altogether, nearly three million Japanese – about 4 per cent
of the population – had perished since the start of the China conflict
in 1937. Another nine million were homeless and 6.5 million soldiers and civilians awaited repatriation from the lost empire. There
were 1.3 million war widows.

Viewed across the vacant lots of midtown Tokyo, distant Mount
Fuji stood out as clearly as in a Hokusai woodblock print. The drone
of the observation planes faded into the distance, leaving a prehis-
toric silence to descend upon the scene. A lone, ox-drawn cart trun-
dled along the once neon-lit Ginza.

Two days later, the correspondents flew into Atsugi air base, near
Yokohama, to cover the deployment of the first of half a million
American troops. The operation proceeded so smoothly – aircraft
touching down every three minutes – it struck one reporter like 'a
well-organized pleasure trip'.[11] Supreme Commander for the Allied
Powers (SCAP) General Douglas MacArthur arrived that afternoon
and was escorted to the Hotel New Grand, on the Yokohama waterfront, where he had last stayed eight years earlier during his honey-
moon. He was welcomed by the elderly owner and shown over his
rooms like a paying guest.

Events were moving rapidly. Washington's initial guidelines for
the occupation had been radioed to MacArthur as he was flying into
Japan. They recommended a hard line: no help with reviving the
economy; no protection for the country's discredited leaders, should
the populace rise against them. A later communication authorised

him to issue a non-fraternisation order if he saw fit.

SCAP had other ideas. Plans to impose full military government – as in occupied Germany – were abandoned in favour of acting through existing Japanese agencies; food aid was rushed in to prevent mass starvation; workers' strikes were initially tolerated, and then suppressed; and no American ban on fraternisation was ever declared (MacArthur told an aide he would not do so 'for all the tea in China').[12]

Hoping his 'pleasure trip' would produce something more newsworthy, Frank Kluckhohn of the *New York Times* boarded a train for Tokyo, revolver at the ready. His questions (in English) to the Japanese passengers were met with 'stony stares' and 'curt answers'. The journey was 'not without strain', he told readers, though 'nothing unfortunate happened'. Arriving at the Imperial Hotel, he was in no mood for the positively cheerful welcome he received from the staff, 'as if there had never been a war'. Within a few days, however, Kluckhohn was pleased to report 'women no longer were shy; children waved to us – some even made the V sign with their fingers'. Thanks to the 'amazing decorum' of the American troops, the Japanese were revealing 'admirable qualities'.[13]

While a far cry from being the feared barbarian invasion, not everything about it was admirable. Within hours of the first landings, two Marines entered a home in Yokosuka and raped a 36-year-old woman and her teenage daughter at gunpoint. Hundreds of crimes were logged during the early weeks. Angered by Japanese press reports of 'despicable incidents', SCAP imposed a strict censorship.[14] Criticism of the occupation would no longer be tolerated. The topics most often targeted by censors, in the years ahead, were sexual fraternisation and mixed-race children.

Comfort without joy

As soon as Emperor Hirohito finished telling his people they must 'bear the unbearable', the government set about making arrangements. The Home Affairs Ministry instructed police across the country to prepare comfort facilities for the foreign troops. Representatives of Tokyo's geisha, restaurant and brothel associations met and, backed by a government-guaranteed loan, formed the Recreation and Amusement Association (RAA).

The initial plan called for the mobilisation of geisha, prostitutes, waitresses, bar hostesses and others experienced in the *mizu shōbai* ('water trade', or entertainments for men). Gathering them proved difficult – Tokyo's brothel quarter, Yoshiwara, was a pile of cinders – so recruiting agents threw out a wider net, using newspapers and billboards to spread the word. One notice read:

> Wanted: Female clerks aged 18 to 25.
> Accommodation, clothing and meals all provided.
> As part of national post-war emergency management, we seek
> the co-operation of new women of Japan for the major project
> of comforting occupation soldiers.[15]

Tens of thousands signed up, driven by hunger, lured by the patriotic sales pitch, out of curiosity or simply in search of a place to belong.

Recruits were urged to join a mission of 'special self-sacrifice', echoing language previously used for the kamikaze squadrons. Another historical model was Okichi, the girl assigned as concubine to the first American consul in the 19th century. At an attestation ceremony in front of the Imperial Palace on 29 August, the women took a pledge:

> We will form a seawall to hold back the madness with human
> pillars of several thousand 'Okichis of Showa' [the imperial

era name]. We will defend and nurture the pure blood of our race for the next one hundred years, while becoming unseen, underground pillars at the foundation of the post-war social order.[16]

The keynotes were the protection of Japanese racial purity and the removal out of sight of sexual contact with the foreign invader. Among those running this state-sponsored enterprise were xenophobic right-wingers who would profit unblushingly from the former enemy.

The first RAA venue, a refurbished restaurant near Tokyo Bay, began with around 30 mainly experienced prostitutes. Once word spread among the occupation troops, raw recruits were rushed in to meet the surging demand. A Yoshiwara madam was hired to instruct and groom the novice 'Okichis'. There were no private rooms, merely partitions. Customers tramped over the straw-mat floors in their boots, pushing down sliding panels mistaken for hinged doors. Naked men 'holding surprisingly thick and long things in both hands, as if supporting a hose, were chasing women', one former RAA employee has recalled.[17] The women averaged 15 customers a day. Sometimes it took several times that amount of 'sacrifice' to clear the 'madness' queuing outside.

A former SCAP official has claimed 'many an American boy was raped during the first year of the Occupation by such Female *Kamikaze*'. If so, the US military provided covering fire: the first penicillin released in Japan went to comfort women; MPs patrolled outside brothels to keep order; Army prophylactic stations were set up nearby; and, in at least one instance, a brothel rate-card was displayed on a quartermaster's bulletin board, warning: 'If you pay more, you spoil it for the rest'.[18]

Not all RAA facilities were intended for prostitution. The 'Oasis of Ginza' was a popular souvenir shop and dance hall operating beneath the bombed remains of the Matsuzakaya department store.

The Armed Forces' newspaper *Pacific Stars and Stripes* published an enthusiastic review: 'You enter to the blare of a perfectly good GI orchestra and walk into a vast room filled with a high percentage of pulchritude and a minimum of gold-and-buck teeth, and service men carrying out their role as conquerors'.[19]

Apostasy

Occupation personnel were treated as honoured guests not merely to flatter them. It also enabled Japanese to play the host. Relieved, more than anything, the war was over, few civilians harboured genuine hatred for long. The half a million letters written to General MacArthur and his command mainly contained expressions of gratitude, polite advice and denunciations of ultra-nationalists. Scores of admiring women went further and offered to have his baby. One letter began: 'My Revered and Beloved Honorable General MacArthur, I long to receive the blessed seed of your child. I am embarrassed to impose upon you when you are so busy, but please come to my residence at the following address …'.[20]

American material abundance worked its magic. Crowds gathered outside Army PXs (Post Exchanges, military general stores), noses to the show windows, eyes coveting the fabulous goods inside. One woman remembers the first thrill of eating chicken off the bone at an American canteen: 'I felt like a savage'.[21] There were crazes for swing jazz, jitterbugging and square dancing. *Call of the Yukon* led the return of American movie culture to the screen. The Japanese-language edition of *Reader's Digest* sold at *above* its cover price. Whatever else they made of the 'Blondie' cartoon-strip, now being syndicated in Japanese newspapers, hungry readers would never forget the sumptuous sandwiches Dagwood consumed.

In a study entitled 'The Enigma of Japanese Friendliness', the distinguished American psychologist Ernest Hilgard considered whether it might be all one big bluff. He discounted the possibility.

There was evidence, he said, of 'deep shame and humiliation at unexpected defeat' and a revulsion against anything military. Feelings towards Americans had switched from fear to dependency.[22]

Many explanations were offered for this apostasy, but the most enduring one portrayed the Japanese as children. It brought together characteristics – changeableness, subservience, credulity, immaturity, propensity to be taught – befitting a simple people misled by bad leaders and recoverable through a benevolent tutelage. This impression was epitomised, for the average GI, by unthreatening contacts with women and children, won over by a chocolate bar or a stick of gum. (Victim status was rarely conceded to Japanese men.)

Women were rendered further child-like by their perceived naivety and ingenuousness. 'Starved for affection, they blossom like flowers under kindness', explained an occupation *Guide to Japan*, 'and many Americans, who are gentle and affectionate with women, frequently wonder how such lovely women can produce such brutes of sons'.[23] The other side of Japanese female frivolity, in this narrative, was her supposed readiness to transfer her affections to others, thus preparing a rationalisation for the serviceman's easy abandonment of such a changeable type.

When Japanese lament their weakness for yielding to Western influences, they often represent it as a feminine trait. Commenting on the occupation in 1953, the critic Naoko Itagaki said the whole nation became 'a kind of prostitute', though women succumbed more easily because they could not 'see through the psychology of most Americans'. In a similar vein, a leading political scientist, Masao Maruyama, described a time when 'people became lethargic and sluttish, nakedly pursuing egoistic ends'. More recently, the historian Rinjirō Sodei has written that Japan 'went to bed with the occupation', and the older generation still felt guilty 'for being seduced too easily'.[24]

Fraternisation

Fraternisation posed a complex challenge for SCAP. Those who believed the Japanese were contrite and ripe for change favoured it. But how did one avoid compromising military discipline and moral authority? Those in the opposite camp saw fraternisation as a way for Japan's old order to undermine the Allies' reformist zeal. But how to remain aloof and still win the population for democracy? These dilemmas were never resolved.

No subject was more prone to dizzying displays of doubletalk. William Worden, correspondent for the *Saturday Evening Post*, assured his readers Japanese women were as ugly as their men were savage. 'There is no chance', he wrote, 'that any great number of Americans will wish to marry Japanese … The flat-chested, button-nosed, splayfooted average Japanese woman is about as attractive to most Americans as a 1000-year-old stone idol'. Frank Kluckhohn reached the same conclusion via the opposite route: 'There are plenty of petite and beautiful women in Japan. But apparently they have no charm for these youngsters, any more, it appears, than these tall, lithe, wise-cracking Americans have charm for the feminine element of Japan'.[25] This would have been an astonishing case of cultural dissonance – had it been true.

Even 'drab women whose pants [*mompe*] gave them the charm of a potato sack' shed their initial lack of appeal. According to one contemporary account, the GI found 'a woman without curves, but a woman nevertheless, and a woman who was willing'.[26] Pacific War veterans were familiar with sexually active 'amateurs' from their R & R days in Australia and New Zealand. Couples managed to clamber over the additional linguistic and cultural hurdles of Japan, by using mime and slapstick humour. A guy could always teach a gal a song. 'You Are My Sunshine', 'Shine On, Harvest Moon' and 'Don't Fence Me In' led the hit parade. Later, a new tune, '*Gomen Nasai*' ('I'm Sorry'), joined the repertoire: the croon of a departing soldier for his deceived lover.

The dating couples' patois of antiquated slang and mispronunciation observed no class barrier. The daughter of a retired diplomat caused a mild sensation at a dinner party when she declared, in a moment of irritation, that she was '*pisto*' ('pissed', slang for 'annoyed').[27] Military phrase books provided servicemen 14 ways of saying 'goodbye'. Encounters with the locals were programmed to be transient.

Early in the occupation, Lieutenant Frank Turner, a Japanese-speaking member of the United States Strategic Bombing Survey, went exploring in downtown Tokyo. He got into conversation with an ex-Army driver named Takebe, who invited him for a drink. Over a bottle of sake, Turner ventured to ask his companion what he thought about fraternisation:

> Takebe did not hesitate to denounce it emphatically. Americans could not be truly interested in Japanese girls, considering the barriers of language, race and war prejudice which prevented such friendships from developing into something permanent. It seemed to him that Americans sought the company of Japanese girls for only one reason, which would become sufficiently apparent, if it were not already, next June when a prodigious crop of 'occupation babies' was brought into the world. For many, many years, these babies would be a constant reminder of American excess and Japanese folly. The men and women in the room all solemnly nodded their assent.[28]

Turner decided the Japanese would need 'a certain resiliency' to get on with the Americans. Not tolerance – with its possibility of understanding or sympathy – but resiliency. Society would have to steel itself for the shock of occupation babies, with no thought of celebrating a new mixed race.

Before the war, social contacts between Japanese women and

foreign men had been confined largely to the upper class: girls attending private Christian schools; wives entertaining for business-men or diplomats; and wealthy women travelling abroad. During the occupation, females of all classes made contact with Westerners, and mostly outside the well-ordered spheres of education, business and diplomacy.

Newspaper editorials, radio broadcasts, posters and leaflets exhorted females to 'maintain dignity'. In November 1945, a politi-cian referred to 'thousands' of women wandering about at night in places like Yokohama Park, earning money: 'We can imagine, by this time next year, girls holding celluloid-doll-like children … striding the streets. Thinking about the future of Japan, the prospect is rather chilling'. The following April, a female candidate campaigned in the general election (in which women could vote and stand for parlia-ment for the first time) on the slogan 'We don't want any blue-eyed babies in Japan'.[29] (She was not elected.)

Around this time, an American missionary approached the head of SCAP's Public Health and Welfare Section, Colonel Crawford Sams, seeking approval to open a special home for the anticipated 'blue-eyed babies'. Sams rejected the proposal. In his opinion, the worst possible thing would be to stigmatise a child by calling it a 'GI baby'. In any case, he said, the Japanese were not a pure race but a hodgepodge of racial influences. 'There've been Eurasians in Japan for many years. They've not been a problem at all. They've all been absorbed very well by the population'.[30]

Sams conveniently overlooked that most Eurasians in pre-war Japan were, or could be presumed to be, the children of white engi-neers, doctors and other professionals – and were not likely to be equated with the offspring of white or black servicemen. As one Japanese commentator put it, the mixed-race citizens of former days were 'romantic … elegant … fragrant', whereas the *konketsuji* of the occupation gave off only a 'dirty smell'.[31]

A week after this unproductive meeting, *Pacific Stars and Stripes* (not subject to pre-publication censorship) ran a report predicting 'at least 14,000 GI babies' would be born to unmarried mothers in the Tokyo–Yokohama area by mid-1946. The source was a senior police official, who based his estimate on information from hospitals, midwives and the pregnant women themselves. The article – the first public airing of the issue – put some powerful noses out of joint. The newspaper ran a denial a week later, quoting Japanese officials as saying the women involved were from 'lower educational levels' and knew perfectly well what they were doing.[32] The subject of GI babies was linked exclusively to an immorality endangering the occupation's reform agenda.

It was as if the human toll of a decade of wartime upheaval and trauma was to be instantly discounted, and a new narrative installed in its place: the conspiracy of female promiscuity.

4

Mitsuyoshi's story

Mitsuyoshi Hanaoka was born in July 1946, 11 months into the occupation. His birth was not registered, however, until October. 'Maybe my mother had to make up her mind' is his rueful comment on this delay.

My mother was 24 when I was born. She was from Hiroshima prefecture. I have a half-brother, three years older than me. His father, it seems, was killed in the war, and my uncle – my mother's brother – adopted him. Aunt and uncle didn't have any children of their own, but they had a proper house; so, this sort of thing was considered commonsense in Japan.

Towards the end of the war, she left Hiroshima and went to Kokura [now part of Kitakyushu]. It seems she chased after a military policeman who was transferred there. If she had stayed in Hiroshima she would have been killed. But Kokura was also a very risky place: it was the original target for the atomic bomb that went to Nagasaki [the B-29 diverted from Kokura due to cloud cover]. If she had died there, this would never have happened. It means I wouldn't have been born. [Tearful.]

Then the American troops came. I heard from my mother that my father was from Pennsylvania. There was a Tamaya department store in Kokura – I presume it's still there – and the Americans commandeered it. He was in a sanitation unit of the US Army. They arrived first and disinfected, preparing the way for the main force. I heard his unit pulled out by Christmas [1945].

His name was John Chominsky – of Polish background. There are various spellings, I don't know precisely. He wasn't an elite. I inherited that line. Blood will out. You can't argue against DNA. [Laughs.] He was a sergeant. It seems he had his own room. In those days there was no food. A woman by herself couldn't do anything. She took up with him. She said to me: 'Your father didn't have any tattoos. He often played the guitar for me'.

Afterwards she came back to her home town. Her belly had become big, so she was in trouble, and she took up with my stepfather. Frankly speaking, that man from Korea – it was called Chōsen in the old days – was used by her. Why would someone bother to take on such a woman? It's different now; but, before and during the war, Koreans were exploited.

Mitsuyoshi's stepfather had left Korea as a teenager to try his luck in South Sakhalin, then part of the Japanese empire. Fortunately for him, he left for Hokkaido before Soviet troops invaded the territory in 1945. Tossing up where to go next, he heard Kure was a dangerous town, best avoided. From his point-of-view, that was a recommendation. He made his living brewing bootleg liquor, and dangerous towns were thirsty towns.

Amid odours of brewer's yeast, pigswill and dung, Mitsuyoshi's mother gave birth in a small, shingle-roofed hut in a village on the outskirts of Kure. A Korean Japanese writer, born in such a village around this time, has described an atmosphere 'constantly seething like a pressure-cooker'. Communal life 'was coloured by roars of laughter and anger, by lawlessness and misery'.[1] Together with the poverty and disorder went an abundance of human warmth, which Mitsuyoshi experienced too – especially from his stepfather. He sheds fresh tears of gratitude remembering him.

In those days, I didn't know he wasn't my father, because he was with me from my birth. He was a very, very, very nice person. He showed me love and cared for me. For example, later on, when food was short, he would say, 'I have sake; it makes me full. So, why don't you go ahead and eat'. I believed him. Only afterwards did I understand.

Mitsuyoshi's mother resented being the subject of gossip and took out her frustration on the boy, frequently scolding him. At one stage, she gave him to a family in another city, but he was returned after a month. Each time his stepfather stepped in to protect him, they grew closer together.

When Mitsuyoshi was four, his mother packed her belongings and left her Korean protector, taking the child with her.

Frankly, she made use of him. Once things had settled down, she left him, and we went away. Just left the house. In fact, we stayed in the same town, 20 or 30 minutes walk away.

I don't know what happened then. But, as you'd expect, living conditions were difficult … And, for me, the most regrettable thing was … she should have put me in a proper place, but … she took me to Kure – from Hiro [the neighbouring town] to Kure – and the most regrettable thing is … she bought me ice cream, something I'd never had before. While I was eating, she said she was going to the toilet. She didn't come back. [He becomes highly emotional.] They found a note in … [He gestures to his top pocket.] That was the situation.

Unable to find work, she had sold off most of her belongings and become desperate. The crying child was found at Kure pier, melted ice cream in hand, and taken into police custody.

I was taken to Hiroshima orphanage tentatively. My story appeared in the newspaper, with a photograph. Then the people in my village … [His emotions spill over.] My photograph … My neighbour cut out the photo and showed everyone. My father [stepfather] couldn't read a newspaper, and his spoken Japanese wasn't good (thanks to that, my school record in Japanese was bad). Eventually, he came to pick me up.

Several months later my mother turned up. She was sticking her nose in things again. [Laughs.] This time I was called to the courthouse. The two of us went: my father and me. My stepfather, that is. I was told to go into the room alone. He had to wait outside. And when I entered, the person I least wanted to see was there: my mother.

I had been called because they had decided to hear the opinion of the person at the centre. Me. The official said, 'Your mother has come to pick you up, but what do you want to do?' I was silent. Because my mother was there, I couldn't say, 'No, I don't want to go with her'. I was struggling. At that moment, the door suddenly opened, and I saw him [my stepfather] peeping in. I instantly decided. I said, 'I will go with my father'. They said OK.

My mother asked, 'Why?'

'That's enough, that's enough', [said the court official.]

It was the last the child saw of his mother, although 'that person', as Mitsuyoshi sometimes refers to her, sent him a bag as a present when he started school and apparently came by the playground occasionally to catch a glimpse of him.

His neighbours in the 'Korean' village were among the poorest in Kure, which meant he was unlikely to develop a sense of inferiority. He was always to be seen playing with other children; adults praised him for being 'a good boy'; and his teachers described him as 'obedient, cheerful and active'.[2] He helped at home, digging the vegetable plot and feeding the pigs.

The appearance at school of the first *konketsuji* in 1953 was a major event in Japan. Mitsuyoshi's class teacher, while pleasantly surprised how 'Japanese' the boy looked, also felt worried because he seemed introverted. Her work diary plotted his progress during the year: second in the running race; happy to be selected a group leader; and silent when asked if he wanted to see his mother. 'At least, for now, he does not have any of the darkness [of temperament] associated with mixed blood', she wrote. 'But what will happen when [he] knows about the real situation of his birth?'

> Immediately after I started third year of junior high school, my stepfather died. Perhaps it was bronchitis; I get that a bit too. It was a very dirty place [where we lived], very dirty. Thinking back, I imagine that was the cause. It wasn't known at the time. He went to hospital, recovered and came back. Then, while visiting a friend, a baker, he collapsed. The man took him to hospital by taxi. I was in school. Someone called me. When I got to the hospital, before I reached the room, the doctor told me he had gone.

For the next four years, Mitsuyoshi lived alone in the hut where he was born. He ran deliveries for a tofu shop to help pay his way through senior high school. His meagre possessions included a study desk hardly bigger than a placemat.

As graduation approached, Mitsuyoshi could not decide what to do next. He thought of training as a chef, so the welfare agency, ISS, lined up a company willing to take him. Nothing came of it. He considered entering the Buddhist priesthood. He tried and failed to enter university. His ISS caseworker criticised him for lacking perseverance and relying on others too much: 'It is more important for him to tough it out in real society than enter university life'.[3] He changed tack again and enrolled at the Kiyosato Farm School.

The Kiyosato Educational Experiment Project (KEEP) was started by an American occupation officer, Paul Rusch, to demonstrate 'how democracy works on a small community level'.[4] Using land in the mountains of Yamanashi prefecture acquired by the

Episcopalian Church before the war, Rusch's experiment grew into the Kiyosato Farm School, which opened in 1963 with 20 students. Some, like Mitsuyoshi, were sent there to prepare for a new life abroad. The students managed a dairy herd, learned to operate and maintain farm machinery, and received Christian instruction.

In a roundabout way, the lessons in animal husbandry provided Mitsuyoshi with confirmation of his origins.

> The neighbours also told me he [my natural father] was American. But maybe that's only what she [my mother] told them. However, if you count back, it's right. It's very simple. With cows, after mating – the same as humans – you subtract three months and add six days. If you make the calculation, you can work out the date of birth. It matches. I got confirmation.

He left Japan in August 1967, intending to work on a cattle property in Brazil. A newspaper quoted him, on his departure: 'Thanks to the love and understanding of those around me, I have become a half-decent person. I am happy my childhood dream is coming true'. The article said he looked forward to inviting Kure's other mixed-race children to join him in Brazil to make 'a bright orchard', free of discrimination.[5] Mitsuyoshi denies having had any such thought.

His high school teacher and the ISS social worker, Yone Itō, were among a handful of people there to see him off. His mother was not present; it is unlikely she even knew he was going.

> Before I went to Brazil, the person who knew me best in the world urged me not to go: 'You'll only be deceived'. He told me: 'The mayor is my relative, so I can arrange to get you a job in the ward office. If it's the civil engineering section, the work is not that hard'. We had that kind of discussion. But I loved nature, and I felt there might be something nice over there.
> When I left by ship for Brazil, as the streamers broke and

trailed away, everyone else was crying. Remembering my teacher's words, not to act shamefully, I struck a heroic pose. [He cocks his arms and puts his hands on his hips.] 'I've done it.' [Laughs.]

Mitsuyoshi emigrated as part of a government-sponsored program. He recalls being interviewed at the Brazilian consulate along with several other candidates. 'Because my face was different from the others, the consul asked whether I could speak English or Spanish. I said no. He asked only me.'

Relating this episode triggers a much earlier memory.

This goes back to before I started primary school. It happened that, if I said, 'Give me money', they [occupation soldiers] would give it to me. I had never before behaved like a beggar. I happened to be near a camp with my friend at the entrance where soldiers were going in and out. Perhaps I was six. I didn't go to kindergarten, so maybe five or four. They gave me a lot. The soldiers stopped, looked at my face and gave me money. I thought it was very strange. I wondered why they gave it only to me. They gave me so much I couldn't even hold it all. Coins with a kangaroo mark – so I didn't bring them back. I left them. Seems someone else picked them up. [Laughs.] That sort of thing happened.

Another time, when I was even younger, I followed some soldiers as they were marching towards the firing range for shooting practice. I did such things. And, another time, when I had a boil on my backside – it was before the last of the soldiers withdrew, so I may have been in the second year of primary school – there was a US Army jeep. It had a rail on which you could hang. When the jeep started, I fell off – onto my boil.

Re-enacting the pain, Mitsuyoshi winces and laughs.

5

Conquering Kure

Back in the helter-skelter days of Japan's early industrialisation, foreign guests eager to observe the country's transformation might be taken to the port of Kure, on the Inland Sea. Few places more dramatically enacted the Meiji-era slogan of 'enrich the nation, strengthen the military'. The Imperial Navy's greatest arsenal lay in a natural amphitheatre screened by islands on the seaward side and backing onto steep hills. Foundries transformed molten metal into cannon, torpedoes and mines; shipyards turned out a new cruiser inside a year, a battleship in two. 'Here indeed the visitor feels that the march of Occidental progress has reached the innermost life of Japan', an American military surgeon wrote during the Russo-Japanese War.[1]

Across from the dockyards, on the island of Etajima, stood the Imperial Naval Academy, modelled on Britain's Dartmouth, down to the imported red bricks and the lock of Admiral Horatio Nelson's hair on display in the museum. The midshipmen it started graduating in the 1890s carried Japan's colours across the world's oceans, returning with tales of exotic places to enliven the geisha hours. The Navy fostered, in this provincial town, a more-than-usual awareness of the outside world.

Inter-service rivalry being what it was, the Japanese Army commander at nearby Hiroshima (a proud castle-town) penned a less flattering portrait of Kure, on the eve of the First World War. With its many migrant workers and outlaws, it resembled a new colony:

'The city appears to be lively, but the people are full of frivolity and fraud'.[2] Wages were good, and the pleasure quarters grew large and prosperous.

At least twice, in the crisis year of 1942, Australian troops confronted marines of the Kure Special Naval Landing Forces: first, on the island of Ambon, in the Dutch East Indies (scene of a notorious massacre of Australian and Dutch prisoners), and then at Milne Bay, on the eastern tip of Papua, where the Allies hurled back an attempted landing. After this unprecedented reversal, Rear Admiral Matome Ugaki paid his opponents a backhanded compliment by blaming older reservists among his attacking force for 'lacking tenacity and fighting spirit'.[3]

Kure's proudest contribution to the war was the 69 000-ton *Yamato*, sheathed in armour half a metre thick, capable of 27 knots, and carrying guns that could fire a shell, the weight of a small truck, more than 40 kilometres. The world's biggest battleship was also the latest thing in naval obsolescence; by the time of her maiden voyage, aircraft carriers, not dreadnoughts, ruled the waves. Held back until the last throw of the dice, she joined the Battle of Okinawa on a suicidal mission.

Those who built her also paid a heavy price. Two thousand Kure residents were killed in air raids during the final months of the war. It might have been a lot worse had the US Army Chief of Staff, General George C Marshall, succeeded in having the atomic bomb targeted on 'a large naval installation'. The mushroom cloud rose on the other side of the hill, and Kure was left to radio the first news of the 'terrific explosion' to Tokyo.[4]

As elsewhere, Hiroshima prefecture obeyed government orders and prepared hundreds of comfort women for the advancing Allies. With Kure's main pleasure quarter destroyed, recruiting agents turned to destitute women. The dialect word for them, '*tobia-gari*', denoted someone reckless and delinquent.[5] They included girls as young as 14. The first American troopships were met at sea before they berthed, and prostitutes went aboard: a variation on a centuries-old commerce entertaining travellers in the Inland Sea.

View from the hills

The British Commonwealth Occupation Force replaced troops of the American Sixth Army, whose withdrawal marked the end of the initial demilitarisation phase. On learning of the impending change, Kure residents assumed that lower-class soldiers, possibly mercenaries, were taking over. Nerves became frayed again.

On a bright, mid-winter day in February 1946, the Liberty Ship *Stamford Victory* entered the Inland Sea. Steering clear of a dozen half-submerged vessels – the graveyard of the Imperial Navy – she brought the first big contingent of Australian troops within sight of their destination. The once-bustling shipyards presented a scene of total destruction: giant cranes, twisted and buckled, crouched over the waterfront; smoke drifted up from a massive coal stack set alight by incendiary bombs (it was still smouldering two years later); low shanty dwellings huddled among piles of rubble. 'The Americans have given us the neck of the chicken in this deal', one soldier wrote in his diary. An Army newspaper tried to raise a smile with a sporting reference: 'Australia takes the Ashes'.[6]

Japanese wartime propaganda had ridiculed Australians as 'sons of convicts'.[7] The tattoos sported by many of the disembarking soldiers seemed to confirm the lawless image. Their dowdy uniforms and strange hats also caught the eye. A local reporter quizzed members of a detachment as they headed to quarters:

'What do you know about Japan?'
'Geisha girls. The beer is good, but not the sake.'
'Do you want to go back home soon?'
'Of course.'
In khaki-coloured uniforms, with big hats like Boy Scouts,

carrying automatic weapons and chewing gum, alighting from the train under powder snow, they shivered again, saying 'very cold'.[8]

Troops from India, the United Kingdom and New Zealand made up the rest of BCOF. These contingents were withdrawn in 1947–48, after which the force became virtually an all-Australian affair. Altogether, in excess of 20 000 Australians took part in the occupation, and many of the 17 000 who served during the Korean War and its aftermath also spent time in Japan.[9]

BCOF assumed responsibility for nine, mainly rural, prefectures in the west of the country. The troops performed garrison duties; helped dispose of war materiel; supervised the repatriation of soldiers and civilians from Japan's former colonies and war zones; and intercepted Koreans trying to enter the country illegally. Parades and guard duty took the luckier men to Tokyo, 18 hours away by special train. SCAP retained control over military government functions, reserving for the Americans the most constructive aspect of the occupation. General Horace ('Red Robbie') Robertson, BCOF's Australian commander, boasted (disingenuously) that he 'steadfastly refused' to take responsibility for aiding or feeding the Japanese.[10]

Another way BCOF set itself apart was by adopting a policy of non-fraternisation. While conceding it was impracticable to issue orders for every contingency, the force commander was specific on one point: 'You must not enter [Japanese] homes or take part in their family life'. The troops were told to keep unofficial dealings with the 'conquered enemy' to a minimum. Kure City's official history is being diplomatic when it says exchanges with the new troops were 'not as expansive and cheerful' as they had been with the Americans.[11] Locals soon learned to step off the footpath to let a BCOF serviceman pass, while taking care not to fall under a speeding jeep or truck, which might not bother to stop.

The troops' inferior spending power compared with the Americans was another sore point – on both sides of the counter.

A Melbourne newspaper complained of the situation under the colour-conscious headline, 'U.S. Negro Soldiers Get Higher Pay'. One impecunious private thought that lowly taxi dancers even 'appeared to look down on us'. A war bride corroborates the impression: 'They opened bars and other places to get money from the Australian soldiers; all smiles – "welcome, welcome" – to get their money. But, behind their backs [she pokes out her tongue], they had another face. That's Kure'. The mixed-race daughter of an Australian soldier recalls an anecdote about her father she heard from a shopkeeper: 'The owner always said my father drank a lot – one case of beer – but he was never drunk. And he was very good at calculating. So, before the owner could tally up the amount, he had worked it out in his head'.[12] The compliment, of course, relied on a *standard* image of the men as uneducated drunks.

Recriminations

Reports began reaching Australia of rampant black marketing ('wogging', as it was called), poor amenities and low morale. Newspapers in London and Chicago were pleased to brand the Australians the 'worst behaved' troops in the occupation. Reputations suffered because of the misdeeds of a minority, who included among them some deeply disturbed individuals. An internal report spoke of 'high rates of neuro-psychiatric invaliding' as a result of a lack of medical screening and personal-history checks.[13]

BCOF recorded 3000 cases of venereal disease within five months of arrival. The head of a veterans' organisation claimed the force was 'morally rotting' due to ineffectual leadership and the corrupting influence of 'depraved Asiatic people'. General Robertson ordered a 'heavy culling' of undisciplined troops and tighter enforcement of the non-fraternisation rules.[14]

The punishment for consorting with a Japanese female could be severe: a fine of £5 and 28 days detention, for example. Even if the soldier were let off with a warning, the woman was likely to be arrested and forced to undergo a gynaecological examination. An Australian doctor has described the procedure:

> The patient had to struggle on to the high cast-iron table, place her legs into stirrups on each side of the table and then put her buttocks over the end of the split table. When she lay down her legs were held widely apart by the stirrups on each side of the bed. She was naked except for her *yukata* [thin cotton gown] pulled up to her waist.[15]

During the examination, she was likely to have to put up with an audience of male MPs and Japanese police.

Kure and its surrounds were dangerous places at night, especially for young women. Teruko Blair was 20 when the Hiroshima bomb blasted her out of the family home. Against her father's wishes, she went to work as a waitress in a BCOF officers' mess. Tiny, even by Japanese standards, she would come to need all her considerable vivacity and courage.

One weekend, Teruko was invited to sing at an out-of-town dance party. Precious potatoes would be distributed afterwards, so she set off, carrying her kimono in her backpack.

> After the show, I changed and was the last to get to the potatoes. I was always slow on those things. Anyway, when it came time to get back to Kure, there was no transport. So two Japanese men said they'd walk back with me. It was dark now. There was a moon. As we went along the road, a group of Indian soldiers – maybe five of them – came up. 'Cigarettes, cigarettes?' Offering them. We said 'No, thank you' and walked on.
>
> A little later, the same group of Indians approached again, and this time it wasn't for cigarettes. They had knives. They held the knives at my companions and forced them into a cave. They

threw me over the guardrail beside the road. I still had on my backpack, full of potatoes. I was knocked out.

But I was lucky; a guardian angel was watching over me. The road ran above the town where the base was. The cool breeze from below blew up under my dress and I woke up. One of the Indians was holding my shoulders. Another was standing by, his arms folded, on guard. Another was trying to get my panties down. But, you see, in those days, elastic was hard to come by, and my panties were tied with a cord. The stupid Indian couldn't work out why they wouldn't come down. And I struggled, kicking my legs – I still had all those potatoes on my back – and I screamed as loud as I could. And, you know, they ran away, tearing off down the hill towards the camp, all of them.[16]

Three hundred cases of rape were reported to Hiroshima prefectural police in 1946 alone.[17] JCOSA chose to withhold information on serious crimes from the Australian public. Prosecutions often did not proceed because victims were too ashamed or frightened to bear witness. It was also not unusual for convictions to be quashed or penalties reduced, on review. Teruko Blair's ordeal was hardly exceptional – apart from her lucky escape.

Stand-off

After years of bombardment and shortages, Japan looked a primitive place. An Australian parliamentarian who visited compared it to 'what England was, say, in the sixteenth century'. Occupation troops readily associated material backwardness with racial inferiority. The sight of women performing heavy manual labour, supervised by men, seemed to confirm the Japanese were uncivilised. John Loughlin told readers of the Melbourne *Argus*, 'no public conscience exists in Japan in regard to the degraded status of women'. George Caiger commented in the *Sydney Morning Herald*: 'Even the bad behaviour of democrats is better than the normal behaviour of Japanese men to Japanese women'. He dismissed any possibility of Australian soldiers forming serious relationships. 'After the initial attraction of strangeness, a man with an outlook of his own will find that robots, with pleasant manners, but no personality, are dull company'.[18]

The first to cast doubt on this reassuring theory was Dorothy Drain, correspondent for the *Australian Women's Weekly*. Drain could see for herself the troops were finding their own company duller than any woman's. 'Jap housegirls, interpreters, clerks, and stenographers seem attractive to me', she alerted readers in May 1946.[19] On the surface, however, the proprieties were being observed, as a reporter for *Pacific Stars and Stripes* comically confirmed:

> The visitor never sees a British soldier in the area strolling a village street with a Japanese girl, in contrast to the frequent sight of the GI walking his girl friend home in the American zone.
>
> In the British area, in the spring the young man's fancy is lightly turned to thoughts of cricket.[20]

Before being granted leave in American-controlled Tokyo, BCOF's cricket-fanciers were lectured on the perils of mixing their 'good English blood with the blood of inferior races'.[21] Though most laughed off the solemn warnings, the spectacle of GIs consorting uninhibitedly with Japanese girls caused genuine surprise.

By June 1947, General Robertson felt it was time to fall more into line with the Americans and sought approval from JCOSA for 'gradual reductions' in the non-fraternisation policy. While the request was pending, tensions and animosities brewing within BCOF erupted into violence one hot and sultry night. An argument between Australian and Indian soldiers over a female companion escalated into a riot in which one Indian soldier was shot dead and several others were wounded. On receiving the findings of the secret inquiry into the 'Battle of Hiro', the BCOF commander withdrew his request.[22]

The occupation tested racial tolerance on many fronts: between Australians and Indians, white and black GIs, foreigner and Japanese. When the popular cartoon strip 'Bluey and Curley' took its knockabout characters to Japan in 1948, the fraternisation issue loomed large. In one episode, Curley is shown gazing at kimono-clad women in the street: 'Gosh! There's no doubt about it, some of those Nip sheilas seem to look whiter every day!' In the next frame, he discovers an African-American GI (drawn with a huge, phallic, cigar in his mouth) doing the same: 'Boy, doze lil Nip gals sure seems to look blacker ebery day!'[23] The joke could be that race and colour are ludicrously relative, except the cartoon also suggests a Japanese female is capable of fitting herself to the eye of any beholder. Caveat emptor.

To lower the risk of temptation, hundreds of Australian wives were allowed to join their servicemen husbands from 1947. An orientation manual, *BCOF Bound*, advised them to prepare for 'a primitive country populated by primitive people'. Kure was all shabbiness, grime and disease. In case that should evoke sympathy, the wives were reminded how a Japanese could change overnight into 'a sadistic monkey, delighting in the torture and murder of helpless people'.[24]

The families moved into a residential enclave, built and paid for by the Japanese, called 'Rainbow Village'. Each new Western-style home was equipped with modern furniture, an electric stove, refrigerator, telephone, vacuum cleaner, steam heating and flush toilet – plus three servants per family. There were dedicated schools, shops, parks and sporting facilities. Visiting repertory companies entertained residents with shows such as 'Hasty Heart' and 'Male Animal', BCOF radio stations relayed descriptions of horseracing and football games from Australia, and families worshipped together at BCOF churches.[25]

White, middle-class domesticity was cultivated inside a walled garden – much like the hygienic vegetables grown for the troops without the addition of indigenous (human) fertiliser. The theme constantly reinforced was that nothing safe or wholesome could be supplied locally. Few individuals took the time to study the language or inform themselves about the country they were living in. This included never learning to pronounce the name of the place: it was KOO-REE or CUE-RAY, instead of the correct KOO-RAY.

Getting to know you

Mutual disdain, however, was by no means universal. The 'larrikin' theme in Australian oral history tends to drown out other voices, and this has been true, too, of occupation memoirs. Some members of BCOF – probably many more than dared show their hand – found the people and the place capable of unexpected charms.

When a camp caught fire, during the first winter of the occupation, the biggest surprise was seeing townspeople rush in to douse the flames and assist the injured. Servicemen learned they could wander the loneliest byways in safety and expect hospitality from the poorest villager. They noticed other things. How children shared any extra food they received; labourers toiled diligently, unsupervised; mothers consoled, rather than scolded, their restless infants; and nudity was unencumbered by embarrassment or immorality. The natural beauty of the countryside, away from bomb-scarred Kure, had similar power to enchant. Many, such as 19-year-old Brian Drover, struggled with mixed feelings of bewilderment and delight: 'To me it was like being on the moon. I couldn't believe that such a place existed'.[26]

One moonscape, in particular, left a profound impression. Former POW Kenneth Harrison was an early visitor to Hiroshima:

We are told that even at Passchendaele the birds still twittered and sang above the shellfire, and that when the artillery barrage in Flanders ceased, men were amazed to hear nightingales. But here at Hiroshima there was only silence. There was no traffic; no trees rustled, no insect chirped, no bird sang. Footsteps were muffled by the ashes, and even the wind found nothing to sigh against.[27]

For Harrison and his companions, 'our hatred of the Japanese was swept away by the enormity of what we had seen'.

Relationships forged with Japanese workmates – whether defusing an unexploded bomb or sharing the hectic routines of a mess kitchen – introduced a richer dimension to the experience. BCOF was paymaster to about 40 000 local employees at one stage, including many female telephonists, typists, interpreters, waitresses and cleaners. Sergeant Tom Hungerford arrived in Japan full of hatred: 'I thought, "I'll give these people bloody curry"'. What he saw changed his thinking: 'I looked down and saw girls, nice rosy cheeks – nothing sexual about it – just nice-looking people, and old mamas waving to us, and I thought, "These aren't murderers"'.[28]

House girls (cleaners and attendants) enjoyed the closest contact with the troops. In the recollections of BCOF veterans, they fall somewhere between surrogate mothers and manipulative pleasure-givers. It was a test of character for men thrust into the unfamiliar position of giving, rather than just taking, orders. Lieutenant Frank Mulhall served as a provost officer with BCOF:

> You take an average bloke off the street, put a uniform on him, send him to Japan and all of a sudden he's a king. For the green recruits, it was great because they were robbing Nips blind: standing over them, having the good life.
>
> But a Japanese wife, pardon me for saying, leaves an Australian wife for dead. You're sitting, thinking, 'I wouldn't mind a cup of tea', and the next minute there's a cup. Absolutely marvellous. They seem to have the ability to think ahead of you and cater to you in such a way.[29]

Little wonder some veterans would forever nurture sweet dreams of their Japanese adventure.

6

Remaking Japanese women

Japanese women were said to have emerged from the war with their authority enhanced by attending to the needs of their families and not succumbing to militarism. Although only partly true (there were plenty of female patriots), this theme turned American press coverage of the occupation on its head. In the *New York Times*, the Kluckhohn line – that the country's willpower and organisation were 'not even dented' – gave way to the upbeat reporting of Lindesay Parrott, who saw change affecting 'the whole Japanese structure'. 'The Japanese woman', Parrott noted, 'never was either such a fool or such a chattel as some have represented her to be'.[1]

While women gained the vote and could now play a role in government, in other ways their lives became harder, not easier. Three million lost jobs to make way for men returning from war service. Their main economic contribution, in the immediate future, would be as unsalaried scroungers and fraternisers. Appealing for public understanding, the Christian politician Kōzō Abe wrote: 'Essentially, there is nothing that separates Japanese Maria Magdalenes [virtuous prostitutes] from women in households who are carrying heavy rucksacks in crowded trains … or working hard every day and night to shore up the family budget'. Abe considered any distinction between prostitute and war victim 'relative, not absolute'.[2]

More inclined to think in terms of absolutes, SCAP botched an important reform. The main effect of banning licensed prostitution, in January 1946, was to change the way sex was sold and weaken its regulation. In place of licensed quarters, red-light districts with 'special cafés' sprang up. After the RAA's comfort facilities were declared off-limits, some employees stayed to cater for Japanese customers, while others moved to street corners and short-stay inns. In consequence, rates of venereal disease soared among American troops – to 50 per cent in some units by mid-1946. Outrage in Congress forced the Eighth Army commander, General Robert Eichelberger, to issue an order prohibiting 'public displays of affection' by troops with Japanese girls. Henceforth, such behaviour would be regarded as disorderly conduct and offenders taken to the stockade.[3]

'Off-limits' signs began popping up wherever troops were stationed, and MPs and Japanese police launched a campaign of hauling young women off the streets for compulsory medical checks. Venereal disease served as a marker to distinguish one kind of Japanese female from another (whereas, for the serviceman, penicillin blurred any moral distinction). Innocent passers-by, with no prior sexual experience, were snared in the round-ups; for them, the trauma of arrest and examination was akin to rape or loss of virginity. These measures, according to one SCAP insider, 'defaced the image of a friendly America' and undid much of the good work of the occupation.[4]

During a four-month period, 2400 women were held for screening at one Tokyo hospital alone. A reporter with the *Tokyo Shimbun* witnessed a war widow begging to be let out so she could spend the night with her children:

'After selling everything, even the furniture, what is there left to sell? I receive a [government] allowance of ¥300 a month, but with three children, what can I do? My eldest tried to stop me, grabbing my sleeve, saying, "It's bad for Daddy". I shook [him or her] off and left the house. People talk about "women of the dark", or "night women". If so, I would like to say: Please return my husband.'[5]

Another danger faced by women who associated with foreign soldiers had been apparent since early in the occupation. On Christmas Eve 1945, a young lieutenant recorded an incident that occurred near his lodgings in Tokyo:

> Three enlisted soldiers walked slowly in, supporting a young Japanese woman by the arms. She had on a green kimono and a *haori* [top gown] of rich red. She seemed about four and a half feet tall and might have been pretty. But she was in terrible agony; her face was twisted with pain.[6]

The soldiers explained that a 'son of a bitch' had come up behind them in the street, struck a low blow to the girl and run off.

Attacks increased in frequency during 1946. According to the *New York Times*, most violent clashes between troops and locals concerned fraternisation. An unknown number of *panpan* streetwalkers – some claimed 'hundreds' (surely an inflated figure) – were killed by vengeful Japanese.[7]

A silent malediction

Japanese men realised that women stood to gain most from the war defeat. Even those who welcomed greater equality of the sexes could not help resenting the ease with which females seemed to enter the post-war milieu from which they felt excluded. The enemy was beating them again, in manners and dress, with dollars and sex appeal.

Fraternising women advertised the shame of surrender and insulted the war dead. Worse still, their sexual freedom threatened the nation's racial integrity. The writer Jun Takami noted the 'clever' remark of a friend: 'Regarding these ugly Japanese women, it's not ignorance, I think, but something in their blood. Whatever you say, Japanese are originally a crossbreed, and the mixed-blood seeks out contact with foreigners'.[8]

Bitterness welled up. Women, it was said, luxuriated 'in the swimming pools of Americanism' or were 'sucked into the mud' of occupation-soaked Japan. One male critic half-joked that they seemed to acquire plumper and shapelier bodies through interracial contact: 'I have asked doctors if this is the result of blood exchange with "tall men in small cars [jeeps]"'.[9]

Jun Ishikawa, the first writer to depict a *panpan* character in fiction, referred to a 'silent malediction' that attached to anyone or anything substituting for the genuine Japanese article, whether demure womanhood or white rice: 'To want something else – be it bread, cake, or doughnuts – is to violate an unspoken taboo. Yes, there is a silent malediction that puts a curse on anything seeking to take its place'.[10] In the eyes of society, *konketsuji* were the end product of a transformative process that *began* when a woman showed a preference for something un-Japanese.

The most conspicuous agents of this betrayal were the *panpan* who chose foreign customers and showed no shame. The mother of a mixed-race child (writing at the end of the occupation) protested at the way anyone in her situation was stigmatised, regardless of the circumstances:

> People in society treat mothers of *konketsuji* the same as *panpan*. But most mothers of *konketsuji* I know are good-natured, and were inexperienced in the ways of the world. People never try to understand the misery of girls who produced babies, dreaming of official marriage in the future, while abandoned by their families and despised by society.
>
> I don't deny ignorant girls were imprudent, lured by soldiers' abundant material goods and white skin. But we were not alone among the servile and defeated who believed all American soldiers were superior to Japanese and adored them.
>
> I wonder if the country's leaders did not teach us this uncritical idolisation of Americans. Why can't [people] blame

Japanese leaders and shameless men, before blaming ignorant us?[11]

The identity assigned to fraternising women shifted like a pattern in a kaleidoscope. The iconic *panpan* was a 'witch', in slinky gown and fire-engine-red lipstick, posing with her Lucky Strike cigarette and aggressively propositioning passers-by.[12] With a turn of the kaleidoscope, she became a tawdry 'clown', with wooden beads around her neck and lines painted on bare legs to simulate stockings. Another turn, and she was the so-called *onrī* (short for *onrī wan*, from the English 'only one'), kept by a single patron in lodgings, food and clothing, with or without hope of marriage. It took just one more turn of the kaleidoscope to include any girl seen strolling alongside a foreigner.

And yet, behind the public's scorn, lay the realisation that, 'thanks to the *panpan*, our daughters are safe'. She was a quixotic indicator of both national decline and survival, simultaneously evoking disdain and fascination. By absorbing foreign impurities, *panpan* performed a role analogous to the sub-caste Japanese of feudal times (now referred to as *burakumin*), who were tasked with slaughtering animals and executing criminals. It explains why they were sometimes contrasted with ordinary Japanese in quasi-racial terms. Prostitutes who kept to their own kind were 'victims of circumstance', whereas those who preferred Westerners were assumed to have character failings (vanity, weak self-control) and low intelligence. *Panpan* became un-Japanese – even anti-Japanese – by wearing colourful clothes and acquiring a foreigner's strange temperament; they failed to be angry 'at what should make them angry' and exhibited 'explosive, momentary emotions'.[13]

A prolific writer on the subject, journalist and government adviser Kiyoshi Kanzaki directed his sharpest attacks at better-educated, middle-class women who worked for the occupation or whose families did business with the Americans: 'Women of these strata drank the cocktail of romantic love and prostitution, were kept as *onrī* and gave birth to *konketsuji*, were abandoned and descended to *batafurai* ['butterflies', or women who flitted between relationships]'.[14] Kanzaki credited *panpan* with having enough sense to avoid giving birth. He was correct, on this point at least, even though the broader public believed the opposite.

Japanese linked *konketsuji* with *panpan* because the one *prefigured* the other: streetwalkers transformed themselves through contact with foreigners, just as mixed-race children transformed the gene pool. 'Who made me such a woman?' went the lyric of a popular song. While the question seemed to require a political or sociological explanation, it also invited another kind of answer, as suggested by the comment of a (fictional) former RAA employee: 'Gradually it seems I have become a woman whose body cannot serve only one man. I wonder whether the blood of various men soaking into my body naturally made me this way'.[15]

Love, possibly

Japanese politicians spent more time arguing over the introduction of a new civil code than they did debating the revolutionary pacifist clause in their American-made constitution. Against conservative objections, SCAP pushed through changes that struck at the heart of the male-dominated social order. These redefined marriage as a condition requiring no more than 'the mutual consent of both sexes' and made the individual, rather than the patrilineal household (*ie*), the basic unit of society.[16]

Whereas anything to do with the military had lost all credibility with the Japanese, on the subject of marriage, at least, 'old patterns' of thinking persisted.[17] Even younger people, who wanted more say in the matter, seldom insisted that their choice of spouse should be based on love alone. The word for 'love' in Japanese, *ai*, covers a wide range of meanings. Another word, *koi*, is used exclusively for romantic love, as in the phrase '*koi o suru*' (to fall in love). The stoicism of women, faced with the sudden departure of their soldier-lovers, reflected a cultural perspective on romance as something to be cherished while it lasted but then forfeited with dignity.

Marriage was a pact between families, which required neither civil nor religious sanction and did not presume to confine the sexual appetite. Until the start of the 20th century, premarital cohabitation had been common, especially in rural areas, and divorce rates high. Only after the modern state began harnessing the family unit to its nation-building objectives did these patterns change. Births outside marriage halved by 1940. The trend went into reverse again during the occupation, partly because the older, more relaxed, view about cohabitation seemed better suited to uncertain times.

Women took up with foreign soldiers for many reasons, the most obvious one being access to material benefits. A GI or Australian boyfriend could easily feed an extended family from his rations and black-market earnings. There was also the lure of an easier life. The daily routine of a Japanese farmer's wife, for example, consisted of eight hours labour in the fields, plus six hours keeping house.

But money and comfort were not everything. Japanese women significantly outnumbered men after the war, causing some to believe they might never have a chance to marry. Underfed and dishevelled Japanese males appeared drab and gloomy in comparison with well-groomed and attentive occupation soldiers. Girls living without parents, due to death or family dislocation, were less constrained from entering an unconventional relationship. For those still at home, dating a Westerner represented a 'democratic' form of rebellion.

A craving for romance undoubtedly led some to misjudge the intentions of their foreign boyfriends. Being trained to serve, the Japanese female supposedly was more easily drawn into an unforeseen commitment. There was, however, another role model for this generation, less often identified by commentators. She was the war widow, who showed independence and determination by choosing to bear a child even though she knew her husband was unlikely to return from the front.

As the personal accounts in this book suggest, it was not uncommon for mothers of *konketsuji* to come from unhappy or broken homes. Some were struggling to readjust to society after returning from one of Japan's lost colonies. In other cases, a feeling of affinity with the outside world – perhaps from having relatives living abroad – led them into a relationship that offered to satisfy their dream. War and occupation uprooted people, and Japanese tended to associate rootlessness with Western culture. The urge to experiment could spring from something as intangible as this.

In the final analysis, these women should not to be equated with the Madame Butterfly courtesans of an earlier era – for whom love and procreation were possible but unlooked for. They were closer, in spirit, to the de facto spouse who rejected her family's plan for an arranged marriage or the self-reliant war widow who accepted the challenge of being a single parent. It was a big step to break with tradition and bind one's future to a Westerner. The choice may be compared to the decision of a Japanese woman today not to marry at all.

GI brides

As early as December 1945, Congress granted European former enemy nationals right of entry to the United States as war brides, outside immigration quotas. Japanese continued to be excluded. This set the parameters for SCAP's policy on marriage: if the prospective spouse was not eligible to enter the United States, permission to marry was refused. GI babies were rendered illegitimate, and subject to the assumption they would stay in Japan, based on their mothers' race. Pregnancy was excluded from the 'unusual circumstances' under which an exception might be granted.[18]

The policy was unpopular among the troops because it infringed on a basic liberty. During a visit to Japan in May 1947, the director of the American Civil Liberties Union, Roger Baldwin, was told of the tragic effects on 'hundreds of girls' who were having abortions. Baldwin complained to SCAP and went public on his return home: 'Over 40 servicemen and civilians in Tokyo alone put up to me pathetic cases of babies and pregnant would-be wives for whom the fathers under the regulations can make no provision whatever'.[19]

Reported rates of infanticide and infant abandonment in Japan were nearly three times higher than a decade before. Abortion was illegal at the time of Baldwin's visit, but women who could raise the money had little difficulty procuring one (some were performed by veterinarians). After the law was changed, a year later, terminations soared – in effect, putting a cap on the number of mixed-race children being born. In 1950, occupied Germany recorded four times as many births to unwed mothers, per capita, as did Japan. It is reasonable to assume most women giving birth to *konketsuji* were willing mothers, who either anticipated marrying the father or had given up hope of marrying one of their own countrymen.[20]

Unable to marry any other way, couples sought out unofficial witnesses. Harold Williams, a long-time resident of Japan (who served in Australian military intelligence between 1941 and 1949) has written disparagingly of these arrangements:

> There were a number of second-rate teahouses that specialised
> in arranging secret Shinto wedding services for the soldiers, and
> in those establishments it was generally the kitchen-boy who
> hastily donned Shinto robes over the top of his kitchen clothes
> and assuming the guise of a Shinto priest mumbled a few inane
> prayers at what was represented to be a legal and valid marriage
> ceremony.[21]

In 1947, Congress revised the Soldier Brides Act to include Japan. The amendment did not necessarily reflect a more liberal attitude to interracial marriage. Its declared purpose was to correct an anomaly that denied Japanese-American veterans a privilege granted to others, like them, who did all their fighting in Europe. Before the amendment could pass, a sunset clause was attached by the Senate – where miscegenation fears remained strong – limiting its effect to 30 days. What previously had been impossible, with due care, now became possible, with indecent haste.

Couples began queuing outside the US consulate in Yokohama at 7 am, until the line stretched into the street. Among the early birds were a former Army lieutenant, Frank White, and his fiancée, Pia Kurusu. Pia's mother, Alice Jay Little, was a clergyman's daughter from New York. The bride's father was the former senior diplomat, Saburō Kurusu, who infamously delivered Japan's final warning to Washington, an hour *after* the surprise attack on Pearl Harbor. The Kurusus' son, a fighter pilot, died defending his father's country; their two daughters both married Americans.[22]

To make it this far, numerous permissions and proofs needed to be obtained, including (for the bride only) a medical certificate, a police clearance and a copy of her household register. There was a moment of comic relief for one hard-pressed consular official, searching through the paperwork of a burly sergeant and his diminutive partner. 'Have you seen her *koseki*?' he asked the soldier. 'Oh no', came the reply, 'I ain't seen nuthin yet'.[23]

Only the groom was required to attest during the five-minute marriage service. But even this was too much for one heavily pregnant bride, who went into labour and had to be rushed to hospital. The Yokohama consulate processed the last couple towards midnight on the final day. The man was congratulated, before being led away by MPs under arrest for speeding on the way there.

More than 820 couples beat the 30-day deadline. Three-quarters of the men were *Nisei* (second generation, foreign-born Japanese). Unsuccessful applicants included residents of American states with laws that prohibited marriages between whites and

Japanese. A former naval officer wired a personal appeal to the Governor of Montana seeking an exemption – without success.[24]

Once the amendment to the Soldier Brides Act lapsed, permission to marry required special dispensation or a private bill sponsored through Congress. The door was opened again in August 1950 and, thereafter, stood ajar for most of the time until a new immigration law was enacted two years later. Between 1947 and 1952, around 11 000 American citizens registered marriages to Japanese, and more than 2000 mixed-race children left for the United States with their parents.[25]

In their choice of marriage partner, the brides showed no obvious colour prejudice: the proportion of African-American husbands was about equal to their representation in the occupation force. (This tends to be overlooked by writers who dwell on the Japanese infatuation with white skin.)

Many more couples exchanged vows, according to Shinto or Christian rites, than ever succeeded in registering their marriage. The rigmarole SCAP superimposed on an otherwise straightforward Japanese procedure could take anything from a couple of months to a couple of years. The dropout rate was high. Hundreds, if not thousands, of relationships foundered because of the Korean War. Overseas deployments split up couples, and the death of a soldier brought a halt to any pending application for his widow's entry to the United States. Unregistered children had no claim on American citizenship. The widow might be lucky enough to receive her husband's back pay, on compassionate grounds, before the case was closed.

The person in his thoughts

The first wave of occupation troops arrived in Japan in a state of war-induced restlessness. Habituated to making and breaking camp, they lived for the moment, without reflection, impermanence their only certainty. Life's journey might seem of no more account than a set of initials scratched above the bunk on a troop ship, destined to disappear under the next coat of paint. It came as a rude shock to discover this latest adventure could leave something meaningful in its wake.

Tom Hungerford's BCOF novel *Sowers of the Wind* (written in 1949 but withheld for five years by a timid publisher) is a scarifying tale of men without a cause. Amid their scamming, fighting and whoring, the only things holding them together are their common hatred of the officer class and their view of the occupation as an ephemeral experience.

When the book's central character, Sergeant Rod McNaughton, rescues a girl (Fumie) from the clutches of a dance-hall tout and sets up house with her in the hills, the serpent in the garden of their pastoral idyll – hinted at in the book's title – is miscegenation. McNaughton resents his mates' frequent warnings not to end up with 'a half-caste bastard tagging along behind'. He is determined not to be one of those men who fathers a child and then fobs off the mother with a handful of yen: "'Fumie had ideas of having a kid, she said she wanted it for when I go home. I went crook at her and she dropped the matter. There's no fear of that ...'".

Notwithstanding his affection for his live-in girlfriend, the soldier sails away from Kure confident he is leaving free of obligations. The wind blows back in his face when an old enemy tells him Fumie is pregnant: 'He saw his son dragging a toy boat in an open Kure sewer, sucking a bit of boiled sweet-potato. Or his daughter married to an ape ... beaten, starved, living and dying in the filth of a Jap fisherman's bed – maybe, if she were lucky, in a brothel'.[26]

The occupation is no longer just another billet to be left and forgotten; the comfort of impermanence has been shattered. McNaughton's vision of mixed-blood misery – with its closed cycle of dirt, poverty and prejudice – serves to condemn him, while, at the same time, distancing him from the object of his regret. The old refrain about Japan being unchanged and unchangeable can be understood to carry an implicit warning against miscegenation.

In Australian accounts of the occupation, without exception, the mixed-race child is an object of horror or pity. Hal Porter has written extravagantly of '*ainoko* (half caste) bastard toddlers [who] lived in alley gutters, and dined from the rubbish-tins'.[27] Joan Haigh, a YMCA organiser, made the following diary entry in September 1947 after visiting a Christian orphanage in Beppu, a hot-spring resort frequented by BCOF troops. In the babies' section, most of the infants were mixed-bloods:

> A number of them were entirely Western in appearance. The nun would say in broken English as we approached the various cots 'Australian baby' or 'American baby' as the case may be. A Japanese nun down on a mat with several babies was holding a ten months old American lad. He was a bull headed Yank if ever there was one and I had to smile when the nun tried to bend him in the middle to make him bow to us in the usual Japanese style. Every inch of Uncle Sam in him rebelled!
>
> … The babies have such thin, poor little arms and yet when we bent over each cot, they would smile and gurgle, all these poor little half-breeds. Life holds very little for a Japanese baby in a Japanese orphanage but to be an Occupation baby must be the lowest rung on the ladder, as nobody wants them: a subject that is taboo in the land of their fathers. Those of us who experienced this visit will never feel quite the same again.[28]

BCOF took an approach to interracial marriage similar to the Americans but prosecuted it more ruthlessly and for longer. An administrative instruction of September 1946 stated that, 'under no circumstances will approval be given for a marriage between a member of BCOF and a Japanese national'. A soldier who defied the ban risked being taken into custody and put on the next boat home. One BCOF veteran recalls seeing a serviceman being led aboard ship in chains: '[His] Japanese wife ... stood motionless on Kure wharf, watching the ship slowly moving, taking her husband away. She made a deep bow ...'. These draconian measures drove some to suicide.[29]

The Japanese authorities were under orders not to register any marriage that involved a member of BCOF. Australian correspondents cultivated the impression such liaisons were both unholy and unlawful. Jack Percival described the 'first' American-Japanese marriage as a 'commercial arrangement'. (Associated Press, on the other hand, called it a love match.) George Caiger, recently returned from BCOF, wrote of women who were 'world champions at inflating men's egos', and soldiers, so disoriented they made 'pets of stray dogs and cats which they would not look at under normal circumstances'.[30]

Commanders felt they had a responsibility to protect young and inexperienced men from themselves. With some exceptions, officers presumed interracial unions were venal, foolish and futile. The deracination of family life proceeded along various lines. Frequent and unannounced VD checks on women who worked for BCOF reminded everyone they were not ordinary employees. Japanese homes were stripped of the normal associations of domestic safety and legitimacy by constant references to them as firetraps and seats of disease. Finally, couples were said to have debased the institution of marriage by turning it into a financial arrangement and submitting to the 'mock' religion of Japanese militarism, Shinto.[31]

Not all *konketsuji*, of course, were conceived with the consent of the mother. The cruelest aspect of any military occupation is the taking of human 'spoils of conquest'. It is a part of the BCOF story many veterans would rather was not told.[32]

7

Mayumi's story

The Kosugis were relatively prosperous before the war. They owned their own house and several parcels of land overlooking the ship-yards at Kure. They watched as the city below burned, during the air raids of summer 1945, relieved to be spared the destruction. Their eldest daughter was already married, and their son was embarked on a solid professional career by the time the occupation began. Only 19-year-old Hisako remained at home.

What happened to Hisako is unclear. Was it true she was seen hanging around with foreign soldiers at Naka-dōri, a notorious strip of bars and pick-up joints? Was she sexually assaulted, as a social worker stated many years afterwards? Was the man, in fact, an Australian? Her mixed-race daughter, Mayumi, realises the answers to these questions lie buried forever.

> My mother always said, 'I don't know your father' and 'You are *ainoko*'. That's the way she put it. I guess it was a casual relationship; a bad expression, but I guess it may have been the case. My auntie told me: 'You don't have a father. Your mother did a stupid thing'. She was always saying these two things. Somehow I felt it was wrong to ask why.
>
> Much later, after I grew up, I learned that many Japanese women were involved with the occupation army, working as maids or making friends with customers who came for drinks at Naka-dōri. In a proper way, some went to live in the men's

country; some went after waiting a long time. On the other hand, some women were raped. That's as much as I know.

Hisako gave birth in December 1948. She never recovered from the ordeal and spent the rest of her life in a cloud of mental illness. Her elder sister, now divorced, moved back to the family home and adopted her mixed-race niece.

Mayumi grew up in an all-female household: 'Not a whiff of a male', as she puts it. Her grandmother was the mainstay, holding things together. When the idea arose, at one point, of sending the child for adoption overseas, she ruled it out.

> I learned life was not easy. There were not a lot of visitors. There were people who spoke ill of us. But we had land, a grass field, a well, a vegetable patch that I weeded, a shed and a goat. I drank goat's milk! They would wake me early in the morning, and I'd help my grandma make straw sandals. My job was to beat and tenderise and stretch the straw rope. When it became time, I'd go to school.
>
> My grandma earned money teaching flower arrangement. We also had a handcart, and we would go around the streets picking up metal rubbish, which fetched good prices in those days. We made our living that way. Yes, keeping the four of us was very hard, I remember. I could not afford to have new clothes very often or go on outings.

As a little girl, Mayumi played happily with the neighbourhood children; the fact she looked different caused her no great anguish. It was when she reached school age that the bullying and discrimination began.

> I was the only mixed-blood child at my school. I was called *ainoko*, *harō-no-ko* [child of 'hello'] and *gaijin* [foreigner]. I hated

these names – even though they were factual. When I was small, walking in the street by myself, if three or four children were walking towards me (adults stared without a second thought) they would pass quietly and nonchalantly. But I imagined they were looking back at me, and when I turned around I always found them staring hard at me. In the case of adults, I could hear them whispering: 'There's that child' or 'That child looks like a *gaijin*'.

At primary school, on occasions when we were told to form in groups of two or three, someone was always left over. I was that person. Pupils still needing to make a pair always looked reluctant to match up with me. Nowadays, I hear they don't do this sort of thing at school. It's more considerate. Always being left alone, I didn't have a proper chance to learn to be sociable.

Mayumi grew tall and slim, with a peaches-and-cream complexion. She felt closest to her grandmother and also got on well with her aunt. On the other hand, when her natural mother turned up at school events, acting oddly, Mayumi felt embarrassed. She struggled against this awkwardness and hated herself for it. She did not understand about schizophrenia.

As property-holders, the Kosugis were not eligible for livelihood assistance, even though city officials rated them 'borderline poor'.[1] The teenager's life took a decided turn for the better after ISS began its welfare program in Kure – and not just for financial reasons.

Where I lived, I was the only one who was mixed-blood. Going to ISS for the first time, I found lots of children like me. I was surprised and a little relieved. Being there made me feel emotionally calmer. I remember this very well. The first occasion [in 1960] was a Christmas camp at Iwakuni [the site of an American military base, in Hiroshima prefecture]. I got a radio as a Christmas present. It was the kind that ran on AC power. My grandma got annoyed with me for listening to it at home, saying it wasted electricity. I felt so sad. [Laughs.]

Until now, Mayumi had taken for granted she had no father. But toys, clothes, school supplies and food donated from Australia invited forbidden thoughts. 'I forced myself to think: "These are possibly from my father". Although it was impossible – I had no hope of finding him. But, to tell you the truth, there were Cinderella moments when I imagined I might see him.'

Following her grandmother's death in 1962, life at home became more difficult. Her mother was admitted to a mental hospital, and her aunt found it hard holding down a job. Bit by bit, the family land was sold off to pay for daily necessities.

During her early teens, Mayumi often felt depressed. The social worker Yone Itō encouraged her: 'She told me, "You have the blood of two races running in you; so you have more potential than others". That helped a lot'. After her aunt began showing signs of mental illness, Mayumi shared with Itō her secret dread of going the same way. She was relieved to hear that her foreign blood reduced the risk. She also learned to stand up to the schoolyard bullies, spraying the taunting boys with water from the washstand and raising her fists if they threatened to hit her.

> I wasn't defeated. From about the age of 14, I tried not to take things in a negative way. In Buddhism, there is a word, *zenchishiki* [total knowledge]. The idea is that, whatever happens, you should look on the positive side. You should look for the good in everything. I became very strong.

With financial help, provided through ISS, Mayumi was able to enter a good senior high school in Hiroshima city, attending as a boarder. A caseworker described her as 'a friendly, active girl': a class leader, a diligent scholar and keen on sport. Because of her seniority, as well as her personality, she naturally assumed a leadership role among the Kure Kids. Group activities bound them together and provided a sense of identity.

In October 1964, following the Tokyo Olympics, members of the Australian swimming team visited Kure for a friendly competition, and ISS organised a party. The buffet menu gave everyone a taste of what they were missing: lamb and tomato sandwiches, boiled eggs, and cheese and biscuits. The older children danced 'The Twist' with the swimmers and sang Beatles songs. A travelling journalist described the event:

> And then, Mayumi, 15, a tall girl in school uniform, stood up on the platform and read the speech she had composed:
> 'Welcome to Kure.
> 'We are very glad to see you again. We are proud of you, Olympic swimmers.
> 'We saw you swimming on television. We are very happy to be with you, Olympic swimmers.
> 'We will never forget about the wonderful memory with you tonight.'
> The Australians, in their green blazers, clapped and cheered her. Thank heavens they cheered her, for the noise made it less unbearably wistful.[2]

Mayumi told the reporter she was learning English and wanted to be an interpreter: '"When I was young, I felt uneasy at school. The children called me a bad name. When Australians come, I feel very happy. I would like to visit Australia, but I do not know if I would be happy to live there"'.

The children understood the main purpose of such media coverage was to trace missing fathers. Occasionally, Mayumi saw contacts renewed and friends leave for overseas, after mothers remarried or adoptions went through. She realised it was not going to happen to her. Denying herself that hope became a drill, a discipline: '[In English] No. [Laughs.] [In Japanese] I didn't. [Laughs.] Never. I didn't expect. [Emphatically] I didn't expect at all. [Quieter] I didn't expect it at all'.

> When reporters asked me about my father, I had nothing to say. No name, no place of birth, no explanation. I felt sick being asked such questions. There was nothing to tell. Nothing. I sometimes wondered whether I was the one always asked to do the media interviews because there was no possibility of my father being identified and, therefore, no risk of a claim for compensation.

During her final year at school, her aunt joined her mother in hospital. Mayumi converted to a day pupil and returned to Kure to keep an eye on the family's dwindling possessions. She lived alone in a small apartment, struggling to pay the rent. School was a two-hour journey away.

Setting off before dawn one morning, she received a sharp reminder of how terribly exposed and alone she was:

> It was still dark when I headed for the bus station. And as I walked along, somebody started throwing stones at me. 'That child.' But I didn't know who it was. I encountered the same person again, twice more. I recognised him, but no one nearby helped me. Instead they ignored it. That was an awful experience.
>
> People in Japan, when they see something unusual enter society, strongly reject it, I think. Many mixed-blood children like us were bullied. Our faces were totally different from ordinary people. Another reason we were bullied was the fact we were children of men from the victor-country of the war.
>
> Many years later, after I grew up, I came across that person. So I glared at him. [Laughs.] That's how I handled it.

As school graduation approached, Mayumi weighed up which direction she should take. Originally, she had planned to attend university and then possibly study in the United States, but the situation at home seemed to demand she start full-time work to earn some money. Yone Itō, though no longer based in Kure, was still watching out for her protégé. She wrote to the new ISS manager:

> I worry about Kosugi-san's future after she graduates from school. She always tends to stay where she is; she cannot make up her mind … I suggest, if possible, that she scale back her part-time job to give herself time to seriously think about her future. As soon as she reduces her working hours she will suffer financially, which means she will need special assistance. Even if a lot of money has to be spent on her for a while, I think it worthwhile.[3]

Itō told Mayumi her mixed-race origins made it doubly important she pursue her education as far as possible, to obtain a respectable place in society. The girl made up her mind and sat the entrance exam for university. She excelled at her studies, topping the class in English. Her tuition and living expenses continued to be met from charitable funds managed by ISS.

> Actually, I wanted to become a schoolteacher. But, when I did a teachers' internship during university, I realised I couldn't go on with it. I was scared. I thought, 'I can't be a schoolteacher'. I was scared of the high school students; I was scared of their eyes. Those eyes, staring at me, were frightening. Maybe it was because I was *hāfu*, or mixed. There were, you see, about 50 children to a class. I did it for two weeks, but that was as much as I could bear. I immediately dropped my dream.

She was encouraged to sit the civil service exam for a position in Kure City Office. Success would earn kudos for ISS and set an example for the younger children. When the ISS manager urged her to '*Gambatte!*' [Try hard!], she replied, 'I will do my best. But please don't expect anything. I will definitely fail'.[4] Nerves got the better of her, and she fulfilled her prediction.

Job-hunting began in earnest. Every time she filled in an application form, she laid her past open to scrutiny. She knew that the slightest doubt in the mind of a recruiter could mean instant rejection – no explanation required. Applying for a position as a receptionist with a big hotel chain, Mayumi expected the worst. The paperwork went through, she was called for an interview and, to her surprise, was hired.

> I was having a very enjoyable time working at the front counter as a hotel clerk. After a month or two, my boss called me over and said: 'You're a *konketsuji* and your appearance is different from ordinary Japanese. You're also very tall. You are not suitable for a hotel receptionist. It's better you work in the back office, taking bookings and handling administrative tasks'.
>
> I was furious. I told him it was unfair. I was fully aware I might be sacked, but I felt I needed to claim my rights. Three or four of my colleagues stood by me. I wouldn't budge. I protested like a machine gun that day, 'Ga, ga, ga, ga, ga!' I had had plenty of practice standing up for myself. He gave way.
>
> Years later, when he was transferring back to Osaka, at his farewell party, he said to me: 'I was wrong'.

Most of Mayumi's friends were in the ISS group, including a boy she particularly liked. 'He told me: "I will absolutely never marry a woman from ISS. You can imagine what the child would look like! It would have a face totally like 'over there' [foreign]". He did not want his offspring to experience what he had gone through.' Years later, Mayumi was driving in Kure when she noticed a child walking along the street. She pulled over and asked whether he was her friend's son.

'This is the pièce de résistance: the kid looked exactly like his father. And he had wanted his children to have a Japanese face!'

There were two men who were interested in me. But when I met the parents, they took a backward step. The conversation would get around to my mother's situation, and they were not accepting.

I had another friend I had known since I was a university student doing part-time work. He ran a shop and was one of my customers. I told him what had happened when I met those families. He said I wasn't suitable for such men: 'With me, however, you can be happy'. His mother had spent her early years in America, and he had lived in Harbin [in Manchuria] during the war. He was 19 years my senior. We had known each other for 11 years, without thinking of marriage. As things turned out, he was right.

Mayumi married at 29. Having changed employers, she was section head at the new hotel where she worked. Her English ability helped in dealing with foreign guests, and those many painful conversations with visiting journalists had built up her confidence. The demons she wrestled with as a girl were under control.

Her chief motivation in life was to prove herself worthy of the help she had received through the kindness of strangers.

If I were not able to go to high school, if I were not able to go to university, without that advantage, I wonder what sort of job I would have ended up in. And if I did not encounter this good person [my husband], there was a possibility my life could have gone in the direction my stepmother [aunt] always worried it would: the wrong way. I can imagine the negative result. Without help, there may have been no choice. Because I was given a scholarship, I can lead a life nobody can point at with a finger of derision.

I once asked the ISS official whether it was OK just to receive money, without repayment. She said it was all right. I asked how I could show my gratitude. She said if I grew up properly to be a fine person, it would be an expression of my thanks. So I live properly. I have done so. Other Japanese children without fathers were not given the chance I was given to go on to higher education. Unless they had outstanding talent, there was no scholarship for them. From this perspective, I was lucky being mixed-blood. I was given the chance.

8

Mixed-blood mythologies

The first Europeans who ventured into Asia, Africa and the New World, 600 years ago, responded to the exotic peoples they encountered according to what best served their political, commercial and religious interests. Other races were judged by their aesthetic values and material accomplishments: in a word, civilisation. The vicissitudes of life at the frontier were similar for native and newcomer. Primitive man could be admired for his survival techniques or maligned for his cunning; loved for his innocence or ridiculed for his ignorance; extolled as Noble Savage or condemned as heathen. Neither practical nor ideological objections single-mindedly drove the races apart.

In New Spain, a territory that took in large parts of North and South America, mestizos (European-Native Indian mixed-bloods) outnumbered Spaniards by as early as 1650. The many kinds and degrees of race mixing led to a proliferation of *castas*, or categories, that mocked the very idea of race. Certificates of whiteness were available for sale; financial means, more than blood, defined who you were. Trappers and fur traders moving into the vast forests of New France (stretching from present-day Canada to Louisiana) also took up with Indian women, and their offspring formed distinct communities. 'Métis Nation' is today an official category of native Canadian.

While practised less often in England's American colonies, racial intermarriage also helped forge alliances, legitimise land claims and pacify hostile natives. The most famous example is the marriage in 1614 of the Jamestown tobacco farmer, John Rolfe, to the Powhatan chieftain's daughter, Pocahontas. By the time of the Boston Tea Party in 1773, as many as 120 000 people of mixed native and European ancestry were living in the English-speaking colonies.

American independence lent a new rationale to this intermingling. President Thomas Jefferson told a delegation of Indians in 1808: 'Your blood will run in our veins, and will spread with us over this great island'.[1] The melting pot would not, however, let itself be called black: laws, dating back to the 1660s, reinforced slavery's chains by punishing black–white sexual intimacy.

As Portuguese colonists spread into Asia, from the 16th century, the crown issued frequent reminders of the need for tolerance; religious conformity was supposed to rank above skin colour as proof of brotherhood. Although newcomers to Goa and Macao tended to look down upon *les mestiços*, as time went by mixed-bloods met fewer obstacles to social advancement. Similarly, Dutch Eurasians were evaluated according to their parents' status – particularly the father – and some took their place among an emerging colonial elite.

When the English arrived on the scene, they also treated interracial marriage as a progressive step. The East India Company gave a gold coin to each native mother in Madras on the day her part-European child was christened. For more than a century, well-connected men of mixed race could aspire to an officer's baton or a senior civil service position.

Making colour count

Scientists in the 18th century began to classify humankind according to a hierarchy of supposedly innate qualities. The Swedish naturalist Carl Linnaeus characterised Europeans as 'inventive' and Africans as 'indolent'. The German physician Johann Blumenbach described 'five varieties' of man – Caucasian, Mongolian, Ethiopian, American and Malay – and gave precedence to the Caucasian, for 'I … esteem it the primeval one'.[2]

The modern idea of race introduced a new narrative to the subject of race mixing. The French savant Georges-Louis Leclerc, Compte de Buffon placed the ideal of human beauty and truth in the latitudes occupied by Europeans. For Buffon, other races represented varying degrees of degeneration from this white-skinned paragon, through the influence of climate and diet. His concept of degeneration reflected a cultural disapproval of mixed things (the mongrel, *le bâtard*), implying not only aesthetic inferiority but also mental and physical coarsening. He valued race mixing as a means of reversing this process – recovering original features (a whiter skin) – not for giving rise to new types of people.

Some found sexual contact between whites and blacks so appalling, social and moral qualms alone could not suffice to explain its taboo. The Philadelphia-born physician Samuel Morton disputed the established dogma that all humans were part of a single species whose racial variety resulted from environmental factors. Seeking proof to the contrary, Morton gathered examples of species-leaping hybrids (some apocryphal) and emphasised the long persistence of physical differences among the races.

The Scottish anthropologist Robert Knox said nature abhorred racial hybrids: 'When they accidentally appear they soon cease to be, for they are either non-productive, or one or other of the pure breeds speedily predominates, and the weaker disappears'. This was proven, according to another American physician, Josiah Nott, by the mulatto's 'inherent tendency to run out, and become eventually extinct when kept apart from the parent stocks'.[3] The French aristocrat Joseph Arthur de Gobineau, seeking to explain why racially different individuals were sexually attracted to each other, came to the gloomy conclusion that, in order for enlightenment to spread to inferior peoples, the white race (to his mind, the only source of civilisation) had to embrace the cause of its own decline.

Even those who considered race mixing a positive force for change, such as the French anthropologist Armand de Quatrefages, conceded that the half-breed was usually suggestive of 'unrestrained debauchery on one side, and servile submission on the other'.[4] The disorder, randomness and carnality associated with race mixing condemned it – as much as its biological success.

During the 19th century, scientists, social critics and clergy, on both sides of the Atlantic, ratcheted up the rhetoric. Biblical authority, previously invoked to emphasise the unity of mankind, was employed with redirected zeal. Had not the perfection of Eden been forfeited through Original Sin? Was not Babel's confusion of tongues proof of a divine purpose? Around the time of the American Civil War, the theory of polygenesis – which attributed a separate origin to each 'primary' race – claimed more adherents. It ushered in science's heyday of skull measurement and teeth mapping, the statistical apparatus of scientific racism.

During Reconstruction, the distinguished zoologist Louis Agassiz was asked whether emancipated blacks and mulattos could be successfully absorbed into the population. Agassiz (who never forgot his visceral reaction to the black waiters he encountered on first arriving from Switzerland) replied: 'The production of half-breeds is as much a sin against nature, as incest in a civilized community is a sin against purity of character … Far from presenting to me a natural solution of our difficulties … I hold it to be a perversion of every natural sentiment'.[5]

To emphasise that miscegenation destroyed the virility of family, nation and race, Agassiz referred to 'the effeminate progeny of mixed races'.[6] A coloured woman, he said, sought sexual contact with a white male in order to raise her social status; the mixed-race child was 'effeminate', therefore, because only the mother wanted it. Madame Butterfly and her genre companions would come to embody a similar inversion of power.

Half-caste treachery

The imperial male (planter, trader, colonial official, soldier, sailor, misfit) acted out the racial hierarchy carried with him from the metropolis. Most European expatriates in remote outposts were bachelor men. Sexual encounters with local women occurred on unequal terms and in circumstances that were – in fact or by assumption – separated from the usual disciplines of family and domesticity.

Race mixing came to be regarded as subversive. Commentators often pointed to the incendiary role played by mulattos during the 18th-century slave rebellion in St Domingue (now Haiti). French colonial leaders in North America lost faith in intermarriage as a means of control. Governors wrote home complaining about the lazy habits Europeans acquired from their native wives.

The retreat of opinion from the earlier tolerance, even encouragement, of progressive intermarriage mirrored the historical transition from imperialism by the few to colonisation by the many. The 18th-century German philosopher Johann Gottfried von Herder famously pronounced that empire and *Volk* were incompatible because colonists grew physically and mentally weaker, until they lost their pre-eminence or were absorbed by the indigenous population. 'Nothing', he wrote, 'appears so directly opposite to the end of government as the unnatural enlargement of states, the wild mixture of various races and nations under one sceptre'.[7] In Herder's analysis, the resiliency of natives and half-breeds derived from their climatic adaptation – the presumed determinant of race.

Alfred Tennyson's poem 'Locksley Hall' (1842) is a classic expression of the 19th-century view of race mixing as being contrary to the spirit of progress. After briefly imagining himself escaping to an island paradise ('I will take some savage woman, she shall rear my dusky race'), the narrator repudiates the idea of mating 'with a squalid savage' and betraying his inheritance: 'Better fifty years of Europe than a cycle of Cathay'.

The same qualities that the East India Company once valued in Eurasians – language skills and local contacts – now awakened mistrust. A peer of the realm warned in 1809 of the 'accumulating evil' of half-caste children in Bengal. 'In every country where this intermediate cast has been permitted to rise', wrote Viscount Valentia, 'it has ultimately tended to the ruin of that country'.[8] Forcing the fathers to pay for the removal of their illicit offspring to Europe, he suggested, would soon encourage self-restraint.

In the altered climate of opinion, Anglo-Indians were excluded from civil and military posts. While formal barriers were later removed, the better jobs in the colonial administration went to new arrivals from Britain. During a parliamentary inquiry in 1853, Lord Ellenborough, a former governor-general of India, interrupted the evidence of a witness sympathetic to the mixed-bloods: 'Are not the generality of Indo-Britons a class of poor weakly-looking persons, very sallow and unhealthy in their appearance, and very small in stature?' he demanded to know.[9]

Every turn of the complex machinery of colonisation – military service, bureaucracy, trade, education, recreation, marriage – threw up issues of racial contact that needed to be formalised and resolved.

White Australia

On a summer evening in 1890, an earnest young couple, walking arm-in-arm, entered the narrow streets of the Rocks, a bare-knuckled neighbourhood at the port of Sydney. The man was Henry Lawson, son of a Norwegian seaman turned prospector, soon to gain fame for his wry stories of campfire, saloon and slum. His companion, the poet Mary Gilmore, would remember their outings together as a kind of awakening:

He used to take me out to see the wrong things, the things repressive of the rights of Australia; the things like a blot on her and which prevented her being herself – the low wage workers, the Chinaman [*sic*] working at treadle-saws in underground cellars lit only by a grating in the street … and last but not least the mixture of blood and the neglected children by the Quay and elsewhere.[10]

It was a time of economic depression. Industrial conflict was rife, from the waterfront to the shearing shed. Many working people felt thwarted and demoralised – and heeded the call of a race-oriented nationalism. Gilmore wrote of 'this pestilential condition of things with which our civilization is so insufficient to cope'.[11] In her nightmare vision, sweatshops, alien arrivals and blood mixing formed an unholy trinity.

As the 19th century came to a close, a fin-de-siècle anxiety about racial conflict was truly global. Influential voices spread the idea that when different races came together there were only two possibilities: degeneracy or war. Charles H Pearson, in his widely read *National Life and Character: A Forecast*, conjured up an image of black and yellow people insinuating themselves into the company of Europeans: 'The citizens of these countries will then be taken up into the social relations of the white races, will throng the English turf, or the salons of Paris, and will be admitted to intermarriage'.[12] Pearson particularly had in mind the marriage of Asian men with white women (always more strenuously condemned than the reverse). If Europeans were not careful, they would hand to the lower races the power to humiliate the West: 'We shall wake to find ourselves elbowed and hustled, and perhaps even thrust aside by peoples whom we looked down upon as servile, and thought of as bound always to our needs'.

Colonial subjects were keen to show the motherland how to prevent this humiliation. The colony of Victoria put a check on Chinese heading for the goldfields in 1855. New South Wales effectively prohibited their entry in 1888. To the cheers of his parliamentary colleagues, the premier, Sir Henry Parkes, declared there could be no admission for those 'who we are not prepared to advance to all our franchises, all our privileges as citizens, and all our social rights, including the right of marriage'.[13]

The threat of competition from a 'coolie' workforce played a part in this agitation – but it was not the paramount concern. Labour Party leader Chris Watson told the first Commonwealth parliament in 1901 his 'main' objection to mixing with 'Asiatics' was the possibility of 'racial contamination'. Prime Minister Edmund Barton wanted Australia preserved forever white: 'The doctrine of the equality of man was never intended to apply to the equality of the Englishman and the Chinaman. There is a deep-set difference, and we see no prospect and no promise of its ever being effaced'.[14]

The world, however, did not stand still. Cities and seaports heaved and roared with the increasingly rapid movement of people and goods. Political battlelines were drawn between free traders and capitalists and their socialist or nationalist opponents, who claimed mercantile liberalism, and the military alliances that protected it, stole bread and peace from white workers. The mixed-race child became emblematic of a travesty perpetrated by one class against another. Mary Gilmore – champion of the poor – was a staunch segregationist by 1908: 'He who would sink him in the sea of another's color, stands in the way of progress, and scuttles the ship that would bear us yet further on'. Gilmore's companion on those walks through the waterside slums of the Rocks, Henry Lawson, also chose a maritime metaphor when he warned: *And watch for other castaways/ On rafts from other wrecks*'.[15]

The *Bulletin* magazine – anti-imperialist and trade-protectionist – railed against the invasion of 'heathenism, tribal wars, leprosy, and Joss' that, it said, threatened to turn Australians into 'a piebald race'. Leprosy – linked in the Bible with sinfulness and believed to be hereditary – was a common metaphor for miscegenation. Lawson depicted the mating of 'white' and 'yellow' as the surrender of 'the pure girl to the leper's kiss'.[16] The odious expression 'racial hygiene' was coined around this time.

The old notion that blood determined heredity left a permanent mark on the language: bloodline, mixed-blood, royal blood, et cetera. It also shaped the way procreation across racial lines was (and, to some extent, still is) conceptualised. Each parent was thought to bestow a semi-identity on the mixed-race child. The blending of two halves did not make a whole, but another fraction, because the focus remained on the putatively unmixed, original parental stock. The parents, in a sense, diminished rather than reproduced themselves. Gilmore took this idea to its extreme: 'Any woman who gives birth to a child whose color is not her own', she told readers of *The Worker*, 'gives birth to a child not wholly hers. It is a graft, a cuckoo born of a foreigner'.[17]

After science disproved any link between blood and heredity, a socio-economic explanation took its place: miscegenation was a lower-class phenomenon conducted in unhealthy, urban slums. The half-caste served as a versatile and potent symbol in journalism, literature and the graphic arts.

'What is that baby?'

American states began expanding their anti-miscegenation laws to include Asians in the 1860s. A broad-based anti-Japanese movement started around 1900, mainly in California, Washington and Idaho. The industrious strawberry farmers and potato growers were getting above themselves, not content with being 'biped domestic animals in the white man's service'. There was a clamour to exclude Japanese students from San Francisco's public schools to prevent them debauching 'the pure maids of California'.[18] (Similar rhetoric accompanied Canada's move to restrict Asian immigration.)

A white farmer, giving evidence before the California state legislature in 1913, denounced a Japanese neighbour occupying a fine piece of land near his:

> 'With that Japanese lives a white woman. In that woman's arms is a baby.
>
> 'What is that baby? It isn't a Japanese. It isn't white. I'll tell you what that baby is. It is a germ of the mightiest problem that ever faced this State; a problem that will make the black problem of the South look white.'[19]

Choruses of approval were heard all the way to Washington, DC. Eventually 11 states outlawed marriages between white Americans and Japanese.

Observing events with a more-than-casual interest was the journalist Kiyoshi Kawakami, who was married to a white American and the father of three children. Having migrated to the United States, attracted by its civic freedoms, he refused to bow to the rising hysteria: 'When I heard a noted agitator shout, in one of his fire-spitting harangues before San Francisco labourers, that "if Japanese and Americans intermarried the result would be a nation of gaspipe thugs and human hyenas," I could not help laughing in spite of the solemn audience about me'.[20]

Kawakami and others, writing in defence of Japanese-American race mixing, kept within the existing discourse. Intermarriage, they said, should remain the exception, rather than the rule, for the time being. It was not essential for assimilation, because Japanese living in America automatically behaved and looked like whites: the Oriental facial type ('stolid, stoical, reserved') gave way to the Occidental type ('vivacious, frank, open').[21] The melting pot imposed its own conformity.

A Bureau of Investigation (later FBI) report of 1922 rode the rhetorical merry-go-round in the opposite direction: 'The Japanese is an undesirable citizen because he does not assimilate. He does not intermarry, nor is it desirable that he should'.[22] A new immigration law would soon exclude all 'aliens ineligible for citizenship' from permanent entry to the United States. The principal target was obvious to everyone.

The melting pot

Early 20th-century America was often imagined as a 'melting pot'. In the famous play of that name, Israel Zangwill had one of his characters proclaim: '"America is God's Crucible, the great Melting-Pot where all the races of Europe are melting and reforming!"'[23] Zangwill's paean to migrant assimilation – in which love, liberty and free enterprise transcended ethnic and religious divisions – was both heroic and heretical. Most Americans still recoiled from unconventional forms of human alchemy.

They looked to the science of eugenics (pioneered by Francis Galton, a cousin of Charles Darwin), which argued that a race's success in the struggle for survival depended on the promotion of 'judicious marriages'.[24] What humanists previously regarded as temporal weaknesses (physical and mental disease, criminality, alcoholism, pauperism and promiscuity), susceptible to material or moral remedies, eugenicists saw as permanent marks of bad inheritance. Because the lower classes bred more prolifically, the seeds of an inexorable decline were being sown, which neither education nor social progress, alone, could reverse.

Although the promotion of biologically preferred characteristics in human reproduction was not, in and of itself, incompatible with race mixing, for many of Galton's followers the overriding concern was racial solidarity. As the mathematician Karl Pearson explained: 'The "solidarity of humanity", so far as it is real, is felt to exist rather between civilised men of European race in the presence of nature and of human barbarism, than between all men on all occasions'.[25] In other words, white civilisation was defined by its ability to close ranks against outsiders.

Biologist Charles Benedict Davenport, a leading American eugenicist, devoted his career to tracking human genetic traits and sorting the 'good' from the 'bad'. Davenport observed the millions of eastern and southern European peasants pouring through the immigration checkpoint at New York's Ellis Island, bringing with them 'the black thread of defective heredity' no melting pot could erase. 'Now we know', he wrote, 'that after a score of generations the given character may still appear unaffected by the repeated union with foreign germ plasm. So the individual, as the bearer of a potentially immortal germ plasm with immutable traits, becomes of the greatest interest'.[26]

Rather than condemn race mixing outright, Davenport emphasised its genetic and social risks. Eurasians were prone to enfeeblement, and mulattos, he claimed, combined 'something of a white man's intelligence and ambition with an insufficient intelligence to realize that ambition'. In hybrids, the most serious defect was 'bad behaviour due to conflicting instincts'.[27]

Thwarted ambition; conflicted instincts: arguments against race mixing were shifting away from measurable, biological characteristics. As evidence piled up that disproved any predictive link between skin colour and intelligence, creativity or moral virtue, segregationists needed another basis for their claims. They put increasing emphasis on the alleged *psychological* incompatibility of different races. The stereotype of the emotionally conflicted mixed-blood was ruthlessly exploited. Courts in the United States, hearing cases brought under anti-miscegenation laws, were invited to consider the need to prevent half-caste misery.[28]

But anxieties over race mixing still drew heavily on physical representations. For the eugenicist Madison Grant, New York was a *'cloaca gentium'* (human sewer) of 'amazing racial hybrids' and 'ethnic horrors'. In his immensely popular book *The Passing of the Great Race*, first published in 1916 and running to many editions, Grant wrote:

When it becomes thoroughly understood that the children of mixed marriages between contrasted races belong to the lower type, the importance of transmitting in unimpaired purity the blood inheritance of ages will be appreciated at its full value and to bring half-breeds into the world will be regarded as a social and racial crime of the first magnitude.

His argument, appreciated at its full value, pointed straight to the gas chamber: 'The laws of nature require the obliteration of the unfit, and human life is valuable only when it is of use to the community or race'.[29]

An era of radical – indeed murderous – racial politics had arrived. Its critique of 'parasitical'[30] urban culture tapped out a drumbeat marching the world towards war and genocide. The apocalyptic vision fixed race mixing as the enemy of civilisation.

Marginal man

Old saws about race mixing being against nature undoubtedly suppressed rates of intermarriage. They were, however, never fully embraced either by science or public opinion.

The phenomenon of heterosis, or hybrid vigour – the tendency of crossbred lines to outperform inbred lines – had been familiar to plant and animal breeders for centuries. It followed that racial interbreeding might be important for humanity's progress and wellbeing. 'Half-castes very generally combine the best attributes of the two races from whence they originate', the English ethnologist Robert Dunn wrote in 1861.[31]

Authorities cited examples from Tasmania to Hawaii – places where a decline in the native population was accompanied by a rise in the number of mixed-bloods – to show that race blending produced 'a type superior in fertility, vitality, and cultural worth to one or both of the parent stocks'. Hawaii, with its highly mixed population of Polynesians, Europeans and Asians, was said to be forging 'a new human type', a potentially 'superior race'. The 'robust, active race' brought forth on Pitcairn Island by the *Bounty* mutineers and their Tahitian wives offered another 'striking instance of the permanently fertile union of two extreme types'.[32]

Lafcadio Hearn's description of the *fille-de-couleur* of the French West Indies is a typical, late 19th-century appreciation of mixed-race beauty:

> She has inherited not only the finer bodily characteristics of either parent race, but a something else belonging originally to neither, and created by special climatic and physical conditions, – a grace, a suppleness of form, a delicacy of extremities (so that all the lines described by the bending of limbs or fingers are parts of clean curves), a satiny smoothness and fruit-tint of skin.[33]

João Batista de Lacerda, director of the National Museum of Rio de Janeiro, in a paper given at the First Universal Races Congress in London in July 1911, suggested the laws of heredity were inadequate to explain the superiority of Brazil's mulattos: 'Some unknown force gives rise in them to an intelligence that is capable of developing to a pitch that neither of the parents could reach'.[34]

What was this 'something else', this 'unknown force'? The American sociologists EB Reuter and Robert E Park ruled out any biological basis for attributing special significance to the crossing of different human stocks – for better or worse. The precocity of mulattos, they decided, must derive from their link to the 'superior [white] cultural group'.[35] Through social and sexual selection, they were equipped to take leadership of black causes.

The mixed-blood's intermediary role lent him a distinct personality type that Park called 'marginal man'. Eurasians fitted the type because, in Reuter's definition, they were 'the result of extra-matrimonial relations between the men of the politically and culturally dominant group and the women of the native or culturally retarded race'. They lived in two worlds, estranged from both. The characteristics of marginal man were 'spiritual instability, intensified self-consciousness, restlessness, and *malaise*'.[36]

Reuter, Park and their followers confined the mixed-blood to a psycho-sociological straitjacket almost as deterministic as the biological straitjacket of race: 'It is only through an identification of himself with the social group to which the social definitions consign him ['the backward group'] that he can find a tolerable life and develop a wholesome personality'. Marginal man might be indispensable to a civilisation renewing itself, but, to adapt Thomas Mann's phrase, he bore the sickness of its 'lascivious form'.[37]

9

The Eurasian malaise

The frustration motif dominated popular and academic representations of race mixing in the early decades of the 20th century. While opinions varied as to whether the Eurasian malaise arose from genetic disharmony or social discrimination, most agreed that mixed-blood exceptionality was inevitable, fascinating and sad.

The Chinese-Canadian author Onoto Watanna (1875–1954) presumably was well-equipped to penetrate the mystery of the half-caste: 'They generally enjoy fine physical constitutions, though they are nervous, highly strung, jealous, conceited, yet humble and self-depreciating and overly modest at times, sarcastic, skeptical, generous and impulsive. It is hard to analyze their natures, because they are so changeable. They are born artists'.[1] By now, surely, the real-life Winnifred Eaton (she assumed the identity of a part-Japanese, apparently as a marketing ploy) was describing her own elusive self.

Kathleen Tamagawa, born in 1893 to an Irish-American mother and a Japanese father, took the opposite approach in her autobiography *Holy Prayers in a Horse's Ear* (the title is a Japanese proverb about wasting words on the ignorant). For Tamagawa, mixed-blood exceptionality lay entirely in the eye of the beholder; all she wanted was to be ordinary. Her story is valuable because it records attitudes to race mixing in both West and East, free of associations with illegitimacy, abandonment or destitution.

Tamagawa's father was a silk trader. Though materially well off, she felt ill at ease growing up in middle-class Chicago.

Neighbourhood children taunted her ('Chink, Chink'), and even close acquaintances treated her like 'a toy'. The family moved to Japan when she was 13; at last, she thought, she could be 'ordinary, inconspicuous'. But Japanese gawked at her in the street, her father's relatives never visited, and his friends seemed to consider her 'a barbarism and a blemish'.

The family retreated to Yokohama's European enclave, the Bluff – only to meet fresh insults. Her father was asked not to accompany his wife and daughter to church because a native face incommoded his fellow Christians. At her convent school, Tamagawa noticed that mixed-race friends with socially prominent fathers were 'usually ignored' by them, whereas sailors and others lower down the social rung gave their offspring 'a name and a home, and even often defended their position'.[2]

The wife of an American merchant, Theodate Geoffrey, considered the Bluff 'perhaps the most extreme example of non-assimilation that the modern world has seen'. The 'gulf of alien civilizations', as she called it, meant most Anglo-Saxons 'not only viewed intermarriage with disapprobation, but visited opprobrium on the children of such marriages'. In Kobe, another Japanese port city, well-to-do foreign merchants made a rule at their social club: 'no shopkeepers, no Eurasians, no mariners'. Imagine their consternation when the Prince of Wales (later King Edward VIII), during a visit to the city in 1922, selected 'a beautiful Eurasian girl' as his dance partner at the welcoming ball.[3]

The Dutch East Indies, French Indochina, Hong Kong, Macao, India and Malaya all had significant Eurasian minorities. HN Ridley – botanist, rubber pioneer and first director of the Singapore Botanic Gardens – categorised them, like some exotic plant, as 'weak in body, short-lived, deficient in energy, and feeble in morals'.[4] Their supposed physical and moral weakness was invoked to justify their social alienation. In comparison with a century before, the discrimination against them was more insidious and cruel.

The poverty to which many of the 200 000 or so Anglo-Indians had been reduced was cited as proof they were 'inherently degenerate and shiftless'.[5] Gertrude Williams's *Understanding India*, published in 1928, conveyed the standard view:

> The most pathetic of India's minority groups are the mixed-bloods … They are ostracised by both English and Indians. They in turn look down on the Indian with a scorn that is acid with hatred, for it is their Indian blood that is their curse. They fawn upon the English and make pitiful advances to them.

Finding some Anglo-Indian women 'almost blond and very pretty', Williams helpfully listed the flaws that gave them away: 'Most of them have an anaemic look. They speak in a metallic falsetto with a curious sing-song accent'.[6]

Mixed-race children learned through bitter experience there were different degrees of British-ness. The son of an Anglo-Indian mother has recalled how she would scrub his face with hydrogen peroxide, trying to erase the mark of her blood:

> Although she was of fair, creamy complexion, it didn't take much time in the sun for her to acquire a tan that advertised that she had 'a touch of the tar brush' to a society where one would rather conceal this fact if one was fair enough to pass for 100 per cent European.[7]

In Hong Kong, influential voices called for miscegenation to be made a punishable offence. A law was never enacted because other means served almost as well. British men recruited into the police and civil service had to sign an undertaking not to marry a Chinese. The Hong Kong Cricket Club might allow a talented player of mixed race to pull on the creams, but it did not mean he would be accepted as a member.

Some Eurasians, according to historian Vicky Lee, were able to join the colonial elite because they could perform or mimic the part of the public Englishman, and 'they also represented – or performed – the Chinese for the English'. This double identity inevitably raised doubts about their loyalty. 'We can rely on nobody except the half-castes', Governor Sir Edward Stubbs complained to the Colonial Office in 1922, 'and even they will throw in their lot with the Chinese if they think they will be on the winning side'.[8]

Previously, an expatriate alone in the tropics might have been excused the occasional foray across the colour line. This was no longer the case. Once white women joined the man's social circle, the question arose: Whom did he really prefer? A planter's display of affection for his sweet-tempered Asian housekeeper was likely to cause more offence than his original carnality. His mixed-race child needed to be packed off to the mission school and hushed up. White relations would lift an eyebrow and suppress a smile whenever they spoke of 'the boodle' (or some such euphemism, meant to call attention to his folly).

Interracial marriages in British Malaya were extremely rare, and the offspring of informal unions found polite society closed to them. 'The most striking feature of European-Eurasian relations', according to historian John Butcher, 'was the lack of social contact between the two groups'.[9] A considerable number of Eurasians found employment in government service, but, in certain other respects, they were worse off than the native Malays.

Sirens and turncoats

In 1938, author Frank Clune travelled to occupied China as a guest of the Japanese government, which hoped to foster a more constructive view of its imperial mission there. The clever Japanese of *Sky High to Shanghai* bear no resemblance to the stupid and uncivilised people Clune would portray in his later book on occupied Japan.

On the contrary, he urged his fellow Australians to learn from the Manchurian experiment, with its high-speed trains and monumental urban-planning: 'Instead of cursing dictators we should put our own house in order'.

At journey's end, relaxing at a cabaret in Shanghai – that notorious potpourri of humanity – Clune found the perfect image to contrast with Manchukuo's order and progress:

> At a table next to mine, a pair of lusty young sailors, one Italian
> and one French, vied for the favours and dances of a red-lipped,
> full-bosomed Eurasian light-o'-love, whose elongated, ox-blooded
> finger-nails glistened like those of the harlots in the halls of King
> Solomon of old.[10]

The Eurasian siren makes her familiar literary entrance.

In plays, musicals, novels, short stories and films, untold numbers of writers have exploited mixed-race stereotypes: seductive, abandoned women; self-conscious, treacherous men. The 'tragic mulatto' – child of the white slave-owner and his Negro mistress – is a familiar character in American fiction; the 'cunning Eurasian' is almost as prominent in the British and European literary canons. From Noël Coward to Eugene O'Neill, Lon Chaney to William Faulkner, examples abound in both serious and popular culture.

The exotic and the erotic have been bedfellows in folklore since biblical times; the modern conceit of the beautiful, promiscuous mixed-blood drew upon this older tradition.[11] Because half-castes appeared at the fringes of society, where looser morals were thought to prevail, it was assumed they inherited a taste for illicit sex – or, at the very least, their parents' unconventionality. They carried a reminder of the biological reality of sex and romance written, as it were, all over their faces. The rootlessness and disorientation associated with mixed-bloods lent the females, in particular, the added appeal of vulnerability. Perceived to have fallen to a lower caste, they must be eager to restore their status by attaching themselves to a white man.

The fictional 'invasion' genre, which reached the height of its popularity between 1900 and 1930, made much of the Eurasian figure of mystery. Equipped with the cultural knowledge of both East and West, he or she made the ideal spy or agent provocateur.

A particularly florid example is MP Shiel's *The Yellow Peril* of 1929, set in London. At the centre of the intrigue (a plot by Japan to invade Australia) is the half-caste spy Oyone, daughter of a P & O ship surgeon and a Nagasaki geisha: 'Tragedy sleeps in those ravishing peepers'. The Chinese master-fiend of the story explains her mission – in terms she, presumably, can understand:

'Nature likes all-of-one-kind! – as the strongest weed in a field either kills or marries the rest. So, in time, one universal world-race – mixed – ruby-coloured – prettier and better than any at present. But before that, we to eat the flesh of half the whites – or they ours.'

The novel's theme of sexual predation is continued in a later description of Oyone at her house in cosmopolitan Regents Park: 'There she put match to lantern, in whose opal glamour she looked a lovely hag in her bedraggled dress and red-hotness'.[12]

It is hard to imagine *The Yellow Peril* being read, then or now, as anything but an absurd confection. And yet, its opalescent vision of the 'lovely hag' shares a cultural and ideological link with Frank Clune's Shanghai siren and the legions of other Eurasian margin-dwellers who have wandered from fiction to fact, and back again.

Modernity

During the inter-war years, the lives of Eurasians residing in Japan did not conform to any single pattern. Some fully assimilated into society, lived comfortably and attained career success. Others were made to suffer. Class, education and family background were the chief determinants of widely varying outcomes.

Immediately following the First World War, there was a quickening in the country's engagement with the West. Japan's diplomats took their places at the Paris Peace Conference as representatives of a major power. Luxury liners, plying new routes across the Pacific, brought foreign celebrities and wealthy tourists to visit the cultural sites, taste raw fish and have their photographs taken with a geisha. Japanese artists and scientists ventured onto the world stage, winning fame and influence.

This increased exchange stimulated a fresh interest in race mixing – imaginatively, at least. Writers rediscovered (or, if necessary, fabricated) the homesick letters of the mixed-race Japanese sent into exile during the distant Tokugawa era. The best known of them, Jagatara Oharu (Jeronima Haru Marino, 1625–97), was celebrated in sentimental verse:

> If the flower should be red, amaryllis is best.
> It is raining at the Dutch mansion,
> Jagatara Oharu is wet and crying.
> She cannot get the departing ship from her mind.
> Oh, the bell rings.
> La, la. The bell rings.[13]

The exotic figure of Oharu entered popular culture at a time when farmers and petite bourgeoisie were being encouraged to resettle in Japan's colonies. Her story conveyed the idea that, while foreign blood might cloud human destinies, it need not obliterate love of country. Being Japanese could now include 'wishing for Japan'.

In the eyes of their elders, young people seemed to be gripped by a severe case of 'foreigner worship' (*gaijin sūhai*). Western fads and physical features – the Eton Crop, the Charleston, Mary Pickford, or any long-legged, White Russian beauty strolling Tokyo's raffish Asakusa district – were pulp to the mill of *ero-guro-nansensu*, a literary coinage (from the English 'erotic', 'grotesque' and 'nonsense') used to describe the vitality, decadence and moral confusion of the era.

The heightened sex appeal of the heroine of Jun'ichirō Tanizaki's 1924 novel *Chijin no ai* ('A Fool's Love', given the title *Naomi* in the English translation) crystallises the moment we meet her: 'Everybody says I look Eurasian'. Naomi's husband is so smitten, he ignores the fact her family runs a brothel. The couple lives in a 'Culture House', a Western-style residence with a front door lockable from the outside – an innovation that allowed housewives to wander.

By the end of the story, the Japanese woman 'with a Western flavor' is unrecognisable to her spouse:

> Whipping off a black garment and tossing it aside, an unfamiliar young Western woman stood there in a pale blue French crepe dress. The exposed arms and shoulders were as white as a fox. Around her fleshy nape, she wore a crystal necklace that glowed like a rainbow; and beneath a black velvet hat pulled low over her eyes, the tips of her nose and chin were visible, terrifyingly, miraculously white. The raw vermilion of her lips stood out in contrast.[14]

She is the 'Eurasian' siren in whom cultural borrowing is as transformative as blood mixing.

The *modan gāru* ('modern girl', often abbreviated to *moga*) was a journalistic favourite of the 1920s and 1930s, arousing excitement and fear with her (mostly imagined) provocative sexuality. She was animated and expressive, dressing flamboyantly in Western clothes or brazenly 'showing arse' by tying the sash of her kimono high on her abdomen. She was a 'surging, great wave' of promise, challenging stuffy traditions or a figure of militancy disturbing the good order of the state, depending on one's point of view.[15]

The *moga* prefigured the notorious *panpan* of the post-war era, whose independence and aggression frustrated a return to normal conditions. Critics of each framed their attacks in similar terms: *panpan* were 'ticks' or 'weeds that kept appearing no matter how often you stamped them down'; *moga* were 'pathogens that poisoned the good and healthy customs of the Japanese Empire'. The trial of a 'vagabond *moga*', accused of murdering her foreign lover, caused a press sensation in 1925. Hollywood helped dress the *modan gāru*, and interracial intimacy added spice and scandal to her public image.[16]

'Asia for the Asians'

In 1920, Prime Minister Takashi Hara gave expression to the nationalist ideal of a perfect union between state and citizen. 'The country and its people are one and the same organism, interdependent, with their lifeblood in common', he wrote. 'Therefore the state of Japan can do no wrong [because its people would not let it].'[17] But how would this organism cope with the foreign blood of empire?

The incorporation of different peoples into a single ethnic group (*minzoku*) began early in the Meiji era with the Ainu of Hokkaido and the Ryūkyū Islanders (Okinawans). Modernisation and enlightenment were promoted through lifestyle reforms that targeted unhygienic practices and primitive customs. Intermarriage was also an approved way of becoming Japanese.

Once Korea and Taiwan came under Japanese control, integration measures were implemented cautiously at first. As a leading advocate of imperial expansion, Shimpei Gotō, liked to say, 'No one can turn a flounder into a sea bream overnight'.[18] This approach later gave way to an aggressive policy of assimilation. Prime Minister Hara encouraged intermarriage and the establishment of mixed settlements, and commentators emphasised the shared ancestry of Koreans and Japanese. A case needed to be made, because Japanese were still more inclined to marry a white American than a Korean.

Once the empire was at war with the West, marriages between Japanese and Koreans increased, albeit from a low base. This was mainly Korean men taking Japanese wives – the reverse of the usual pattern in which males of the dominant culture married subject females, and not what policymakers had in mind. A eugenic study undertaken in 1941 concluded that, if the Korean partner were a 'superb' type, there should be nothing to fear concerning the children. But, in view of the fact most Koreans entering Japan were unskilled labourers, the researchers recommended controls be put in place to protect the 'endowments of the Yamato *minzoku*' from dysgenic intermarriage.[19] ('Yamato', a place name, was synonymous with 'pure Japanese'.)

Similar contradictions bedevilled social relations in the new state Japan carved out in eastern China. While Manchukuo was meant to showcase a superior Asian model of ethnic harmony and mutual support, the reality was different. Japanese colonists in urban areas formed their own enclaves; and, although farmer-settlers socialised to a greater extent with other ethnic groups, their additional role, defending Japanese strategic interests in remote areas, encouraged a jaundiced view of the majority Han Chinese. A small elite assumed leadership in an ethnic hierarchy hardly less rigid than the European one it supplanted. Policy guidelines for Manchukuo issued in 1942 stipulated that 'the mixing of even a single drop of [Japanese] blood should not be allowed'.[20]

The following year, the Welfare Ministry produced a voluminous document entitled 'A Study of World Policy Centred on the Yamato *Minzoku*'. The report warned against allowing Japanese colonists to intermarry with races 'at a lower stage of cultural development', because this would threaten the unity of the *minzoku*. Persons willing to cohabit with members of another race, it said, were usually 'inferior in social status and intelligence', which amounted to 'reverse selection' in eugenic terms. *Konketsuji* were described as 'dependent, obsequious, irresponsible and weak-willed, with a tendency to be nihilistic and self-destructive'.[21] These views were supported by numerous references to Western scientific literature.

Not all influential Japanese agreed. A senior administrator in Korea, for instance, condemned the influence of 'chauvinists with a mania for Germany'. To adopt a 'pure blood policy' in the colony, he warned, would be courting 'disaster'. Apart from denying Korea's place in the empire, treating Koreans like Jews ignored the fact Japan was 'the most mixed of all Asian nations'. The Japanese general who led the invasion of Java also invoked the 'mixed nation' argument when proclaiming 'brotherhood' with the local population.[22]

Policymakers could never decide whether the slogan 'Asia for the Asians' meant association (Japanese leadership of different ethnic groups retaining their identities) or assimilation (making all imperial subjects Japanese). The sort of amalgamation preferred in Korea seemed utterly impracticable at the periphery of empire. Hidemi Kon, a member of an Army propaganda unit, felt 'strange' hearing people in the Philippines identify themselves as mixed-bloods rather than Filipinos. Kon also noted that many *konketsuji* were respected members of the nation's elite. The novelist and future head of Japan's Cultural Affairs Agency doubted it would be possible to instil 'Asian consciousness' in a population with so much Spanish and Chinese blood.[23]

In Army-occupied Singapore, Eurasians were exhorted to give up feelings of superiority at being 'blood relatives' of the British.[24] In the former Dutch East Indies, an effort was made to gain their co-operation by issuing mixed-bloods separate identity cards from Europeans and not interning them. But, once the war situation deteriorated, Eurasian youths were required to swear a loyalty oath, and those who refused were detained.

Far from remaining aloof from the natives, the Japanese left tens of thousands of mixed-race children in occupied Asia.

Enemy blood

The campaign of cultural purification unleashed in Japan in the 1930s, with its attendant claims of racial superiority, cast a slur on anyone sullied by foreign blood. Life changed for every mixed-race Japanese as loyalties came under suspicion.

Not long after arriving in Tokyo in 1938, the Englishman John Morris began having trouble with his servant. When he sought help from the police to sack the 'wretch', they disclosed the nature of the problem. 'I am glad to say that he was certainly not a typical Japanese servant', wrote Morris. 'Although possessed of a Japanese name and completely Japanese in appearance, he was as a matter of fact Eurasian'. The journalist did not question how the police came to know so much about the man: the son of a German father of British nationality who had visited Japan from Ceylon on a Buddhist pilgrimage. Morris was simply pleased to be rid of him. 'The fruit of a temporary liaison, he was, in fact, what in his more drunken moments he had often called me.'[25]

During these darkening days, state security was forever sniffing out enemy blood. Imao Hirano was one of a number of mixed-race Japanese (his father was French American) to hear the knock on the door. Hirano has described being tortured by the police: 'I was hung upside down or hit with a wooden sword. Simply because I am "*ainoko*"'.[26]

Social position afforded only limited protection. Tomisaburō Kuraba (Glover), the son of a famous 19th-century Scottish trader and his courtesan, was a graduate of Japan's most elite school and a respected businessman. The Glover mansion, with its commanding view of Nagasaki harbour, symbolised the romance of a bygone era (it remains a popular tourist attraction today). He should have had nothing to fear. But, by 1939, a 'foreign' house overlooking the Mitsubishi shipyards was considered a liability. The company stepped in to acquire the property, obliging the aged Tomisaburō and his mixed-race wife to take up residence further down the hill. They were spied on by the military police (*kempei*), and any person meeting them was liable to be visited afterwards and interrogated.

By the time the A-bomb arrived over Nagasaki, Tomisaburō was living alone. His wife was dead; there were no children. To whom did he answer now: victor or vanquished? As the occupation troops were preparing to come ashore, the old man strangled his pet dogs and hanged himself.[27] His suicide was an ill omen for what lay ahead.

10

George's story

A young woman squats on the floor behind a small child, running a comb through his hair. Both are looking up at the camera. His hair and skin are fairer than hers; he carries the features of his Australian father. The room is bare, except for a dressing mirror and a few cushions: a cheap rental in a shabby building, hard up against a stormwater canal. There is a faint glimmer in the mother's eyes. Is it fear or misgiving? George's father has gone forever. Soon she will be leaving too.

Sachiko Tsutsumi was working as a bar hostess in Kure when she met George's father. According to a social worker's report, they married at a church in Hiroshima in 1949. The Korean War broke out a year later.

> I was born in 1950, and my father was killed in the Korean War in 1951 – within half a year. Talking about my father, I have tears; but, in a real sense, I don't have any memory.
>
> She [my mother] said, '*Yume makura ni tatsu*' [The spirit of the dead appears in a dream]. I guess she received no notice or report from the military because she [the marriage] wasn't registered. They were not recognised as having an official relationship. Maybe she heard from someone else.

A note of scepticism creeps into George Tsutsumi's voice whenever he speaks of his mother. He seems uncertain what to believe, whom to trust. It is there, again, when he mentions Sachiko's home town in Kyushu.

> The permanent address is there. There are a lot of Tsutsumis there. Throw a stone and you'll hit a Tsutsumi. I don't know why she came [to Kure].

George's wife, Hatsue, is sitting with him during the interview and chimes in: 'She seems to have been a nurse at the time'.

> She said various things. A self-declaration. If it comes to that, you can say that you're Miss Universe.

'She looks attractive?' I suggest.

> I wonder.

He picks up another battered photograph. She is standing in the street, a broad smile on her face, in front of a poster advertising the movie *Ben-Hur*.

> Where is it? By that time she's not with me – almost from when I was born. Maybe [I was] an obstacle when she was working.

George was only a year old when Sachiko deposited him with an elderly couple she once worked for – 'Mr and Mrs T' – and went away. According to an ISS case report, she 'moved with soldiers from one place to another', sending back money and making occasional return visits to Kure. (George has no memory of them.) Contact ceased altogether when he was seven.

Sachiko's former boss died soon afterwards. The boy remained with the man's widow, occupying a windowless, three-mat (five-square-metre) room at a disreputable inn.

Well, in those days, everyone was poor! But we were among the poorest. When things were at their worst, our only electric appliance was a single, 20-watt light bulb. No radio. Television, of course, was in a dream world. It was truly appalling.

I was a big eater. I was hardly ever full. It's no exaggeration to say, I was raised on the free, school luncheon program. The reconstituted milk others hated, I relished.

School fed George. It also thrust him into the glare of unwanted publicity.

In Year One, a stepladder was suddenly brought into the classroom. My photograph was taken. Perhaps it was the *Chugoku Shimbun* [a local newspaper]. And I remember the front page said, 'Let's look for the father of this boy'. After that, wherever I went, I was asked: 'So, you don't have a father? You don't have a mother?' For a while I was 'famous' in the local area. I didn't feel particularly good!

According to a social worker's report:

When George was ten years old, ISS tried to place him for adoption with a good family, as he wished. But Mrs. T. disagreed, and the adoption could not go through. He wanted to join the Boy Scouts but could not enter without the group's co-operation. People had prejudice toward such children of mixed parentage.[1]

Repeated experiences of being rejected led George to feel he could take control only by getting in first and repudiating all ties.

Rather than adoption, I think it would have been better if I had been put in an orphanage. Better than being half-baked. I often thought so. Because, you see, it was a burden for me to have to take into account those who were looking after me. There was a point when it would have been better to go to a place where there were no ties.

Other children called him 'Big George'. By the age of 12, he was 173 centimetres tall and weighed 64 kilograms. He stood out because of his size and features. Strangers glared at him in the street. He became intensely self-conscious.

> The [mixed-race] children's faces were the faces of those who, not so long ago, were dropping bombs. The faces, by themselves, provoked animosity. For those who had been educated to hate, I guess it was natural to feel hatred when they saw miniatures of their enemy hanging around. Perhaps some were able to grasp the real situation, intellectually, but their emotions could not accept it. I understand this now. But, at the time, I wondered why I was singled out for bullying.

George was featured in a press campaign in Australia calling for the mixed-bloods to be admitted for adoption: 'These children, begging for love, whose are they? Ours!'[2] He pinned his hopes on a change for the better – and felt betrayed when it all came to nothing.

> We were told everyone was to go. But the Australian government would not let us in. Emotionally, I was highly offended. I thought we were rejected because we were poor. I resolved then, whatever happened in the future, I would never set foot in Australia.

People noticed a sudden change in George's personality: the once congenial, outgoing boy became destructive. He fought with school-mates at the least provocation and acquired a bad reputation. Because 'Mrs T' worked nights, he was frequently left alone and developed a habit of staying out late. Among the female social workers, he went from pin-up boy to villain: peeping up their dresses, smoking on the roof of the ISS building, and even threatening a newspaper reporter with a knife. The day he tossed an explosive into the office stove, George came to blows with the manager, Yone Itō.

> I thought Itō-sensei [he uses the most respectful honorific] was advertising herself. The worst time, I told her: 'Aren't you trading human beings? You sell children to get money!' By adoption is what I meant – because she was also arranging that. Maybe I was jealous. Perhaps I thought those children were better off.

The notorious 'Tsutsumi of Wassho' (the name of his junior high school) spent more time wandering the streets or hiding out in abandoned air-raid shelters with members of his gang than attending class. A conscientious teacher would come looking for him, but George usually managed to stay one step ahead. He did not lack the ability to learn – his IQ scores were above average – what he lacked, utterly, was the motivation.

> Even if I went to school, it was no use learning. There was nothing to look forward to in the future: no plan to go higher, no possibility of dropping lower. That was my view of life. I didn't want to do anything.

Itō resisted suggestions the boy be placed in an institution. His violent behaviour, she said, was a bid for attention and would pass once he gained confidence. His relatives were eager for someone to adopt him, though the chances of finding a suitable home were now remote. The ISS manager decided George should join Mitsuyoshi Hanaoka to train as a farmer, in preparation for migrating to Brazil. Before the Kiyosato Farm School would accept him, however, he needed to show he was in earnest by gaining work experience on a real farm. Realising this would involve a long daily commute, George refused: 'How could I be so enthusiastic?' His attitude forced Itō to reassess the amount of time and money being devoted to his case.

He left school at the minimum age, without prospects. Neither his grandparents nor an aunt living in Kure were willing or able to look after him. Before long, he was in the hands of the police and bound for a reformatory – unless someone took responsibility. So, at the age of 17, he was reunited with his mother.

> There was a time she was working as a hostess, when she was young. But she couldn't continue doing that forever. I don't think she ever got married. When I went to Yokosuka [a naval base near Yokohama], she was working as a cleaner at a club [cabaret]. There are a lot of clubs with [American] military as clients. She was cleaning at those places.
>
> The first week was a novelty for both of us. But, because we have the same personality, I guess the other side [my mother] also felt it became rather trying. I had no feeling whatever for her. As far as I was concerned, she was just the person who gave birth to me.

They stuck it out together for six months. Once re-established, however, the link was never completely severed again. George asked about his father and, several times, felt the barb of her tongue: 'He wasn't like you. He didn't drink, or smoke, or sing in his cups!' He learned that his mother had had two miscarriages before giving birth, so it seemed his parents had been together for a while.

> After she got old and settled down, she found the name [of my father] at a cemetery in South Korea. She said she cried. He had been that close to her, she said.

'His name was Joseph, Joe?' I ask.

Is it Joseph? Joe Ritchie. I heard only 'J'. Joe. J-something.

'Where in Australia was he from?'

All I know is that it was several kilometres to his nearest
neighbour. And he didn't know, until he came to Japan, that the
sea was salty. It was so remote. It may be different today.

Throughout the summer of 1945, drought refused to release its grip
on the land. Monstrous dust storms charged across outback South
Australia. Crops failed again in many parts of New South Wales.
Across the border, in Victoria, dams were reduced to sun-bleached
craters; farmers there had been carting water for months.

The Murray River, down to its lees, could barely creep past the
thirsty peach orchards at Mooroopna, the small Victorian town
where Joseph Ritchie was born.

Early summer: 60 years later.

Swallowing the bitterness of a lifetime, George Tsutsumi has
embarked on the journey a recalcitrant government refused to let
him make as a child – to his father's birthplace, his *furusato*, his
home town.

The big man's long legs are stiff and unsteady after the six-hour
drive from Melbourne to Mooroopna. He is unsteady in spirit, too,
lacking bearings and stunned to silence by the unfamiliar topography. He feels awkward and conspicuous, all over again. Surely, he
remarks, the locals must take note of every car that stops on their
dusty main street.

Where to begin? How to connect with this odd-named speck
on a map, shrinking to nothing before his sun-dazzled eyes? The
newsagent tries to be helpful: sells George a pamphlet on the town's

history and points out the small hospital where his grandmother probably gave birth. The cannery is worth a visit; tourists like the prices at the Co-op next door. Right now, though, people are feeling pretty shaken up after last week's dreadful weather: 'The hailstorm wiped out the entire cherry crop and half the apricots'.

Wandering an overgrown cemetery, George scans the pitted headstones for other possible Ritchies. Finds none.

Joe Ritchie left school at the age of 14, the year the war reached the Pacific. He knocked about the Riverina district, working as a station hand. The seasons were lean but, with so many men away at the fighting, help was always needed.

Fatherless and an only child himself, he was soon sporting a tattoo on his right arm: a swallow with a ribbon in its beak, bearing the motto 'Mother'. They made a note of it at the Army recruitment centre in Albury – a mark of identification – when he signed up at 18:

Religion: Presbyterian
Medical classification: A1
5' 4", 134 lbs
Hazel eyes, fair hair.

Date of birth? There was no way he was going to tell them April the 1st, 'April Fool's Day', so he pushed it forward a bit.

At the National Archives in Melbourne, George and Hatsue are shown into a private viewing room. A musty scent of old paper rises as his father's Army records – blotchy, handwritten entries; strange acronyms; a patchwork of teasing, obscure details – tumble from the folder. Having sustained himself this long on crumbs of information, he finds the exotic feast set before him unappetising.

He picks over the papers without enthusiasm, until his eyes light upon something. He lifts a small photograph out of the pile. It must have been taken soon after his father enlisted. George studies it intently and then says, in a new tone of voice, 'He's smiling. It's the first time I see him smiling'.

Private Ritchie looked pleased to be in uniform, setting his slouch hat at a jaunty angle. It is conceivable he expressed disappointment on VP Day – 'the show's over before I can do my bit' – with all the bravado of the unblooded recruit.

Army life agreed with him: he put on weight and grew a couple of inches. With no particular job beckoning, back in civilian life, Joe volunteered for service in occupied Japan and sailed aboard the troopship *Kanimbla* in August 1947. Was he really surprised to taste the salt of the sea? Or was that a bit of blarney put about to impress the Japanese girls?

The troops embarked from mid-winter Sydney; a fortnight later they disembarked in mid-summer Kure. Before he could begin to adjust to the topsy-turvy place, Joe found himself flat on his back in hospital with a severe case of mumps, contracted during the voyage. He was soon up and about again, but the infection may have permanently weakened his constitution.

He had better luck with his work detail: assigned to a canteen unit. Kure was a hungry town, where a can of food served as hard currency. At the end of a year, he was ready to sign up for an extended tour of duty. Was it simply because he was enjoying the adventure – or did he have a more substantial reason for staying?

In the studio portrait, Sachiko holds three-month-old George in her lap. Joe is seated beside them dressed in a civilian suit and tie.

It was not an occasion for smiles: the non-fraternisation rules still applied, and they were taking a risk just being together. The week before, Joe had been picked up by MPs for travelling 'out of bounds' on a tram. Having no permission to marry, he needed to conceal his likely reason for being there. Fine: 10 shillings.

Time was precious. The BCOF brigade was getting ready to join the Korean War. The Australian War Memorial holds a photograph of Private Joe Ritchie with a group of soldiers examining a captured, Russian-made machine gun. A month after this publicity shot was taken, he and his mates embarked by ship for Pusan with the 3rd Royal Australian Regiment. Well-wishers who came to see them off – Sachiko and George presumably among them – were caught in a blinding downpour.

The troops went into action almost immediately, joining a major offensive with other units of the American-led United Nations Command. Whether Joe saw combat is not recorded; in any case, he was already a sick man. George remembers his mother telling him about his father's habit of gulping down whole mouthfuls of sugar. The meaning of this strange craving is revealed in the Army records.[3] He had undiagnosed diabetes.

The records also yield the name of George's grandmother – Lucy Irene Ritchie – and an address in Melbourne. It is the next stop on his journey. The quiet street in South Yarra runs through a fashionable residential neighbourhood. Before the smart set moved in, these narrow, semi-detached dwellings were called 'workingmen's cottages'. The one he is looking for, almost hidden behind an old melaleuca tree, appears to be in original condition, apart from a fresh coat of paint. There is no answer to the knock on the door.

Mid-winter Korea is savagely cold. Joe Ritchie's war has lasted three months. When they bring him to hospital, he is suffering from malnutrition and hypertension. He cannot walk because of pains in his legs.

A little after six, on the morning of 24 January 1951, a delivery boy knocks at the cottage in South Yarra, bearing an urgent telegram addressed to Mrs Lucy Ritchie:

> IT IS WITH DEEP REGRET THAT I HAVE LEARNED THAT YOUR SON 3/1925 PRIVATE JOSEPH RITCHIE DIED OF DIABETES MELLITUS ON 23 JANUARY AT 4 AMERICAN FIELD HOSPITAL TAEGU KOREA STOP I DESIRE TO CONVEY TO YOU MY SINCERE PERSONAL SYMPATHY AS WELL AS THAT OF THE GOVERNMENT OF THE COMMONWEALTH OF AUSTRALIA.

Six months later, a 'Mothers and Widows' badge will arrive in the mail.

There is nothing to suggest Mrs Ritchie knew of her son's wife – or the grandson, who pauses today at the tear-stained doorstep.

11

Occupational hazards

Ted Weatherstone was an ex-RAAF intelligence officer who had polished his language skills interrogating prisoners in the Pacific. As Australia's first post-war consul in Japan, he found himself at a different sort of battlefront, where history and prejudice pinned down the lives and loves of former enemies.[1]

Two years into the occupation, a young BCOF lance corporal came to Weatherstone seeking a visa for his fiancée. The application ground to a halt at the desk of the Immigration Minister, Arthur Calwell, who wrote on a departmental memorandum: '*No* Japanese women, or any half castes either, will be admitted to Australia whether they be Japanese nationals or the nationals of any other country. They are simply not wanted & are *permanently* undesirable'. Calwell told parliament that, owing to the brutalities committed by their soldiers during the war, 'Japanese men and women should not be allowed to pollute these shores'.[2]

A severe fate awaited any serviceman who defied orders. Signalman John Henderson, a former prisoner of war of the Japanese, arrived in Kure in April 1946. He took up with a well-educated young woman by the name of Mary Abe. They exchanged vows in a Shinto ceremony, and she was pregnant by the time he applied to take her to Australia the following year.

BCOF headquarters decided to act. Henderson's company commander carried out the arrest order: 'He was a thin, frail-looking lad, very red-haired and close to tears. We could not risk giving him leave – he might have finished up on a charge of desertion'. Back in Australia, the Wallsend coalminer's son appealed for help to the Legion of Ex-Servicemen. None was forthcoming. Faced with a choice between defending the White Australia policy or the civil liberties of a colleague, veterans' groups generally put race first. Five years later, Mary Abe was reportedly seen in Kure soliciting for prostitution to support her mixed-race daughter.[3]

Australian public opinion split over the marriage issue. Some letters to the press condemned Calwell's stand as dictatorial and un-Christian. Others countered with warnings about Japanese whores and half-castes sullying the bloodline. The Minister for the Army, Cyril Chambers, probably expressed the majority view: 'I cannot understand the mental attitude of soldiers who choose Japanese wives in preference to Australian girls'.[4] Determined to discredit one persistent ex-soldier, Chambers went so far as to read compromising details of the man's medical history into the parliamentary record.

In March 1949, the troopship HMAS *Duntroon* returned to Sydney carrying several hundred BCOF personnel, including around 20 men forced to leave wives and children behind. Keith Morrison, a civilian, had stowed away to Japan and spent a year with his partner, working as a fisherman, until his arrest and deportation. Morrison wanted to wipe the slate clean so he could return to her legally: 'She's a great girl and much better than the average Australian girl'.[5]

We also know something about two others who disembarked from *Duntroon* that day. Private Ken Gibbons of Melbourne took his discharge and hid away aboard a freighter heading north. He was caught, held for six months and deported. He returned to Japan as a merchant seaman, jumped ship, and spent several months with his family before surrendering to police. The occupation authorities vetoed his application for permanent residence and sentenced him to three years jail, partly suspended on condition he never attempted to return. Gibbons's repeated requests to bring his family to Australia were turned down by successive governments. 'All I want is to live peacefully with my wife and baby girl', he pleaded in 1951.[6]

Private Pat Stapylton of Sydney fared no better. All he could offer his wife and child, back in Kure, were letters pledging his fidelity:

> I miss you very much. I still don't know when I will be able to see you. I wish I was still with you. I am very lonely. I have not changed, my heart is still the same. I love you always. You are my only wife & I love you so much.[7]

Stapylton never saw his wife again. His daughter was still searching for some trace of him 60 years later.

A tangled web

Men who refused to take responsibility for their actions deserve to be condemned. It is more difficult, however, sorting out men of weak resolve or vague intentions from genuine cases of unrewarded perseverance. Appearances can be deceptive. Chance, health, family pressure, social position or a mother's determination to keep her child in Japan: any number of factors can obscure our retrospective view. No case better illustrates the risks of rushing to judgment than Frank Loyal Weaver.

One night in April 1952, a car came speeding through the streets of Tokyo's Shinagawa ward with American MPs in pursuit. The stolen Buick missed a bend and slammed into a telegraph pole. Weaver, a 26-year-old Australian, was dragged from the wreckage badly concussed. So ended the latest escapade of a man celebrated by some as a romantic hero and condemned by others as an unholy menace.

Frank Weaver (who also took the name Tetsu Ichiro Utaka Kitagawa) had a long record of petty crime going back to his youth in Western Australia. After being sent home from BCOF in 1947 – judged unfit to plead, 'on grounds of insanity', to charges of arson and theft – he contrived to illegally re-enter Japan no fewer than *seven* times. This latest appearance, surviving car wrecks and dodging MPs' bullets, so angered the Australian Head of Mission, Roy 'Hoddy' Hodgson, he drafted a cable to Prime Minister Menzies suggesting he sever military ties with the Americans, because 'they can't shoot straight'. Hodgson thought better of it in the morning.[8]

The object of Weaver's affection was Sachiko Kitagawa, whom he married in a Christian ceremony in 1950. However, she, too, had second thoughts and departed the scene later with another man. This gave the Japanese press a further reason to sympathise with the handsome foreigner whose exploits discredited the White Australia policy and put other, less resolute, men to shame. It took something as absurd as the ban on Japanese brides to create the extraordinary Frank Loyal Weaver.

A change of heart?

By 1948, BCOF was essentially an all-Australian affair. With the departure of the other Commonwealth contingents, force strength fell to around 2500. Living conditions and amenities had vastly improved, and troop rotations became less frequent – inadvertently removing the best means of preventing soldiers forming long-term attachments.

In September 1949, BCOF's Australian commander, General Robertson, cabled the Defence Department advising of a new situation:

> For some months there has been growing attendance of Japanese
> nationals largely female at church services and matrimonial
> entanglements appear inevitable. Policy of most chaplains appears
> to be that if soldier forms attachment and particularly if he gets
> girl into trouble he should marry her irrespective of nationality.
> With extended social contact these problems will multiply.[9]

SCAP had recently announced a major shift in policy 'from the stern rigidity of a military occupation to the friendly guidance of a protective force', and General MacArthur expected the Australians to fall into line. Robertson believed BCOF should either comply or get out of Japan.

The government's Defence Committee favoured dispensing with the non-fraternisation policy. Cabinet did not. With a weather eye fixed on an approaching election, it set the matter aside. The chairman of the Commonwealth Immigration Advisory Council, Les Haylen, fretted about a 'flood of Orientals' leading to a 'brindled population'.[10]

Although no longer strictly enforced, the non-fraternisation policy was never rescinded – a situation one senior officer described as 'morally horrible'.[11] A Japanese woman could date a serviceman at less risk of harassment by MPs, but, more than ever, she laid herself open to trouble. She could walk down the aisle of a BCOF church with her partner, but the marriage still could not be registered. For another three years, the Liberal–Country Party government (which took power from Labor in December 1949) winked at a situation steeped in hypocrisy, leading people on, while being fully prepared to let them down.

Divided lives

The head of the Immigration Department, Tasman Heyes, urged the government to hold the line: 'I feel … we would almost certainly be courting a prolonged and heated attack if we decided so soon after the war crimes trials to admit Japanese'.[12] Australia was still executing enemy combatants for war crimes as late as June 1951. The media gave more attention to this issue than all other aspects of relations with Japan combined.

Married servicemen had few options open to them once they were discharged from the military. Some tried to take up Arthur

Calwell's cynical offer of a passport and one-way passage back to Japan, only to find SCAP refused to let them in. Others departed for Canada, which had eased entry restrictions for non-Europeans. Several applied to take their wives to the United Kingdom, alerting officials to a possible backdoor route to Australia. Lives were turned into lotteries. Best mates who threw in their lots together were sorted into winners and losers more by luck than fair dealing. It deserves to be remembered as a shameful and tragic episode in Australian history.

Paul Gray and his friend Harry Sarre trained together in the Allied Translator and Interpreter Service (ATIS). Both had Japanese sweethearts, and both received their recall notices in late 1949. Desperate to stay, they tried to obtain local employment. 'Harry and I tramped the streets of Tokyo', Paul recalls. 'We wore the leather off our shoes. But work was impossible to find.'[13] Leaving behind their de facto wives – both pregnant – one returned to Perth and the other to Melbourne.

At the outbreak of the Korean War in June 1950, Paul grabbed the first opportunity to get back to Japan with the RAAF. He was able to stay long enough this time to obtain permission to marry. He and his wife, Eiko, went on to raise five children and enjoy retirement together on the north coast of New South Wales.

Harry Sarre, still back in Perth, kept faith with his Kazue, waiting in Hiroshima, by sending regular sums of money. Their daughter, Mariko, was seven when the letters stopped. Harry had died. Almost immediately, a second blow struck: Kazue's father's timber business was destroyed by fire. The single mother took in sewing and worked as a factory hand to make ends meet. Then, crossing the road one day, she was hit by a car and seriously injured. Losing hope, she began to drink heavily.

Kazue was now offered a way out: a proposal of marriage from another Australian man much older than her. Perhaps she did not care for him; perhaps the offer came too late. She ran away, leaving behind a mountain of debts. Mariko, conspicuously mixed-race with 'light-brown hair and blue eyes', was 19 when this happened.[14] She spent her college years living by herself in a rented room, working part-time to pay back what her mother owed.

The war bride Teruko Blair was working as a tour guide in Canberra in 1995 when she picked up a Japanese couple from the airport one day. The first thing she noticed about the woman in the back seat was her fair complexion. Driving into town, they struck up a conversation. 'She asked me how I came to be in Australia and whether I had any children of my own. As I was explaining, she started to cry. She said she had had an Australian father once …'[15] Harry Sarre's daughter had come to see what her life might have been like.

Brian Drover, the young soldier who thought he had landed on the moon when he arrived in Japan, was still there five years later. Having married a Japanese, he might as well have been living on another planet.

Drover appealed for help to the Minister for External Affairs, Richard Casey, when he visited Japan in August 1951. The 23-year-old protested against a policy 'which makes exiles out of individuals who choose a mate from a "non-white" race'.[16] He accepted that 'mass immigration of Asiatics' was undesirable but could not understand what this had to do with the wife of an Australian citizen. A colleague also stranded in Tokyo, Robert Robinson, laid before the minister impeccable patriotic credentials: the scion of a pioneering family in Geelong, who had served his nation under arms for more than seven years. 'At this moment', wrote Robinson, 'I have an equal chance of becoming an asset, once again, to my country, or forever remaining a "moral exile"'.

Neither knew that the government had received a recommendation from the Immigration Advisory Council in favour of admitting Japanese war brides. Representations had been lodged on behalf of 38 women and children, and veterans' groups no longer opposed the move. The same week Casey was in Tokyo, Cabinet considered – and *rejected* – the proposal.

The reasons given for Cabinet's refusal were the depth of anti-Japanese feeling in the community and the need to protect troops stationed abroad from contracting ill-advised marriages.[17] (Ministers ignored advice from BCOF headquarters that a policy change was unlikely to result in a spate of hasty nuptials.) Nobody needed to mention the disqualification of race, as it conditioned the entire immigration program.

Peace dividend

The government was grappling with two related issues at the time. One was the increasing resentment being shown in Asia towards the White Australia policy (which Casey experienced first-hand during his travels). The other, and more immediate, problem was obtaining ratification for an unpopular peace treaty with Japan. A majority of Australians, according to a Gallup poll, expected a rearmed Japan to pose a renewed threat within a few decades.[18]

During the treaty debate, Labor's Les Haylen condemned the settlement because it would 'write finis to the experiment which has been called "White Australia"'. The Liberal MP and future Immigration Minister Alexander Downer, Sr was even more vehemently opposed, calling it 'an act of folly, a myopic blunder'. The former Changi prisoner of war crossed the floor of parliament to vote (unsuccessfully) against ratification.[19]

With emphasis on the negative, the Immigration Minister, Harold Holt, announced in March 1952 that the government could no longer 'justifiably continue' blocking the entry of Japanese wives of servicemen and ex-servicemen.[20] He did not say so, but the peace treaty made the situation untenable.

A thin welcome mat was laid out. The wives needed to satisfy tests of health, character and security; they were not granted permanent resident status immediately; and no family members, apart from children, could accompany them. The minister retained total discretion applying criteria as broad and vague as, whether she was 'of a type who would be accepted by the Australian community'.[21]

In satisfying the twin objectives of softening public feeling towards the Japanese and answering critics of White Australia, officials could not have done better than start with Gordon and Cherry Parker and their two fair-haired daughters. A migration officer rated Gordon 'a good type';[22] his petite and pretty wife was an orphan of the atomic bomb (no family to worry about); and the children were baptised Christians. It also helped that Gordon's father was active in the Liberal Party and influential politicians took up his cause.

In complaining about his own situation, Parker was careful to avoid general criticism of immigration policy. Rather, he portrayed the Japanese as the villains: hostile to women who married foreigners and eager to take revenge on their mixed-race children. Cherry Parker sounded like a political refugee when she stepped off the plane at Essendon Airport into a barrage of camera flashes and reporters' questions: 'I was alone in Japan. Now not frightened any more'.[23]

New hairdo, fresh make-up and a tasteful frock completed the repackaging of the sweet-sounding Cherry (her given name was Nobuko) as the fully Westernised wife and mother – a long way from the 'Jap tart' Gordon's sister had envisaged.[24] While of limited comfort to the Parkers – still dealing with hate mail and abusive phone calls – a new opinion poll indicated most Australians favoured admitting the war brides.

Their marriage endured, producing four more children within six years. On a visit to Kure in 1995, I asked Cherry whether she had any regrets. There was just the slightest hesitation before she replied: 'No regrets'.

Going, ready or not

The government felt confident few servicemen would want to bring home Japanese wives. In pursuit of this objective, officials refrained from contacting any man previously denied permission; the Embassy in Tokyo withheld public announcement of the policy change; and engaged couples were warned, during screening interviews, that international marriages had a poor success rate. The Immigration Department started out with just 14 applications.[25] Hundreds followed.

It took courage to defy history and leap into the unknown. Adding to the strain, bride and groom each approached the decision from a different perspective. He looked into the bureaucratic abyss, while wondering how the marriage would affect his standing among family and friends. For her, the anxiety of facing exile to a life among strangers was mixed with relief at avoiding the shame of being one of those women left behind.

The journey that would eventually lead Fumika Itō to Australia began in a moment of indecision. A girlfriend invited her to a sukiyaki party, a real treat in those days. She hesitated about going because BCOF soldiers would be there, and she preferred to avoid their company. Recalling the episode, Fumika smiles ruefully: 'That was bad luck'. Bad luck? 'Because I didn't get to choose.'

Private John Clifford took a fancy to the pretty 21-year-old. Several nights later, Fumika was awakened by the sound of pebbles striking her bedroom window. Johnny was in the street below. Terrified her father would wake up – and forced into a corner again – she agreed to a date.

After they became intimate, Fumika moved out of the family home. She pondered what would happen if she got pregnant. Friends warned her to be careful, not let things go too far. But, having taken up with this man, she decided she would never marry another. Was it because of society? 'No, because of me.' Her landlady, an old woman with no children, was the only one to offer encouragement:

'She told me, "I made the mistake of not taking the step; don't miss your chance". I thought, "Even if nothing else happens, I want to leave something of my blood in the world. I want a child"'.

When Johnny joined the fighting in Korea, in December 1950, Fumika was already pregnant. He returned a few weeks later severely wounded, shot through the chest and missing a lung. Following a long stay in hospital, he was sent to the Japanese seaside to recuperate.

Mary, their daughter, was born. A year went by. Johnny no longer talked about the future. Fumika read about the Parkers going to Australia and decided to bring matters to a head. 'Please listen to me. Please listen.' Shy by nature, she struggled to express her feelings, in his language. 'Maybe what I say goes into your ear and out the other side. But, no matter, I say it. When are you going to marry me?' He listened in silence, tears flowing down his face.

He obtained a posting nearer Kure and began making preparations. Then, with a day's notice, she was told to get ready for the wedding; she had no time to gather friends, buy a new dress or have her hair done. And, by the way, could she organise a ring? 'Isn't the man supposed to do that?' she asked. The day after they were married Johnny took ship for home. Fumika followed later, among the first big group of war brides, aboard the *New Australia*.

Their union did not prosper. Her husband's bad temper, painful injuries and financial irresponsibility piled up unhappy memories. For a long time, after his death, Fumika would not let herself utter a bad word against him. Hearing her more candid self talk of the past, she asks for his forgiveness – and takes the story back to their wedding day. As Johnny reached for her hand to slip on the ring, she instinctively pulled back. One of her fingers was slightly deformed. 'Don't be embarrassed', he said. 'Don't hide it. There's nothing wrong.' She thought, 'This person will not disparage me'.[26]

They were among 161 Australian-Japanese couples to register marriages at Kure City Office in 1952. Over the next four years the number would rise to 650.[27]

Farewell to Kure

Following the peace settlement, BCOF seamlessly evolved into the British Commonwealth Forces Korea (BCFK), which continued using Kure for its headquarters. The new war brought other Commonwealth troops back to Japan (including from Canada this time).

The Korean armistice of July 1953 was still holding, three years later, when the Australian military drew up 'secret' plans for the final withdrawal from Japan: 'Operation Greygoose' prepared for the flight south.[28] The belated departure prompted this bitter eulogy in a Kure newspaper:

> It began in 1946 with occupation soldiers in broad-brimmed hats like cowboys … Then, in the absence of a peace treaty, the city became known as a 'town of violence', and the subject was taken up in parliament … And, during the Korean War … Kure R & R Centre supplied 10 000 supplemental UN troops [Japanese workers], comfort women and training (or was it an export campaign?) for international war brides.[29]

Japanese media reports on Kure's prostitution problem routinely lumped together *onri* and *panpan*. The official barriers that had prevented marriages and divided families attracted little comment. The public's attitude to the war brides was ambivalent, exemplified by the 'export campaign' comparison in the editorial just quoted.

Contrary to expectations, the brides did not fit any single bill of lading. They ranged from city-bred college graduates to farmers' daughters with no more than a primary school education, from girls of 19 to mature-aged women. Confounding the Madame Butterfly stereotype was the 38-year-old widow who married a sergeant 13 years her junior. Nearly half the couples had met in the workplace – and not only at entertainment places.

The first reports to reach Kure on the war brides' reception in

Australia carried mixed messages. Some accounts spoke of an encouraging lack of prejudice, others emphasised problems of adjustment. A few wives cancelled departure plans and filed for divorce as a result of what they heard. Within three years, at least ten women had left their husbands and returned to Japan, including one who complained of being treated like 'an unpaid maid'.[30] But they were a small minority; most persevered.

On 4 November 1956, a thousand people thronged the Kure docks to farewell the last of the Australian troops, embarking aboard the MV *Anshun*. A Japanese Navy band played 'Auld Lang Syne', and a blizzard of streamers, billowing on the autumn breeze, tangled with the eager souls who ran beside the ship as it pulled away.[31] The only genuine unknown about the withdrawal from Japan – absent from BCFK's 'secret' plan – was who would turn out for the mothers and children being cast adrift?

Prior to embarkation, the Army chaplains were asked to look into the matter. They managed to identify just two deserted wives. One, described as 'an excellent type', had been issued a British passport. The other, having spent six years in a relationship with a man and borne him a son, was 'apparently a fairly good type', according to the chaplains' report. A third woman was stranded because her fiancé had died while in the process of applying to bring her and their child to Australia.[32] These perfunctory inquiries, with their subjective judgments, ceased once BCFK disbanded. The business was filed away, with every intention of being forgotten.

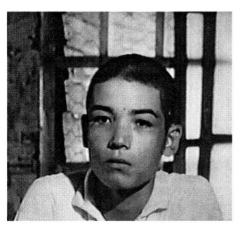

Top left Karumi (Kumi) and Jōji Inoue were living in squalor after their mothers married and moved away.
Film still from *Our Mixed Bloods in Japan* (1962). Courtesy Yone Itō.

Top right Mixed-race orphans taken into care were not as numerous as they were made to appear.
Photograph by Kōyō Kageyama. Courtesy Tomohiro Kageyama.

Above Official rations supplied only half the minimum calories considered necessary for survival early in the occupation.
AWM: P01205.012

Left Social workers described American-fathered Mitsuyoshi Hanaoka as 'gentle and cheerful'.
Film still from *Our Mixed Bloods in Japan* (1962). Courtesy Yone Itō.

Top Air raids in 1945 left much of Kure in ruins.
AWM: P05223.004

Above Female BCOF employees found to be infected with venereal disease were paraded before the camera.
AWM: 132118

Top BCOF was Kure's biggest employer.
AWM: P01205.004

Above Many friendships were struck up in the workplace.
AWM: 147482

Top left Mayumi Kosugi's aunt looked after her from an early age.
Mayumi Okamoto (née Kosugi)

Top right The photograph is inscribed 'Kawaii Jōji' (Cute Jōji, or George), but George Tsutsumi's mother would soon leave him.
George Tsutsumi

Above A family portrait had to serve in place of a marriage certificate: Joe Ritchie with Sachiko and George Tsutsumi.
George Tsutsumi

Above Pilot Officer Ted
Weatherstone (centre), official
interpreter at the Japanese surrender
on Timor, September 1945
AWM: OG3479

Left Arthur Calwell greeting the
100 000th British post-war migrant
NLA: 944770

Top BCOF commander Lt Gen Sir Horace Robertson with Australian Prime Minister Robert Menzies in Kure, August 1950
AWM: HOBJ1154

Above Courting on the quiet: Paul Gray and his fiancée (later wife), Eiko, at Hagi in 1948
Paul Gray

Top left Teruko Blair and her husband (deceased) raised three children in Australia.
Walter Hamilton

Top right Johnny and Fumika Clifford at their commitment ceremony before he left for the fighting in Korea
AWM: P08339.002

Above Miki Sawada's segregation policy was controversial.
Photograph by Kōyō Kageyama.
Courtesy Tomohiro Kageyama

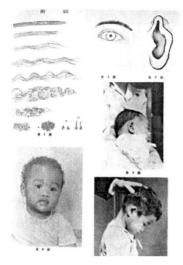

Top left Konketsuji research papers were still being produced in the 1980s.
Minzoku Eisei [Race Hygiene], April 1953

Top right Japanese public schools promoted assimilation of *konketsuji*: Masaaki Usui (Johnny Akiyama) in 1957.
Pix, 17 August 1957

Right Charles Nation was one of the few ex-servicemen to remain behind in Japan with his family.
Kiyotaka Kawasaki

Top left Alexander Downer, Sr (Immigration Minister 1958–63) opposed bringing the Kure Kids to Australia.
NAA: A12111, 1/1958/25/1

Top right ISS Australia founding director Constance Moffit made little headway against the White Australia policy.
NAA: A12111, 1/1955/13/4

Above Yone Itō with the children's chief benefactor, Melbourne businessman Alex Ferguson, in 1962
ISSJ

Top left Fr Tony Glynn spent 42 years working for reconciliation between Australians and Japanese.
Fr Paul Glynn

Top right Mitsuko Yoshida, like many women after the war, enjoyed her newfound freedom.
Kazumi Purvis (née Yoshida)

Left Kazumi Yoshida was her mother's 'treasure'.
Kazumi Purvis (née Yoshida)

The brilliant Suzuo with his mother
and half-sister in Kure, 1957
Pix, 17 August 1957

Top left Kanayo and her son, John, did all they could to make themselves Australian.
John Pate

Top right Junko Shintani (neé Fukuhara) is married, with one daughter, and still lives in Kure.
Walter Hamilton

Left John and Sharon Pate with daughter Cassie at home in Sunbury, Victoria
Walter Hamilton

Left Eddy Evans worried what lay ahead for his wife, Kazue, in Australia.
Barbara Chamberlain (née Evans)

Below Barbara Chamberlain (née Evans) and husband Duncan at home in Goolwa, South Australia
Walter Hamilton

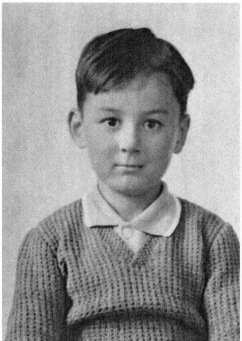

Top left Tetsuko Kellehear on her wedding day, Kure 1954
Allan Kellehear

Top right Allan Kellehear: 'I learned not to expect ready acceptance'.
Allan Kellehear

Above left Terry Huxtable was a father to Johnny for six years.
Johnny Akiyama

Above right Johnny and Mamiko Akiyama have two married children and divide their lives between Japan and Australia.
Walter Hamilton

Above left Kumi Inoue: 'Look what I have achieved' as an Australian.
Walter Hamilton

Above right Mitsuyoshi Hanaoka is retired and living in São Paulo.
Walter Hamilton

Left George Tsutsumi, after a long stevedoring shift on the Nagoya docks
Walter Hamilton

Top Kiyotaka Kawasaki and his
family have resettled in Brisbane.
Walter Hamilton

Above Three generations: Mitsuko
Yoshida with daughter Kazumi, and
granddaughter Mayumi, in Melbourne
Walter Hamilton

12

Enemies in miniature

As Miki Sawada tells the story, she was on a night train heading towards Kyoto in February 1947 when police came through looking for black-market contraband. They took down an unclaimed parcel from a luggage rack near her seat and, inside, discovered the body of a dark-skinned infant.

'Dumb *pansuke* [prostitute]! You're getting off at the next station.' To her surprise, Sawada found the policeman was addressing her. 'Perhaps it was because I was wearing Western dress and carrying an English book. Or perhaps he saw my shock when the wrapping was opened. Though it is weird to think how an old woman in her fifties [she was 45] could bear a baby …'[1] Suspicion quickly shifted away from the outraged Sawada, but the episode – with its dramatic touches and vindication for the heroine – would pass into modern folklore.

Sawada was the granddaughter of Yatarō Iwasaki, founder of the Mitsubishi business conglomerate. The Iwasaki fortune included a seaside estate at Ōiso, in Kanagawa prefecture – or had, until the property was taken over by the government in lieu of taxes. Sawada resolved to raise enough money to buy back the estate for a children's refuge. The Elizabeth Saunders Home was named for the English governess whose bequest to the Anglican Episcopal Church in Japan (*Nippon Sei Ko Kai*) got the project started.[2]

No individual did more to define the *konketsuji* issue than Miki Sawada. She retailed anecdotes suggesting an epidemic of abandonment: bodies dumped in rivers and drains, a massive legacy of unwanted children. To her, they were a race apart, with a limited future in Japan. For this, she blamed the immorality of the parents more than Japanese racial prejudice: 'The only way by which the terrible stigma on these unfortunate children, who must shoulder the fearful guilt of their parents, can be washed off is not by training them to become merely clever, but by training them to become men of worth – gentlemanlike and ladylike'.[3]

The entrance to the Ōiso estate from the public road was through a long tunnel, and infants were sometimes abandoned there. One visitor to the Home felt this transition point had a 'wonderful psychological effect':

Nature is beautiful around the Saunders Home ... The air is clean. Vulgar society is held at bay by the tunnel, and on the huge lawn children of seven races are playing. It is an odd scene that moves us to sorrow and curiosity. It is neither East nor West; it is the 'lawn of a wonderland'.[4]

Among the first to play on this magical lawn was the son of an Australian soldier. The child's mother, a dancer, had looked after him for a year, before making the journey to Ōiso.[5] In another case, years later, a war widow wrote to Sawada from Osaka describing an afternoon she had spent with a 'young and handsome' Australian:

I want to tell about that time, about the child who was produced in three hours. I really wish my child could see his father. When I look at his eyes and the colour of his skin, and hear people admire his beautiful face, I always think about his Australian father.

Sawada urged her to give up her little boy: 'She and her mother talked it over. Even though they knew it was for the best, emotion prevented them from releasing the child whom they had raised to the age of seven. I went home empty-handed'.[6]

Sawada's policy of removing the *konketsuji* from society was strongly opposed in some quarters. A prominent American missionary, Charles Iglehart, claimed she was engaged in 'an experiment in genetic development'. For Iglehart, the children's best hope lay 'in anonymity, and, where this is impossible, in following a completely conventional social pattern until a conventional acceptance has been won and established'.[7] The Episcopal Church in the United States, after initially supporting Sawada, suspended funding in 1953 because of her autocratic methods. Be that as it may, she got things done, and her efforts undoubtedly saved many lives.

Forbidden fruit

In his acclaimed 1949 film *Late Spring*, director Yasujirō Ozu keeps references to the occupation to a minimum: a Coca-Cola sign; a train carriage bearing the words 'Allied Personnel'; and a murmured comment. Two young women are discussing a mutual friend who is heavily pregnant and unmarried. One leans across and whispers something to the other. 'That's awful!' the listener exclaims. 'These things happen', says her companion. 'Divine providence, you know.'[8]

The awful secret ostentatiously kept from the audience was easily guessed. Everyone was discussing the subject, usually in hushed tones. Ten months after the surrender, a radio announcer was reportedly sacked, on SCAP'S orders, for referring to the arrival of the 'first occupation present'. Censors even deleted references to *konketsuji* from medical journals. The few articles that made it into print employed euphemisms, such as 'blonde' or 'blue-eyed babies', or put the SCAP-approved case that no problem existed.[9]

Foreign correspondents were harder to control. The first in-depth story, by former war correspondent Darrell Berrigan, appeared in the *Saturday Evening Post* in June 1948. Berrigan wrote sympathetically of 'bewildered mothers [who] are not hardened prostitutes' and 'lonely young men feeling the full force of manhood'. In his opinion, the main reason most Japanese refused to see it this way was not racial prejudice or the children's illegitimacy. It was something else. People usually concealed what they truly felt about the occupation, but 'vilification of these innocents is safe – and satisfying'.

Nobody knew how many *konketsuji* existed, and no official count would be attempted, said Berrigan, 'so long as the Allied authorities have anything to say about it'. His conservative estimate of between 1000 and 4000 was accompanied by the claim that most babies were 'either killed outright before or after birth, abandoned or left at an orphanage'.[10]

Miki Sawada was just getting underway when he visited; infants were crowded into a bedroom at the estate, awaiting the completion of nursery facilities. Another orphanage, Our Lady of Lourdes Baby Home (*Seibo Aiji-en*), under the Bluff at Yokohama, held 130 mixed-race children. The nuns there also favoured removing them from society, because they were so physically outstanding: 'We want to keep them segregated from the pure Japanese, send them to English-speaking schools and, if possible, send them back [*sic*] to the United States and Britain later'. SCAP and Japanese government officials insisted the children would be better off left in the community. On one thing, however, all agreed: the need to prevent the *konketsuji* becoming 'unhappy misfits' like the Eurasians of India, Indonesia and Indochina.

Welfare settings

For many a repatriated Japanese soldier, the first sight of filthy war orphans begging in railway stations drove home the reality of defeat. The entire nation was hungry and bewildered, but the young were especially vulnerable. The average 12-year-old weighed 20 per cent less than a decade before.[11]

The emergency called for state intervention on an unprecedented scale. A new child welfare law set minimum standards and state subsidies for the country's hundreds of private orphanages. There was a general tightening up of a chaotic situation – highlighted by the discovery of the bodies of more than 100 infants at a Tokyo maternity hospital (it is not known whether any were *konketsuji*). Father Edward Flanagan of Boys Town fame was engaged as an adviser by SCAP, and the American Licensed Agencies for Relief in Asia (LARA) directed the lion's share of its food, clothing and medical supplies to tens of thousands of needy children.[12]

Only a small proportion of war orphans were waifs, in need of institutional care. Ninety per cent lived with relatives or guardians.[13] The same was true of the country's fatherless *konketsuji* – contrary to popular belief. The real situation was hard to grasp because, rather than seek public assistance, Japanese preferred to hide their shame. Also, in the not-so-distant past, welfare entitlements were assessed by the police, and they weeded out claimants considered morally unfit. Little wonder mothers of mixed-blood children avoided scrutiny.

Another way the children might have come to light, through local adoption, was effectively closed off. Japanese were familiar with the practice of adopting a member of their extended family or a son-in-law to secure a male heir, but it was rarely used to rescue an unknown child. A proverb went: 'One does not know from which horse the bone has come'. In May 1952, the *Tokyo Shimbun* reported on what it said was 'the only blue-eyed boy' in the capital with a Japanese foster-parent.[14]

At the end of the occupation, there were just 482 *konketsuji* (78 per cent 'white' and 22 per cent 'black') under institutional care. Half were lodged at either the Elizabeth Saunders Home or Our Lady of Lourdes Baby Home. The rest were scattered across scores of public and private orphanages.[15]

Social researchers by now had gathered a considerable amount of data on mothers of *konketsuji*. The main reasons women gave for surrendering custody of their children were desertion by the father, financial hardship and family opposition. Two-thirds had been through some form of marriage ceremony, and one-third had worked for the occupation forces (a proportion that declined after 1950). The researchers identified 10–15 per cent as 'mistresses' (*onri*) and 5–10 per cent as prostitutes.[16] The figures do not provide a complete picture (mothers who abandoned infants anonymously could not be questioned), but they are worth contemplating before plunging into the vortex of the public's imagination.

Numbers game

Lifting censorship from the *konketsuji* issue was like driving a stick into an anthill: wild claims and speculations poured out; anger and prejudice overran commonsense.

In April 1952, a week before the peace treaty came into effect, the president of the Japanese YWCA, Tamaki Uemura, addressed an open letter to the wife of General Matthew Ridgway (the new SCAP). She claimed that hosts of ignorant, immature Japanese women had been seduced by occupation troops and turned into prostitutes: 'These girls have reportedly mothered 200 000 illegitimate children, and deserted many of them during the past six and a half years'.[17]

Uemura was well known and respected on both sides of the Pacific, and her letter received wide publicity. The '200 000' figure gained credence before Japan's Welfare Ministry could undertake the first serious attempt to quantify the problem. It distributed questionnaires to every registered obstetrician and midwife in the country, asking them how many mixed-race children they had delivered. The tally, announced that December, shocked everyone: just 5013.[18]

Recognising that the survey had shortcomings – for example, low tallies for births prior to 1949 suggested lapses in record keeping or memory – the ministry followed up with field interviews. The main concentrations of *konketsuji* were in Tokyo and neighbouring Kanagawa prefecture, as expected, though some were found in every part of the country (including 130 in Hiroshima). Officials identified 3490 children living with mothers or guardians. When added to the number in institutional care, the total came to less than 4000.

Assuming a considerable amount of under-reporting (for reasons already discussed), informed observers estimated the true number of *konketsuji* to be around 10000, including those who had already left Japan with their parents. It was also assumed many times this number had died from natural causes, neglect, infanticide or abortion. In place of anecdotes and alarmist claims, a somewhat clearer picture was emerging.[19]

Hybrid hype

To help frame a policy response, the government assembled an expert panel that included Mrs Sawada, social critics Kiyoshi Kanzaki and Sōichi Ōya, and specialists in psychology, sociology, paediatrics and education.[20] The convenor was the head of the National Institute of Public Health, Yoshio Koya, a medical scientist whose eugenic views on race mixing were influential during Japan's colonial era.

Koya insisted on looking beyond the 'sentimental' issue of child protection. He worried about the tendency of Eurasians to form a 'foreign stratum' in society, prone to exploitation by 'communists or nationalists'. Koya also anticipated problems resulting from the 'disharmony of genes', although he could not decide how serious this might be. While he warned that the genetic 'stamp' of black fathers would last for generations, in the next breath, he celebrated the power of a subjugated race to 'take revenge on the armed conqueror' by swallowing up his alien blood.[21]

Such erratic views were of little help to officials trying to devise practical countermeasures. Perhaps the doctors and anthropologists making empirical studies of the mixed-bloods could supply answers?

By every conceivable means – body measurements, teeth casts, X-rays, tests of sensory and emotional response, analysis of artistic expression and patterns of play, and even post-mortem examinations – they searched for deviations from the Japanese norm. The resulting academic papers, with their imposing charts and mug shots of bewildered children, make for depressing reading. *Konketsuji* were sized up against unphotographed and unnumbered 'pure Japanese' and inevitably found wanting.[22]

The testing regimes represented a significant intrusion on the lives of their unhappy subjects – for little scientific gain. By focusing on institutionalised children, whose delayed development could be due to environmental factors, much of the research was hopelessly flawed. This did not prevent irresponsible commentators spreading alarm about differences in IQ and sociability scores between 'pure Japanese' and mixed-bloods in early age groups, while ignoring data that showed little difference between these two groups of institutionalised children by the age of four or five. One professor of medicine wrote in a major newspaper: 'The inundation of future *konketsuji* could be more significant for Japan's racial history than the atomic bomb'. He considered it fortunate that a new abortion law would limit their number.[23]

In response to appeals from private institutions, the Welfare Ministry drew up a plan to build five special schools for *konketsuji*. The scheme immediately ran into opposition from the left-wing Japan Teachers' Union, as well as from government officials who felt it would be incompatible with a new 'Children's Charter' that guaranteed equality of education and opportunity. The Education Ministry settled the question by declaring that all children registered as Japanese should attend regular public schools.[24]

Many *konketsuji*, however, were not registered as Japanese: that is, not listed in anyone's *koseki*. They were stateless. Mothers hesitated to register them because a *koseki* was a semi-public document in those days, and a blank space where the father's name should appear could blight a person's prospects for life. One way around the dilemma was for the child to be registered as the offspring of a married family member (another reason officials could never identify them all). Aware some mothers lacked the necessary family support, the mixed-race author Imao Hirano publicised his willingness to become a nominal father and reportedly 'adopted' 16 children this way.[25]

The government did finally allow two institutions to operate special schools, but most *konketsuji* took their places alongside other Japanese youngsters. Teachers were instructed to spread them across their classes, taking care to gain the co-operation of parents of any child seated beside one. Other parents were to be warned to refrain from 'careless talk' likely to encourage bullying.[26] Nothing was left to chance as schools prepared in the spring of 1953 to receive the first 430 mixed-race pupils – out of a primary school population of 11 million.

Black and white

One image more than any other dramatised the nation's anxiety about its lost cultural and political sovereignty: the black Japanese. People did not know whether to laugh or cry over anecdotes about black mixed-bloods trying to scrub the colour from their bodies and mothers secretly swapping them for other children at public baths. It was widely assumed that sexual encounters involving black soldiers were violent, perverted or strictly commercial and black offspring alienated the affections of their unfortunate mothers.

Our Lady of Lourdes Baby Home plumbed the depths of prejudice after it built a new facility for 39 *konketsuji* (mostly with African-American fathers) in Yamato City, near Atsugi airbase. The local primary school refused to admit the children, forcing the institution to purchase a bus and transport them to and from Yokohama, a daily, two-hour round trip. Three years later, the school agreed to take some of the boys but abandoned the trial after parents complained they were disruptive. Another three years went by, and the orphanage applied again. The school board suggested confining the *konketsuji* to a special class, as if they were handicapped, but staff refused to countenance further discrimination. This was in 1960. Soon after the issue had been resolved, a female teacher made the following entry in her work diary:

> When I was tidying a shelf, a [mixed-race] child called me, '*Sensei*' [Teacher or Miss], in a fawn-like voice. I pretended not to notice. Then the child called me in a low voice, '*Okā-san, Okā-san*' [Mother, Mother]. I wondered if this was because the child had heard the word '*Okā-san*' in conversation with classmates and wanted to experience using it once.[27]

Every mixed-race child learned to expect taunts of *ainoko* or *harō-no-ko* (child of 'hello'). The black child also heard cries of *kurombo* (nigger) or *dojin* (earth person, aborigine). Media commentators based predictions about mixed-blood behaviour on skin colour: whites would be bossy, due to feelings of superiority; blacks would be destructive, because of society's hostility or, some suggested, their 'savage' ancestry.[28]

A preoccupation with externals blinded observers to the true inner life of the children: the anguish from witnessing a mother's pain; the guilt at causing a family feud; or, for those sent abroad for adoption, the sadness of giving up friends and familiar surroundings – stopping being Japanese. The son of a black *konketsuji* has expressed this well: 'My mother loved Japan, but Japan did not love my mother'. They were never, as imagined or depicted, intrinsically separate from society. Regarding themselves as Japanese, they were constantly forgetting and being reminded of their other, perceived, identity. 'Only when I saw my reflection in a mirror or in a train window at night', said one young woman, 'I knew I was different'.[29]

Offspring of war

The writings of two government advisers illustrate how difficult it was to overcome prejudice.

The commentator Sōichi Ōya could be liberal-minded. 'It's useless appealing to the "purity of racial blood", like the Nazis', he insisted. 'There is no such thing as a "Japanese race", only a "Japanese ethnic group". If Anglo-Saxons or Negroes have been added recently, what's the problem?' He could also be bigoted. Another article, published under his name, referred to black *konketsuji* as 'miniature King Kongs' and confined the employment prospects of mixed-bloods to sport and entertainment: 'We should not expect a lot to become academics or succeed in endeavours requiring brain power'.[30]

Kiyoshi Kanzaki was equally ambivalent. He wanted society to overcome prejudice and give the children a happy life, outside institutions: 'That way Japan can truly be a great and tolerant world citizen'. However, he consistently saw the issue through a filter of disdain for the American military and their camp followers, who give birth to *konketsuji* 'like methane gas'.[31] Teachers with mixed-bloods in their class, Kanzaki believed, faced a conflict between promoting humanitarian values and fostering an independent national spirit. In other words, by treating all children the same they risked sending an unwholesome message.

The issue became more vexed as the occupation gave way to a permanent American military presence. In December 1953, the welfare scholar and Socialist parliamentarian Katsuo Takenaka described a nation gripped by fear:

> People see their homeland turning into something like a colony and sense a *panpan*-like change appearing among female Japanese nationals. Blood purity is becoming cloudy … gentle and strong Japanese women are giving birth to black and white children.

I wonder if we are not witnessing the pollution of Japan's heritage and race, leading to their eventual ruin.[32]

This theme dominated books and films on the *konketsuji* issue. The first was written by Setsuko Takasaki, a welfare officer in Kanagawa prefecture, whose beat took in the 'three top mixed-blood children's bases', Yokohama, Yokosuka and Zama. These places, wrote Takasaki, gave off a 'dirty smell' that caused Japanese to gag. She described one neighbourhood where *konketsuji* congregated in fetid alleyways:

> They see blood dripping out of the arms of street urchins as they inject drugs. A one-eyed, pregnant beggar *panpan* holds on her swollen belly a black-skinned, mixed-blood boy, his face covered with spots. Others include: a blonde boy, about five years old, crawling under a food-stall; a blue-eyed child eating a ten-yen bowl of rice porridge; and the familiar face of a cheerful girl, about seven, with braided blonde hair, loudly singing a pop song.

Although the author sympathised with the children, she could not conceal a deeper pain: 'General Tōjō never dreamt the war would produce not only white but also black Japanese'.[33]

A soybean solution

The controversy formed part of a larger debate about the lessons Japan should take from the war and what kind of society was needed to secure the peace. Some commentators saw a way of proving to the world Japanese were a mature and responsible people. 'We don't need to copy the heartlessness of their fathers', remarked the novelist Taiko Hirabayashi. 'Raising the mixed-blood children is a task for the Japanese.' Black *konketsuji* were said to be better off in Japan, because Americans were even worse racists (similar comments were made about Australians, in relation to white *konketsuji*). The critic Fumiko Matsuda was succinct: 'We need to have the attitude not to make any unhappy Japanese'.[34]

Did this mean tolerating greater diversity or incorporating all citizens within a single ethnic identity? The editor Keiichi Aoki took the latter view. Let the *konketsuji* eat *natto* (fermented soybeans) or miso soup, he declared. 'All we have to do is to raise them as members of the same racial family.'[35] An editorial in a leading daily, the *Yomiuri Shimbun*, straddled both positions:

> At a time when society is going backwards and revealing a narrow-minded nationalism, there is a risk that hatred engendered by the war will exact an unseen revenge [on the mixed-bloods] … Real nationalism equals humanitarian love and [the recognition that] race mixing often produces good results. It is definitely not a negative thing for tolerant-hearted Japanese to let *konketsuji* melt into the population.[36]

Once the children began entering the education system, 'melting' seemed a realistic possibility. Under the influence of a largely sympathetic teaching profession, the watchword became 'non-discrimination', and analysis that treated them as different was discouraged. Emphasis shifted from guiding the mixed-bloods to guiding society towards a more enlightened view.

But all the miso soup in the world could not turn *konketsuji* into mainstream Japanese. Within a few years it was apparent even seemingly well-adjusted individuals needed help. In a major departure from the case-by-case approach favoured by social workers, a developmental psychologist at Hiroshima University, Mitsuya Yamauchi, analysed the *konketsuji* as a distinct minority, defined not by skin colour or family background but by a shared experience of discrimination. His analysis was able to explain certain puzzling behaviour: why, for instance, the children were so clingy with their teachers.

They were using them, Yamauchi said, to 'restore their privileges' when excluded from the majority group.[37]

Yamauchi believed it was essential to lead *konketsuji* towards an objective understanding of why they were different. Nothing would be gained by trying to ignore the fact. This inconvenient truth challenged those who imagined prejudice could be defeated while still clinging to a homogeneous ethnic identity.

The American connection

Washington observed with alarm the anti-American backlash that followed the occupation. Assessing the situation in 1954, the US military Joint Chiefs thought that if Southeast Asia went communist, so would Japan. In *The Great Seduction*, Richard Deverall, a former senior SCAP official, described how leftists were exploiting the *konketsuji* issue to discredit the American presence. The 'peculiar and dangerous' Japanese aversion to race mixing, said Deverall, made them vulnerable to subversion by 'Red China'.[38]

The American government was not prepared to accept responsibility for thousands of GI babies; that would be an admission too far for an imperial power with bases dotting the globe. Instead, it tried to take some heat out of the issue by indirect means. Return passage to Japan was arranged for 100 servicemen willing to assume responsibility for their offspring; with encouragement from the State Department, expatriate business, church and veterans' groups in Tokyo formed the Joint Committee for Assisting Japanese-American Orphans, which directed financial aid to the most needy cases; and, most importantly, the 1953 Refugee Relief Act allocated a visa quota to foreign orphans, regardless of nationality, clearing the way for 1700 Japanese children – mainly *konketsuji* – to be adopted by American families by 1957. (After this date, orphans entered free of numerical quotas.)[39]

The shift of emphasis towards inter-country adoption was a

major change of direction. Only a few years earlier, Charles Iglehart, the Methodist missionary and SCAP adviser, had dismissed proposals for sending the children to America as 'fantastically impracticable'.[40] According to Iglehart, Americans were no more tolerant of Eurasians than Japanese were, and 'tearing' children from their mothers would be 'inhumane' (a view he no longer espoused by 1957).

There were, indeed, good reasons for proceeding cautiously – although they became apparent only after hundreds of placements had been completed. Many early adoptions from Japan were arranged by proxy – in which a legal agent acted on behalf of a foreign client – without proper checks on the receiving family. An investigation turned up 'instances … of physical abuse of children, breakdown of adoptive homes, adoption of children by persons who were unstable or mentally ill or who had serious physical illness, and placements of upset or emotionally disturbed children with persons unprepared or unable to help them'. Another study concluded that a quarter of all adoptions up to 1955 should not have proceeded in the way they did.[41]

The American Joint Committee turned for help to International Social Service. The Geneva-based ISS had taken over work begun by the YWCA in the 1920s, assisting migrants, refugees and displaced persons. The unacknowledged children of foreign servicemen in Europe and Asia represented a new challenge for the expanding network of ISS national branch offices. In 1955, soon after helping establish an office in Australia, Far East Representative Florence Boester arrived in Tokyo and put together a team of social workers, paid for by the US government.[42]

ISS's preferred method was to send a child to an approved family in the United States on a trial basis, before completing the adoption locally. The organisation co-operated with state welfare bodies, which would need to take charge of the child if the placement did not work out. Boester and her colleagues found Japanese orphanages were unused to waiting for 'home studies' to be completed on prospective adoptive parents, and any delay in selecting a family could result in an impatient mother or institution accepting a better offer. As a result, ISS placed a large proportion of mixed-bloods with American military families based in Japan.

ISS America worried that not enough children would be left for its stateside clients. Boester tried to boost her enrolment by soliciting referrals from prefectural welfare offices and urging institutions to release children before the Refugee Relief Act expired at the end of 1956. Orphanages proved reluctant to forgo the income they obtained from adoptions, and local officials preferred to deal directly with American families because they could obtain a 'personal benefit' (Boester's phrase). The Elizabeth Saunders Home declined to co-operate with ISS, and each came to hold the other in low regard.

Nevertheless, by 1958, American families had adopted around 2000 *konketsuji*, and ISS was handling a major share of new placements. As the pressure valve was released, Florence Boester noticed a marked improvement in the tone of Japanese press coverage of the children and a reduction in public animosity towards them.[43]

13

Kiyotaka's story

Corporal Charles Nation, a gangly, fair-haired, 26-year-old Australian veteran of the Borneo campaign, joined BCOF in 1947 and was assigned as an orderly-room clerk. Yoshie Kawasaki, a former film actress, was a war widow with a young son, struggling on a housemaid's wage. She jumped at the chance of earning three times more as a BCOF typist. And so they met. In March 1948, they exchanged marriage vows in a Shinto ceremony.

After the birth of their son, Kiyotaka, Charles supported his family by trading on the black market. Several times a week, dodging police surveillance, he bicycled between his camp and the house they kept in Yoshiura, a suburb of Kure. It was another four years before he and Yoshie could register their marriage.

Charles's relations, back in the Victorian country town of Echuca, remained none the wiser. Interviewed late in life, he explained his reluctance to pass on the news:

> Our young bloke came along in July 1950. It took a couple of
> hard years' work to manufacture him. It wasn't until he was nearly
> three years old that I wrote home and told the folks that I'm an
> old married man and a father.
>
> Well, the poor old lady she just about went into hysterics. She
> couldn't believe that her youngest boy had got himself married to
> a foreigner, least of all a Japanese.
>
> I had a pretty general idea of the feeling of Australians at

that time, and immediately after. And I thought, it would be no hardship for me to take her home and reside in Australia, but there'd be a hardship imposed on her. So that was the genesis of my thinking of remaining in Japan. The only reason I remained in Japan was because of my wife. Since I believe I married the most wonderful woman in the world, why need I embrace anything else?[1]

'They loved each other and were very close', says Kiyotaka, 'but they fought all the time'. He mimics his father: 'Australia, number one! Japan, number ten!' Then he acts his mother, in high dudgeon: 'My government surrendered to your government. But I never surrendered to you! Go home! Go back to Australia'. Charles would try to pacify her: 'OK, Yoshie. OK'. He knew the storm had passed once she expelled a final 'Humph!'

Charles never mastered Japanese and does not seem to have made close friends outside his family's immediate circle. Kiyotaka reckons his father never got beyond his first impression of a broken, ugly country.

When he came to Japan in 1947, at that time everything was monochrome: black and white – no colour. Everything was dirty. The air was dirty. The water was dirty. The food was dirty. That's why he always complained: 'I hate Japanese'. Everything had to be perfect. He wanted perfection, but he was not a perfect man. I was scared of him. Just before he died, he told me: 'I like today's young Japanese, but I still hate the ones my own age'.

His behaviour was outrageous. Whenever we went out to a restaurant, he'd complain: 'Are you going to charge for this?' My mother would get angry. 'You'd never do it in Australia. Why? Because you simply don't like Japan.' 'I love Japan', he'd say. 'No, you'd never do this in Australia!' Nobody in Australia, you see, would take his sort of behaviour seriously. But people in Japan say 'sorry, sorry'. Maybe he was happy to hear that. It made him feel good. He was odd. [Laughs.]

Once Charles finally got around to breaking the news to Echuca, Aunt Kitty was dispatched north on an inspection tour. She sent back word that he was the 'King of Yoshiura' (or, as Kiyotaka jokingly puts it, 'the black-market king').

Charles's access to goods and services, unavailable to ordinary Japanese proved a godsend when Yoshie's first son fell ill.

> My half-brother was really sick, nearly died, and Poppa took him to the occupation hospital and got injections, and thankfully he lived. After that, my mother never opposed my father.

The couple earned the gratitude of neighbours the same way.

> They looked after many people in Yoshiura. They loaned people money. For instance, one man was injured, and gangrene got into the wound. He nearly died because he had no money to go to hospital. Father said: 'You go, we pay'. They cut off the leg, but he lived. Many poor people … My father looked after them. At that time I didn't understand why! Because he was usually saying, 'I hate Japanese'. The fact was, everyone knew 'Charlie-san' in Yoshiura.

At the end of the occupation, Charles took his discharge from the Army and found work at an American PX near Yokohama. He transferred later to a commissary in Seoul, South Korea. From that point on, he was able to get back to Yoshiura only twice a year. Kiyotaka was six when these long absences began.

> Each time his visit lasted two weeks. I never forget. Mummy cried every time. 'This is final. This is final.' Going to Korea, carrying a

big bag. 'No come home.' But he always came back.

Mummy told me that when he first left Japan I could speak English properly. 'Your Japanese was funny', she said. But, by the time I finished primary school, I could not understand English at all.

Kiyotaka was bigger than other children his own age. He formed a gang and (in the memory of one fellow student) was a bit of a bully. In Year Six, his teacher discovered him squeezing classmates for donations – 'to pay for treatment for an injured dog', as Kiyotaka recalls.

> I was beaten because this was considered very impertinent. Another time, the same teacher caught me fooling about in a school storeroom and beat me again. He said, as he hit me, 'Do you know how many Japanese soldiers were killed by soldiers of your father's country?' So I came to the limit of my patience – I snapped. I picked up a piece of broken furniture and hit him. That's why I wasn't able to stay at that primary school. At my next school, I was marked out as a 'bad boy'.

At ISS activities, Kiyotaka stood out for a different reason. He remembers feeling guilty when other children remarked how nice it must be to have a father. 'That was very hard to hear.' Even though his father was absent most of the time, at least he knew who he was. He preferred to stay away from ISS, unless it was a special event. His father did not like him attending for a different reason: he felt it brought shame on the family.

Looking back on those days, growing up in Kure, Kiyotaka comically eschews any rosy nostalgia.

> I said to Mayumi [Kosugi] recently, 'We were punks'. Everyone a punk (except for one or two): just punks; little shits; brats,

shitty brats; gangsters, boy gangsters. [Laughs.] We were bad. Mayumi-chan [the honorific used for a child], honestly speaking, she wasn't a good girl. [Laughs.] Don't you think? They were delinquents. They were objects of contempt. Whenever something happened, we were criticised. If I do something: 'Gross monster!' Comments like that.

I was a punk. Like, fighting. I was often in fights. I remember starting school, and there was this boy, and he beat me. I came home crying. [Emotional.] And my mother and father said, 'Go back, and don't come home crying again'. I started from that day: 'I must do something'. I might not win every time. [Laughs.] But if somebody called me a name, I'd fight him.

On the roof of the ISS building – which, as you know, was in front of the former BCOF headquarters – everybody was smoking. We played up and were always being singled out by the police.

Kiyotaka twice came under police guidance, which meant being detained and having his parents summoned.

For nothing, just walking. There was a soba shop run by my mother's niece's husband, so I often went there to eat or help out. Walking to the bus stop, I was picked on by this Mamma Police [female delinquency officer] who scolded me: 'What are you doing at this time of day?' I wasn't old enough to properly explain myself, so we argued. I screamed, 'I just came to eat soba'.

One day, the Mamma Police visited the soba shop when my mother and I were helping out, and demanded to know, 'What are you doing here? Are you working? I'll report this to your school!' It started again. My mother was furious and challenged her to step outside. She complained that the police repeatedly arrested her son for no good reason: 'I'll make it an international incident, if necessary'. She often got into fights over me.

By the time he was in junior high school, Kiyotaka was 192 centimetres tall. Naturally, he tried out for the high jump. One day, during athletics practice, his friend threw a wild discus, which thudded onto the ground nearby.

> I yelled, 'What are you doing, you bastard!' I picked up the discus and hurled it back. It sailed over his head. The coach was watching and called me over: 'Listen to me …'. My results in the high jump, hurdles, et cetera, were all poor. Here was my chance to get to [senior] high school. So I said, 'OK, I'll give it a try'.

His skill with the discus transformed Kiyotaka from 'bad boy' to 'number-one draft pick' when the time came for admissions to senior high school. He continued throwing further and further, into university and beyond, representing his country at international competitions and setting a national mark not bettered more than 30 years later. It is the longest-standing record on the books of the Japan Association of Athletics Federations.

Competition took him to Australia. He remembers attending a reception in Brisbane and meeting a former BCOF soldier. The man was handing around photographs from his days in the occupation, including some taken in Yoshiura. The moment that Kiyotaka mentioned he came from there, the veteran put the snaps away.

> I still remember his face: the look of surprise. There is a Japanese expression, 'sune ni kizumotsu hito' ['a shin-sore person', meaning someone with a guilty conscience]. There must be a lot in Australia. He was an official. He said he'd be attending the competition the next day. We shook hands: 'See you tomorrow'. But he didn't come. He didn't come to the farewell party either.

Kiyotaka knew, from what his father had told him, the occupation soldiers were no saints. Older Kure residents, he says, remember the rapes: 'This is not well understood by Australians'. His wife concurs. They also acknowledge the other side of the equation: mothers who abandoned or rejected their mixed-race offspring. He cites the case of a friend who, on attending his mother's funeral, was assigned the seat of 'the least important person'.

After completing university, Kiyotaka took a job with a paper manufacturer in Nagoya, where he met his future wife. He practised English by listening to American Forces Radio and kept up with athletics, competing in Montreal the year he started work.

After he had put away the discus for the last time, he returned to Kure and opened a health club. The business was located on a street leading to a once-notorious neighbourhood. It was the Vietnam War era.

> Whenever a visiting navy ship arrived from Australia or the UK, I saw a lot of sailors walking up the hill towards Aga. Perhaps their fathers had been to Japan and told them, 'Why don't you go to *ju-san-chome* [13th street], there's a nice place there.' [Laughs.] But the street no longer existed. They'd return complaining: 'Useless information'.
>
> I said to my father, 'Maybe their parents or seniors told them. They were really marching!'
>
> 'Could be, could be', he said.

Charles, by now, was working at a nearby American military base and living back in Yoshiura. He still hesitated about taking his family to Australia and attended his mother's funeral alone. It seems she never forgave him for marrying a Japanese – or so he believed. When Yoshie eventually accompanied him on a visit to Echuca, she dressed in formal black kimono and *zori* (traditional sandals) and apologised at Mrs Nation's grave: 'I'm sorry I took your son'. She was pleasantly surprised by the way Charles's family treated her. She found a new method of teasing him: 'Even we divorce, I go back to Australia. Uncle Eric look after me, Uncle Archie look after me'.

Yoshie died in 1991. Despite his constant complaints, Charles was still in no hurry to leave Japan. The house at Yoshiura held too many happy memories. His health gradually deteriorated to the point where he needed a wheelchair. By now it was too late to return to Echuca – nobody was left to look after him. So he went to his sister in Brisbane.

Charles's death, at the turn of a new century, left Kiyotaka with his own life-changing decision to make.

14

Plausible deniability

On 5 May 1952 ('Children's Day', a public holiday), a Kure news-paper reported the arrest of a 29-year-old woman – the mother of two mixed-race children – who had been caught stealing clothes and a blanket. According to the *Chugoku Nippo*, a small local newspaper, as the mother was being questioned by police, her four-year-old son amused himself by 'singing decadent popular songs and dancing'. It was said to be a typical case of a woman promised marriage, and then 'thrown away like rubbish'. Not long afterwards, the attempted murder-suicide of an unemployed mother with a mixed-race boy made the news.[1]

Over the next 12 months, the main occupation-related topics in the *Chugoku Nippo* were *konketsuji* and foreign soldiers' crimes. By contrast, in the same period, the *Chugoku Shimbun*, a more respected regional newspaper, devoted only two stories to the children. It paid more attention to soldiers' crimes, war brides, prostitution and the post-occupation economy.

The contrast in approach was most evident when the mixed-bloods began their education. The *Chugoku Nippo* expressed sur-prise at how little fuss was being made: 'It seems good children of blond hair and blue eyes are innocently going to school'. Ignoring the wishes of teachers not to draw attention to them, the paper went ahead and published the personal details of several *konketsuji*. In reporting the results of a personality test, which rated them 'friendly' but 'easily angered', it struck a self-satisfied note: 'They observe well how society regards them and have rebellious spirits'.[2]

Kure City Education Board established a *konketsuji* advisory council and commissioned Hiroshima University researcher Mitsuya Yamauchi to prepare guidance manuals. Yamauchi urged teachers to identify each child's special talent and instruct students not to judge people by skin colour. He attributed the prejudice against the *konketsuji* to several causes – dysfunctional family life, low socio-economic status and social isolation – and not race alone. Kure began to gain a progressive reputation among welfare professionals by demonstrating the advantages of raising mixed-bloods outside institutions. A headline in the *Chugoku Shimbun* in May 1955 celebrated the attainments of '23 Integrated Children'.[3]

Integrated, perhaps. Popular? No. Despite the fact (or possibly because) they scored well on intelligence tests and were physically bigger and linguistically more precocious than their peers, two out of three of Kure's *konketsuji* were rated 'unpopular' at school. They were also said to be 'emotionally aggressive' – though, again, was this the cause or the result of their unpopularity? Looking on the bright side – to the one-third who were managing better – some observers concluded that 'if one does not feel prejudice as prejudice, it naturally disappears'. Yamauchi was not among the optimists. 'Prejudice runs at such a deep emotional level', he warned, 'using words and logic, persuasion and public relations may be insufficient to change attitudes'. People in Kure judged the mothers first, and this determined how they felt about the children.[4]

Out of sight

The Australian public remained blissfully unaware of the Kure Kids for the duration of the occupation: not a single photograph appeared in the press; not one case was brought to light. A March 1948 newspaper report confined Japan's abandoned half-castes to the Tokyo–Yokohama area (exclusively with American fathers). An editorial around this time denied any Australian servicemen were involved – apart from making (purely charitable) donations to a foundling home. A report on Hiroshima's orphanages in the services magazine *Gen*, in September 1950, failed to mention the mixed-blood children who were present.[5]

Jennie Woods, a BCOF officer's wife, saw behind the khaki veil of silence. Episodes of rape and sexual exploitation are prominent in her occupation memoir, written late in life. She has described an encounter with the mother of an 18-month-old boy (fathered by an Australian military policeman), who offered her the child for adoption. Woods inquired at BCOF headquarters about the possibility and was told 'such a child could never be considered Australian, either by adoption or any other means'.[6]

By the time Sergeant Ron Jamieson arrived in Kure, several years later, the children were a common sight. He heard at an orphanage there were 200–300 *konketsuji* in the area. Jamieson also wanted to adopt a little boy but, on this occasion, it was the mother who declined. She was sure her 'Jim' would do the right thing and come back for them. Her fortitude inspired Jamieson to launch the 'Eurasian Children's Appeal', with the aim of building a refuge where the women and children could stay until they were reunited with the fathers. On his return to Sydney in 1955, he wrote to the Minister for the Army: 'I have been confronted by them, in the streets, begging and their mothers doing even worse to support their child, until their de facto servicemen husbands return. They should not be forced to these lengths'.[7]

When the issue was raised in parliament, in February 1956, the minister, Sir Eric Harrison, thought it 'rather strange' for such an allegation to be presumed correct. He agreed to 'have a look' whether an investigation was warranted. The problem might not be 'legally ours', commented the Melbourne *Herald*, but on the grounds of 'national pride and human sympathy', it should not be ignored. The Sydney *Telegraph* took a similar line. The troublesome

Sergeant Jamieson, meanwhile, was put out of business. Acting on a complaint from a veteran's group, the New South Wales police ordered him to abandon the fundraising appeal. He was charged with stealing Army stationery and 'severely reprimanded'.[8] No serious attempt was made to investigate his claims.

None of this deterred Corporal George Budworth – a quietly spoken, quick-fisted soldier who achieved what others merely talked about. One evening in 1954, Budworth encountered Fusako Tsuruta in Kure's entertainment district carrying a mixed-race infant on her back. They began a relationship. Over the next two years, George formed a close bond with her son, Hideki: the pair were frequently seen going about together, on and off base.

In March 1956, as George's departure loomed, Fusako formally consented to his adopting Hideki, who took the name Peter Budworth. With the connivance of sympathetic BCFK officers and consular officials, the soldier obtained approval to take the boy to Australia. Permission was also granted later for Fusako to join them, but this was never followed through. Budworth apparently convinced the authorities he was Peter's natural father, even though documents showed he had arrived in Japan *after* the child was conceived. This deception may explain why he delayed having the adoption confirmed by an Australian court, as was required before the Immigration Department would grant Peter permanent residence.

Army headquarters grew suspicious and began making life difficult for the soldier. Fearing the worst, he deserted and took to the road, tramping the rural backblocks of New South Wales, with his 'Japanese shiralee' (swag or bundle) by his side. Finally, in 1962, the boy's naturalisation papers came through: 'It's the first time I've ever seen him cry. George cried, but he was happy, and he said, "I can keep you, you can stay"', recalls Peter Budworth. The child who beat the odds would go on to become a decorated senior officer in the Australian Federal Police.[9]

Combating compassion

Like the nursery rhyme's 'man who wasn't there', the Kure Kids refused to go away. Over the three next decades, the government's secret file on 'the bastards of Australian troops' would accumulate more than a thousand pages of memoranda, letters and clippings. An early contributor blamed Japanese communists for whipping up the controversy. The Americans were the only ones in the spotlight, this official claimed, and they might be embarrassed if Australia took the initiative. He advised against making inquiries with the Japanese authorities – in case they asked for help.[10]

The subject remained suspended between calculated ignorance and vague appeals to a moral dilemma until a Salvation Army chaplain, just back from Japan, shaped it into a cause worthy of a Christian response. In place of bastards and bar girls, Pastor 'Jock' Geddes substituted an image of honesty, poverty and maternal devotion. 'Nearly all Japanese mothers', Geddes declared, 'love their children so passionately they would work like slaves rather than neglect them'. He wanted the Australian Council of Churches to push for an adoption 'repatriation' scheme.[11]

Humanitarian or moral considerations were outweighed, for the government, by a desire to hold the line against Asian immigration. In pursuit of this objective, officials were adept at using contrived policy instruments. The most notorious was the dictation test, a means by which non-European migrants were excluded under the pretence of maintaining literacy standards.[12] In similar fashion, officials now deployed child welfare rhetoric to head off an adoption campaign for the Kure Kids.

In July 1956, the Immigration Department admitted, on 'humanitarian' grounds, a few children already adopted or under the care of Australians living in Japan (one of them being Peter Budworth). In the process, it established a basis for denying the same right to other citizens keen to adopt as yet unseen Japanese children. (The first person refused was an Australian nurse in Korea who wished to take home an Amerasian child. News reports on the thousands of Korean orphans being adopted by American families stimulated interest in Australia.)[13]

This is how the policy was justified, in confidence, to the Commonwealth Immigration Advisory Council:

> Departmentally, it is considered that to permit Australians to adopt and bring here Japanese children with whom they have never had any close association, would constitute a very awkward precedent. There are thousands of children available for adoption in Japan as a result of alliances between Japanese women and occupation troops. The plight of these children would appeal to the compassion of many Australians in a position to adopt them, but their entry in considerable numbers would be directly contrary to established immigration policy.[14]

While ministers were publicly downplaying the size of the problem to discourage interest, officials were busily inflating it to 'thousands of children' to conjure up a threat to the White Australia policy. The 'plight' of the children, in this briefing note, does not amount to a welfare concern but a liability, requiring a barrier to be erected between them and the compassion of those in a position to help. It is breathtaking in its cynicism.

The Advisory Council endorsed the department's formula, which prescribed that a Japanese or mixed-race child needed to have spent 'some time' (administratively interpreted to mean six to nine months) in the personal care of the prospective adoptive parents *prior* to being eligible for admission to Australia. This prohibitive requirement waited like a spider in a shoe for the next unsuspecting foot.

'Story of Shame'

A year later, in August 1957, the tabloid magazine *Pix* published the first detailed account of families in Kure enduring a 'life of poverty and hopelessness'.[15] Large-format photographs showed boys and girls, 'typically Australian in appearance and mannerisms', outstanding amid their Japanese surroundings. The 'Story of Shame' thrust the issue before the public in a way that ensured it would not be forgotten.

Journalists Shinichi Takeda and Peter Robinson described the case of a young woman with two mixed-race children, the first born allegedly as the result of rape, the second fathered by an Australian serviceman to whom she was legally married. This man, after returning home, had sent money for a while and then broken off contact. Unable to work, due to illness, the woman was living with her son and daughter in a slum on the city's outskirts. A photograph showed her wrists bandaged, following what was said to be a suicide attempt.

Another woman was weeding paddy fields and humping rocks in a road gang to support her family. 'The past is a bad memory and so long as I'm tied to it, I lose all strength to go on living', she said. 'My daughter is my only hope for the future.' (Ironically, the harder she worked, the less she came to resemble her little girl. There were whispers of a secret adoption; acquaintances refused to believe the dainty, blonde child could share the same blood as ran through this woman's weather-beaten face. True or false, the girl repaid her mother's sacrifices with a lifelong devotion.)[16]

The mixed-race children attending school in Kure were described as 'a gay, happy-go-lucky bunch of kids'. More emphasis was put on their poverty than on problems of discrimination. The reporting was mostly restrained and accurate, except when it relied on Miki Sawada's estimate of 200 000 occupation pregnancies ('births' had become 'pregnancies' by now) to posit an Australian share 'almost certainly over the 1,000 mark'. Not necessarily false, just impossible to prove.

The article, and references to it in the Japanese press, angered Ambassador Alan Watt. He doubted the mothers were 'paragons of virtue' and complained to Canberra that no mention was made of Japan's wartime 'record of cruelty and rapine'.[17] He felt sure Tokyo would try to exploit the issue. (It never did.) Once he had calmed down, Watt suggested there might be a case for a 'few' adoptions and private charitable donations.

The mayor of Kure, contacted by Australian church leaders, confirmed the 'children and their mothers have been living a life of such extreme poverty and destitution that we cannot bear to think of their condition without deep sorrow'.[18] According to a survey by city officials, just one family in seven was receiving any financial support from the absent father. Most mothers or guardians, however, wanted to keep their children, and no more than a dozen were immediately available for adoption.

First aid

A month after the *Pix* article, the Department of External Affairs – still unaware of the policy decision taken by Immigration – reassessed the case for government involvement. The head of the East Asia division felt some sort of 'gesture' was appropriate because 'a real human and tragic problem exists and cannot be forever shirked'.[19] He pointed to a direct line of responsibility going back to the 'rigidity' of the BCOF policy on marriages.

External Affairs was also concerned to prevent a public outcry over the children's treatment in Japan damaging bilateral relations.[20] Having just signed an historic Commerce Agreement and seen an end to the last of the wartime restrictions on trade, neither country wanted unfinished business from the occupation invading the diplomatic agenda. If, at the same time, Australia could improve its international image by admitting some of the Kure Kids for adoption, so much the better.

The Tokyo Embassy began moving in this direction. The task fell to Ted Weatherstone – the same official involved in the initial skirmishing over occupation marriages. Weatherstone wrote to a German Jesuit missionary in Kure, Father Peter Koop, seeking information. In his reply, the celebrated atomic bomb survivor (Fr Koop's story is told in John Hersey's bestseller *Hiroshima*) made clear he was interested in deeds, not 'deliberations'. If the Embassy came to see the situation for itself, he was ready to offer 'every kind of help', but he would not engage in 'a useless answering of questions'.[21]

Weatherstone persisted with the indirect approach by linking up with ISS in Tokyo. Following a meeting with Florence Boester, a proposal went to Canberra for ISS to undertake an investigation, at a cost to the public purse of £75 (about A$2000 in current values). The plan found few friends within the bureaucracy. Consider the 'precedent that will be set', the Secretary of the Department of the Army cautioned his counterpart in Defence.[22] Father Koop was right to suspect a lack of will. For the next five years, the deeds he invoked would be left up to others.

The narrow road

The Australian Council of Churches spent 18 months mulling over Pastor Geddes's appeal for help. Wary of anti-Japanese sentiment in the community, it began moving only after the *Pix* article flushed out dozens of Australians willing to adopt, and the way ahead seemed more secure. Prominent among the couples stepping forward were BCOF ex-servicemen with Japanese wives. One veteran saw it as a means of expressing his gratitude for having his life saved by a Japanese soldier during the war.[23]

The Council tried the shoe on for size, as it were, by putting a hypothetical case to the Immigration Department: If one of the Kure Kids were selected for adoption, would the child be allowed into the country? The department couched its negative reply in terms of 'the absence of any strong compassionate circumstances', leading the churchmen to believe each case would be treated on its merits.[24] Officials failed to explain they meant the 'compassionate circumstances' of the applicant, not the child. The point remained obscure for another year.

In the meantime, Alexander Downer, Sr took over as Minister for Immigration. As well as being a former wartime prisoner of the Japanese, Downer was a staunch defender of Australia's Anglo-Saxon heritage. He revealed the sting in the adoption policy in May 1958: 'The illegitimate children of servicemen in Japan are not generally eligible for admission to Australia'.[25] His statement made no mention of deserted wives – *all* the children were 'illegitimate'.

In defending the decision, he began by declaring a humanitarian concern – it would be cruel to subject the children to 'possibly insurmountable' assimilation problems – and ended by disparaging the mothers: 'willing accomplices of the fathers'. 'A bid for the children is a bid for the mothers', Downer told parliament, 'and by the time the whole operation were carried out, quite a small colony of Japanese migrants would be coming into this country'. In private correspondence with colleagues, he was blunt: 'We do not want the children here'.[26]

In addition to the assimilation concern, doubts were raised about whether an Australian court would recognise an adoption order issued in Japan. This was an issue only because the government declined to endorse the inter-country adoption method favoured by ISS, which involved assessing a child's need for adoption, conducting a 'home study' of the candidate family to ensure suitability, and then monitoring the placement for several months prior to finalising the adoption under local laws. The necessary legal and welfare framework already existed in Australia; the alleged difficulty stemmed from the government's requirement, in effect, that a placement be completed *before* the child became eligible to enter the country.[27]

Every argument, every rationalisation, was distorted in the circus mirror of race. The Kure Kids tapped into a deep-seated anxiety about half-castes that influenced policy-making in myriad other ways. These included the notorious practice of forcibly removing part-Aborigines from their Indigenous families (the Stolen Generations) and measures that variously encouraged (to 'breed out colour') or prohibited (to prevent 'alarming throw-backs') half-caste Aboriginal women marrying white men. It even emerged in security assessments of the half-castes of Australian-controlled Papua and New Guinea, who were described by ASIO as a 'ready-made and most useful "fifth column"' for a possible Indonesian invasion.[28]

Brothels and bells

There was no official discrimination against *konketsuji* in Japan. They had the same entitlements to livelihood assistance, for instance, as other citizens. Welfare payments, however, were never sufficient to live on, and the poor relied on networks of relatives and friends for support. This was what a single mother often lacked. The fact that only one in four eligible Kure families with a mixed-blood child applied for public aid underscores how paltry the payments were and the reluctance of mothers to be identified.

City officials blamed language difficulties for their inability to contact missing fathers to obtain maintenance for deserted wives. In less guarded moments, they conceded interest in the issue was 'not very deep'.[29] Kure had too many other problems. It was still feeling the effects of BCFK's departure, which had put 9000 people out of work, including nearly 2000 women. At 16 per cent, the city's unemployment rate was among the highest in Japan. The struggles of a few score families, out of a population of 200 000, were dwarfed in the bigger picture.

News that Australian church groups were gathering 'an enormous amount' of aid (£50 000) for the mixed-race children caused a flurry of excitement.[30] As it turned out, the money ISS needed to begin relief work in the city was supplied from a different source: the American Lutheran mission. ISS concentrated on arranging adoptions to the United States and planning for the distribution of charitable donations promised from Australia.

It also lodged another bid with Canberra for financial support – and was again refused. The Secretary of the Department of Air, AB McFarlane, believed Australia had discharged its 'moral responsibility' in 1946 with the non-fraternisation policy.[31] In the margins of this memo, a bureaucrat at External Affairs has written: 'At one stage, an official brothel was set up at Bofu by the RAAF!' On the memo from Tasman Heyes at Immigration, ruling out help from that quarter, the same dissenting official has penned the comment, 'Never send to know for whom the bell tolls ...'. The head of the Defence Department nailed the foregone conclusion: 'We should be chary about doing anything that could be taken as an acceptance of Australian guilt and responsibility'.

Tilting at White Australia

The regulations giving effect to Australia's restrictive immigration policy were riddled with contradictions and anomalies. Rather than trade in the rickety machine for something better, politicians of all stripes preferred to exchange insults about its backfires and breakdowns. The task called for rhetorical gusto, a thick skin and a faulty memory.

Labor's parliamentary firebrand, Eddie Ward, took the lead in agitating for the Kure Kids, portraying them as a chosen people suffering in Babylonian exile. He claimed they were 'walking the streets with placards round their necks reading, "My father is an Australian", and begging for alms to maintain themselves'. Another crusader was the Member for Parkes, Les Haylen: 'Somewhere in their cosmic make-up, in their genes, in their Australianism which has been transmitted to them through their fathers, they must feel a tug towards their homeland'.[32] This was the same Les Haylen who, when in government, had rebuffed a direct appeal on behalf of the mothers and children.

More influential, in the long run, was a younger cohort of Labor politicians with no allegiance to the party's racial ideology. Left-wing Victorian MP Jim Cairns took up the cause of the Kure Kids and risked disciplinary action by publicly advocating immigration reform. His New South Wales colleague, Gough Whitlam, also used the controversy to advance his leadership ambitions. His break with Arthur Calwell on the issue signalled a willingness to take the party in a new direction.

Having failed with the Immigration Department, the Council of Churches 'reluctantly, and with shame' paid for eight of Kure's mixed-bloods to be adopted by American families.[33] It also contributed £1200 a year towards putting a full-time ISS social worker in the city. The next task was to materialise the long-promised £50 000 rescue fund. The Reverend Harvey Perkins, general-secretary of the Council, wrote to Prime Minister Robert Menzies requesting £10 000 to get the ball rolling. The money was needed, Perkins said, to save the children 'from the worst forms of discrimination which is the lot of the depressed classes of Japan'.

The request hung in the balance for several months. To carry the day, it needed a demonstration of public feeling. While media interest was keen, community responses remained muted. Had any of the powerful veterans' groups expressed sympathy, the outcome might have been different. The RSL's national executive received a resolution from its New South Wales branch, calling for action, but chose to set it aside. Legacy, a body dedicated to assisting the families of veterans, also turned down an appeal for help. Mrs Jessie Vasey of the War Widows Guild told the press the children were 'undoubtedly from an undesirable class and would not make good migrants'.[34]

The outcome depended on Menzies. The social lioness and philanthropist Dame Mabel Brookes exhorted her friend to show compassion: 'I know Japan and the Japanese way of life, and if these children are called their "social dust" you can take it nothing but degradation and starvation lies ahead of them'. Though Menzies assured her the government wanted to find a solution to 'this distressing problem', he told Cabinet there was 'no case' for Commonwealth assistance. It 'might easily lead to pressures for assistance in other places where Australian troops are stationed'. His submission made no allowance for the fact the occupation was essentially a peacekeeping assignment (an argument a later government would use to deny BCOF veterans full war-service entitlements) or that some of the children were born to unions blessed by BCOF chaplains. Official aid was ruled out, paradoxically, because the fathers had been engaged in the service of their country. During the discussion, reference was made to the attitude the government should take towards adoptions. This was deemed a 'hypothetical question' and set aside.[35]

Cabinet's decision effectively killed off the rescue campaign. From the beginning, the Council of Churches had been reluctant to lead from the front on the issue, preferring instead to coax out public opinion. It found less controversial uses for its money in Japan, such as a dairy project that the Ambassador would have no hesitation in dedicating.[36]

15

Our mixed-bloods

Yone Itō had been away from Japan for five years when she stepped off the ship in Yokohama in March 1959. 'After the war', she recalls, 'when cities were levelled and the victims of war were seen everywhere, it seemed natural for me to study social welfare'. She had taken a degree in social work from the University of Louisville, Kentucky, and gained experience working with families of psychiatric patients in Chicago. Twenty-nine and single, Itō joined ISS to lead the Kure Project: 'I was already a stranger in Japan when I came back. So I could do whatever I liked'. In the absence of a settled opinion on the best approach to the *konketsuji*, she would need to devise practical solutions to a unique set of problems. 'I, myself, could not help feeling a sense of mingled pride and humility.'[1]

Nobody knows precisely how many children of Australian fathers were left in Japan. A realistic estimate would be in the low hundreds. In 1952, the Welfare Ministry counted 116 *konketsuji* born or raised in Kure (not all fathered by Australians). At the time, city officials put the number at nearer 150–160.[2] The BCOF troops were not confined to one place, however; they visited many parts of Japan, performing duties or on leave, and left offspring wherever they went. By 1956, almost as many children identified as being of Australian paternity were attending school outside Hiroshima prefecture as inside.

Itō arrived in Kure knowing almost nothing about the place apart from its fame as a naval stronghold. For the next decade, her residence would be the local YWCA. Venturing alone, on foot, into the many small neighbourhoods dispersed through the hills, she found 'the mentality of people living in an enclosed area tends to be confined in a hard shell; to be exclusive and suspicious of strangers'.[3]

By the time of her first progress report, Itō had identified 88 *konketsuji* in need of help, including 52 with Australian fathers. Many were entering a critical phase in their emotional development, between the ages of nine and 12:

> Encountering social prejudice, they feel they are the greatest victims in the world and make themselves out to be heroes of anguish and emotional instability. For those ones with a strong inferiority complex, proper support and careful guidance are necessary. Forty-five per cent of the children are in a situation where they cannot even live with their natural mothers. Frustration and social pressure often lead them in an evil direction.

While the children come across as overwrought and wayward, in Itō's account, the mothers are portrayed in almost heroic terms. She especially admired them for trying to impart a positive image of the fathers to their offspring. An element of self-justification in this nostalgia did not make it less admirable. Itō thus upended the prevailing view within ISS (and the wider community) of 'pathological' mothers versus 'innocent' children.

Many families were showing signs of mental stress. Mothers struggled to find decent employment; one in four had moved house within the past year. Kure residents were unsympathetic and warned Itō against showing solidarity with the mothers. 'While we were enduring shortages, these women lived luxuriously', one shopkeeper told her. 'Now the soldiers have gone, why should we help them?'[4] To have any hope of success, the Kure Project would need high-level endorsement. This came with the establishment in 1961 of the Hiroshima *Konketsuji* Rescue Advisory Committee, under the auspices of the prefectural governor.

Inter-country adoption

Although ISS hoped to obtain funding for an ongoing welfare program in Kure, it started out with only enough money to put through a small number of inter-country adoptions.

One of Itō's first cases was Steven, the freckle-faced son of an Australian soldier. The boy lived with an alcoholic stepfather and often could be seen wandering the streets in a dirty kimono, the nearest thing to a waif among the Kure Kids. Caught shoplifting 'presents' for older boys, Steven ended up in an institution. At the age of 12, the 'straightforward, gentle child' went to a new home in the United States. Two months later, Itō received a letter from his adoptive mother:

> We can put your mind at ease about Steven adjusting here. He seems to like it very much, has a grin on his face from morning to night, and has made many friends, both boys and girls. Our house usually has three or four after school every day, watching TV, listening to records and eating cookies.[5]

A radio documentary, made with Itō's help, told another upbeat story about an 11-year-old girl named Kaoru. Her father had been sent back to Australia before her mother – a BCOF waitress – gave birth in 1949. He returned to Japan as a stowaway but was arrested and deported. Kaoru grew up 'an outstandingly beautiful child, with white skin and clear brown eyes'. Her teacher admired her lust for life: '[Kaoru] does not have any ill-natured, coarse, or violent side, often observed in the children of poor families. There's no poverty of heart in [her]'.

When boys teased her, she confided in her diary, 'I hate the fact

I look like my daddy. I especially hate being called *Nisei*'. She started skipping school and wandering far from home: a common *konketsuji* response to discovering why they were different. Among the Kure Kids, this crisis tended to be delayed because mothers shielded them from the truth. Kaoru was placed with an American military family and was said to be settling in well, learning English and playing confidently with her new stepbrother, Chuck.[6]

The desire to rescue mixed-race children from prejudice in their country of birth was a major factor behind the growth of inter-country adoption after the Second World War. It led practitioners to break with established practices, such as matching children with couples of the same race or religion. In the case of the *konketsuji*, there was also a preparedness to place older children for adoption. Once they began reaching school age, more were sent to new homes abroad, not fewer. Strict age limits seemed to make little sense if a major factor affecting the wellbeing of a child did not crystallise until the onset of adolescence. Itō believed 'the most important consideration is whether the child is capable of benefiting from adoption'.[7]

The American author and philanthropist Pearl Buck, a leading proponent of inter-country adoption (the term 'trans-racial adoption' came into use later), claimed vested interests used age limits and 'matching' criteria to keep children in institutions: 'These are the citizens of my new world, the children without parents and the parents without children, pressing eagerly toward each other, and yet unable to reach each other'. Buck insisted a child's right to be loved should outweigh the right of a negligent parent to maintain custody. On the opposite side of the argument were national welfare establishments sceptical as to 'whether a child should be altogether uprooted from his traditional background'.[8] ISS stood somewhere in the middle: committed to careful screening of clients and opposed to proxy adoptions, but also keen to limit the number of children in institutional care.

Itō completed the last of 15 adoptions from Kure in 1965. All but one of the children went to American families.

The list

When the first director of ISS Australia, Constance Moffit, learned about the Kure Kids in 1957, she saw an opportunity to lift the work of her branch from the obscurity that was starving it of public donations. She consulted with Florence Boester about starting an inter-country adoption program along the lines of ISS America. Boester encouraged her to take on the 'repugnant' White Australia policy: 'It is really a battle of principle you are fighting'. Though her heart was in the right place, Moffit was not up for the fight. She readily fell in with the view, put to her by External Affairs, that there were numerous 'difficulties' in the way of doing anything.[9]

Three years later, the Benevolent Society of New South Wales – Australia's oldest charity, with special expertise in adoption – took up the cudgels. The Society's treasurer, Victor Segal, returned to Sydney in March 1960, after inspecting the situation in Kure, and condemned the government for its inaction. Segal committed a blunder, however, by implying he had obtained a list of the names and addresses of delinquent fathers.

Naming and shaming was not a strategy likely to impress anyone. The government kept such information under close wraps. Appeals from desperate women that entered the file usually stopped there. 'I loved him and lived with him, aiming at marriage, in spite of my parents' opposition', wrote a mother of two children. 'Were I as old as I am now, I might have known a little better.' She enclosed a photograph of the smiling father, in his RAAF uniform, along with a copy of his birth certificate. 'Please help and find him for us.'[10] She was told it was a private matter in which the government had no standing.

Segal's veiled threat drew an angry response. 'Don't rake over old embers and talk of lists', protested a Sydney alderman. 'The Society would be wise … to put his list in the incinerator.'[11] Segal insisted he had been misquoted, and there was no name-list, but the damage had been done. Minister Downer refused to meet him to hear his arguments why the children should be admitted for adoption.

Constance Moffit was horrified to see ISS named as the source of Segal's information. She immediately wrote to Downer laying out a case for why *none* of the Kure Kids would benefit from adoption to Australia: 'We do not think that the poverty of the mothers, even "dire" poverty, constitutes in itself a sufficiently grave reason for removing these children from their mothers'. (This was a furphy; mixed-bloods were never 'removed' from their mothers.) The emotional damage they had already suffered, she added, would be compounded by the strains of adjustment to the 'vastly different Australian way of life'. Her 'expert opinion' was widely publicised.[12] It convinced key pressure groups to give up on the adoption remedy and armed the government with a weapon to use against its critics.

Prior to 1965, Australia would admit just three or four mixed-race children from Japan (apart from those accompanying war brides or fathers). None was allowed to enter the country for placement with an adoptive family. During the same period, the United States accepted well over 2000 for adoption.

Reforming zeal

Just as it seemed the Kure Kids were a lost cause, signs began to appear of a shift in public opinion. New pressure groups began to assail the government's hard line on Asian immigration. The best organised was a Melbourne-based coalition of mainly lawyers, academics and clerics called the Immigration Reform Group. The government's 'callous' treatment of the mixed-race children, it said, demonstrated that unfair laws could not be administered fairly.[13]

Founding members of the Immigration Reform Group included Margaret Kelso (who replaced Moffit as ISS director) and the barrister John Dynon, whose wife, Moira, was also a prominent social activist. Moira Dynon encouraged the Australian-Asian Association of Victoria to take up the cause. The association – dedicated to improving cross-cultural ties – was an important player, in good standing with External Affairs. The expanding network of shared interest included the powerful Melbourne *Herald* newspaper group, whose Asia correspondent, Denis Warner, produced a steady stream of articles on the Kure Kids.

Mrs Dynon prepared a report that faulted the government for labelling the mixed-bloods 'illegitimate'.[14] She pointed out that the legality of the Shinto or Christian marriages gone through in Japan had never been challenged. Some children (particularly those born prior to 1949, when the Nationality and Citizenship Act came into effect) were entitled to recognition as British subjects. On the matter of adoption, however, Mrs Dynon deferred to the Moffit opinion. She would change her mind later, when she knew better, but with every passing year this option became less viable.

The Australian-Asian Association concentrated on collecting money and clothing for the Kure Project. In January 1961, press photographers were invited to the Embassy in Tokyo to record Ambassador Laurence McIntyre handing over the first cheque to Kimi Tamura, director of ISS Japan. It was not the only new money finding its way to the Japan branch. Just as Australians were being told that inter-country adoption would do more harm than good, the Japanese government began paying ISS a subsidy to help find *konketsuji* new homes abroad.[15] The then Welfare Minister, Masa Nakayama, was the mixed-race daughter of a 19th-century American merchant.

Father Tony and 'AJ'

They were unlikely comrades: AJ (Alex) Ferguson, an irascible Melbourne businessman, with a flair for publicity, and Father Tony Glynn, a Marist priest toiling in the low-yielding vineyard of the Japanese mission. By coincidence, both first set foot in Japan in

April 1952, arriving aboard different ships within days of each other. Ferguson was on a health cruise and scouting for business opportunities; Tony Glynn was fulfilling a promise made to a former POW chaplain to join the work of post-war reconciliation.

Father Glynn was shocked by what he found in Kure. It shamed him to think American families were stepping in to help Australian-fathered children, whom 'we ought to look after'.[16] During a two-year sabbatical, back in Australia, he encouraged couples interested in adoption and prayed for the sparks of public concern to catch fire. The controversy was fully alight by the time he returned to Japan in 1959 and met Alex Ferguson, now semi-retired and still indulging a passion for travel. The priest described the situation in Kure, expressing frustration at the lack of progress. Nothing galvanised the impulsive Ferguson more than the word 'no'. The cause was also a tonic of sorts for someone coming to terms with his own mortality.

Tony Glynn and his brother, John, a Marist priest in Sydney, raised money through junior chambers of commerce and community service clubs and maintained pressure for the children to be allowed into Australia (one idea was to build a welfare home to receive them).[17] Tony provided the Embassy in Tokyo with written advice from Japan's Welfare Ministry in favour of adoption. 'Owing to their peculiar circumstances', the document stated, 'difficulties may arise about employment, marriage and so forth in the future. In view of this, it is considered that the children may become happier if they are adopted by proper supporters who are not prejudiced'.[18] Despite this, the Embassy would later claim the ministry *opposed* the adoption of older-age children.

Back in Melbourne, Alex Ferguson launched the Japanese-Australian Children's 'Adoption' Fund, which invited companies and individuals to financially 'adopt' a child, a technique used in the United States in the 1930s to channel aid to China. By encouraging contact with the children, and giving each a personal story, the campaign brought them closer to the Australian public. Some of the

Kure Kids, Ferguson said, were starving: 'Their plight is terrible'. Margaret Kelso came away from a meeting with the businessman deeply impressed, telling a colleague in Geneva: 'He is a person of singleness of purpose and great determination'.[19]

The 'Adoption' Fund's first instalment of £900 (¥700 000) reached Yone Itō by Christmas 1960. Father Glynn was on hand to see cash and school stationery distributed to 57 children. The next task, he declared, was to break down the White Australia barrier. A local newspaper, presumably meaning well, dubbed the priest 'The Father of Mixed-Blood Children'. More adroit was Ferguson's title for Itō: 'The Angel of Kure'.[20]

What the camera saw

To attract sizable donations from corporations, Ferguson needed his appeal to be tax-deductible. He wrote several times to Prime Minister Menzies asking for the concession, without success. Rejection goaded Ferguson into a renewed effort to have the children admitted for adoption.

He arrived back in Japan aboard the *Arcadia* in the summer of 1962 determined to take his campaign to a new level. Illness had delayed the trip for several months (he nursed a heart condition and suffered from migraines). Father Glynn urged him to be careful: 'You are too valuable to get sick'.[21] The first task 'AJ' set himself was to persuade the social workers to allow direct access to the children. Margaret Kelso thought her colleague, Kimi Tamura, had agreed to keep sponsors at arm's length, but Ferguson threatened to bypass ISS if it refused to co-operate, and Tamura gave way. Kelso was already feeling nervous about Ferguson's high-octane assault on public opinion – she now began to resent his influence over her Japanese colleagues.

Mr and Mrs Ferguson and Tony Glynn were guests-of-honour at a party organised by Yone Itō for 60 children and mothers. The youngsters (whose average age was 11) ate ice cream, played charades and sang songs, while a film crew recorded the happy event. Ferguson presented another generous cheque (mostly his own money) and asked the assembled children, 'Who wants to go to Australia?' Nearly all shot up their hands. The film crew followed Itō into the hills around Kure and captured potent images of innocent 'Western' faces in poor, seemingly alien, surroundings.

Ferguson's short documentary *Our Mixed Bloods in Japan* became a siege-gun trained on the battlements of government policy. It was exhibited at public rallies, aired in television news bulletins and discussed on radio talk shows. Celebrities – from the formidable political activist BA Santamaria ('to maintain this sacred cow [the White Australia policy] we, as a nation, refuse to recognise our responsibilities') to the laconic screen star Chips Rafferty ('give the poor little devils a fair go') – joined in rousing the nation's conscience.[22]

Ferguson provided the press with photographs and personal profiles of several children, including George Tsutsumi, Karumi Inoue and Mitsuyoshi Hanaoka. The so-called 'Dossier of Tragedy' portrayed them as outcasts (he used the word '*eta*', a taboo term for Japan's former untouchables), 'rubbish to be jeered at and beaten and misused'. It was the kind of publicity External Affairs had always feared. Japanese diplomats objected to claims the *konketsuji* were being systematically mistreated.[23]

The controversy fed off a conviction that Japanese were a cruel, backward and racist people. Two decades of POW atrocity stories hovered behind the image, in the tabloid press, of children awaiting rescue from 'a sort of Japanese concentration camp without barbed wire'. The 'waifs' were being 'treated worse than aboriginals are treated in Australia', blared the Melbourne *Truth*. The Sydney *Daily Mirror* filled its entire front page with a photograph of a pretty, mixed-race girl, under the headline 'CONDEMNED!' The paper went on: 'Many of them will continue to forage in the gutters and garbage until they are old enough to live by crime'.[24]

The more Alex Ferguson resorted to claims of Japanese perfidy, the more attention he got. He was seriously ill and increasingly desperate. 'I'll boom this into the biggest controversy in Australia for 30 years if I have to', he vowed in a bedside interview:

> Mr. Ferguson closed his eyes again and tried to sleep. He breathed deeply for a minute – almost drained of strength – and then he opened his eyes again.
>
> 'There's a little girl of 12,' he said, 'who works in a pick-up joint selling beer at night. One of the loveliest children you will ever meet.
>
> 'How long has she got before she is tainted? Two years? Two minutes?'[25]

As the siege-gun roared, the ALP took an historic step away from White Australia. The Labor Caucus voted to demand a joint parliamentary inquiry: a personal rebuff to party leader Arthur Calwell, who spoke against the resolution.[26] Among supporters of the motion, brought by Senator Pat Kennelly of Victoria, was Calwell's deputy, Gough Whitlam. Political commentators identified the first breach in Labor's hitherto rigid stance against Asian immigration.

Alexander Downer had little time to enjoy Calwell's embarrassment. Zell Rabin, live-wire editor of Sydney's *Sunday Mirror*, penned a sardonic profile of the Anglophile minister ensconced at his family estate in the Adelaide Hills – deer park, chapel, Georgian-style mansion and all. 'He dislikes the Japanese … His attitude towards other Asians is slightly patronising and condescending.' Rabin sensed Downer relied on none of the fathers acknowledging their half-caste children, 'because deep down he has doubts about the integrity of any man who would sleep with an Asian woman'. With opinion running heavily against him, Downer realised he needed to do something to defuse the issue. He agreed to meet Ferguson and view his film.[27]

In typical fashion, 'AJ' kept a trump card up his sleeve: a plan to sponsor a mixed-race girl to live at his Melbourne home and attend school for six months (the longest stay permitted on a temporary entry visa). Before he could play the card, he needed to deal with a potential flanking opponent. At the ISS office, Ferguson confronted Margaret Kelso and accused his one-time admirer of lying about her colleagues' attitude to contact with the children: 'You're the only problem'.[28] He was now ready for the showdown in Canberra.

'AJ' never made it. His exertions overstrained his heart. Four days later, the 67-year-old was dead.[29]

Death of a salesman

The funeral drew an overflow crowd to Ivanhoe Methodist Church in Melbourne. The Council of Churches' Reverend Frank Byatt led the tributes: 'He made no claims to be an Angel. Yet he was engaged on "angels' work below" … We must not break faith with Alexander Ferguson and his pledge on our behalf for these children of our kith and kin'.[30]

News of his death hit hard in Japan. The 'Angel of Kure' was in tears, mourning the loss of 'a person deeply precious to the children'. Sixteen-year-old Mitsuyoshi Hanaoka wrote to Ferguson's widow: 'We must persevere in order to live up to his expectations'. Mayumi Kosugi told her: 'I felt as if he were my own father. No, he was closer than a father to us'.[31] Another girl sent a drawing of herself praying to Ferguson's image in the sky. The Kure Kids would forever feel indebted to him.

Tony Glynn plunged into a 'personal crisis … of solitude and fatigue'. Fearing the campaign was about to collapse, he appealed to his friend the novelist Morris West to write a book on the subject. West – who was already sponsoring one of the children – doubted a frontal attack on the White Australia policy would succeed. 'Our only hope', he wrote back, 'rests on the slow creation of a climate of self interest, in which Australians will begin to understand that they can no longer live in the illusion fostered by ancient prejudices and heretical opinion'.[32]

Perhaps a changing of the guard at Immigration would speed this process. In 1961, Sir Tasman Heyes (knighted the previous year) retired and was replaced as Permanent Secretary by Sir Peter Heydon, a former senior official at External Affairs. The ever-vigilant Arthur Calwell took the opportunity of Heyes's farewell party to deliver the new man an 'unbroken exhortation' on the need to preserve Australia's 'racial purity'.[33]

He was right to be wary. In his previous job, Heydon had sought to persuade Heyes to allow the Kure Kids to come to Australia. Such a small intake, he argued, would have no effect on the nation's racial composition.[34] Did he change his mind? Or did he fail to persuade his new minister? Immigration would develop a fresh approach to the issue under Heydon, without making any immediate concession on adoption.

Downer and Heydon met Ferguson's son, Noel, and viewed the film *Our Mixed Bloods in Japan*. It made a powerful impression. Downer, however, was not ready to receive a delegation from the Australian-Asian Association of Victoria. The celebrated POW surgeon EE 'Weary' Dunlop, Moira Dynon and Frank Byatt were made to wait another month before being able to present their bid for a grant of £85 000, tax deductibility for private donations and the lifting of all entry restrictions on the children.[35] They were not to know the minister had finalised his submission to Cabinet the week before.

Citing advice from ISS Australia (the Moffit opinion) and Japan's Welfare Ministry (misrepresenting its view), the submission ruled out adoption as contrary to the children's best interests, 'even if it were practicable'.[36] Downer proposed instead making a grant to ISS of £20 000 over five years (about A$500 000 in today's terms). The government would avoid conceding direct responsibility, he said, by requiring ISS to use the money to assist all mixed-bloods in Japan, regardless of paternity. Cabinet endorsed the plan on 28 November 1962.

According to a press statement, only children whose natural fathers acknowledged paternity would be eligible for entry to Australia. This was even less flexible than the previous policy, and hardly the 'sympathetic treatment' Mrs Dynon remembered Downer as promising. She felt betrayed and vented her anger in public. One or two ex-servicemen emerged to arrange entry for their offspring, but other inquiries were parried away by officials.[37]

The Australian Embassy in Tokyo invited Tamura and Itō to join a discussion on ways of minimising publicity for the Kure Project.[38] The government was getting ready to reject Labor's call for a parliamentary inquiry. Tamura decided it would be futile to persist with the adoption campaign (though she never gave up on the principle). It was unfair, she told Tony Glynn, to keep raising the hopes of eager couples. Perhaps, when the children got older, they might be invited to study in Australia, and then, if they wanted to stay, they should be allowed to become citizens.

Ferguson and his supporters had fallen short of their goal. For the rest of his life, Father Glynn would look back on their efforts as a 'failure'.[39] Without them, however, it is unlikely the Kure Project would have received vital public funding – something the government resisted for five years. Regardless of statements to the contrary, the nation *had* accepted responsibility. Officials knew full well the grant created a 'precedent' and continued to fret about it.[40]

Little by little, working with a succession of new ministers during the 1960s, Peter Heydon relaxed entry conditions for non-Europeans.[41] At least another five mixed-race children were admitted from Japan between 1963 and 1967, including one child who came for adoption. Although the abolition of Australia's race-based immigration policy would await a change of government in 1972, these reforms paved the way. The Kure Kids were a shadowy presence at the dawn of enlightened self-interest.

16

Kazumi's story

Unlike some of the Kure Kids, Kazumi Purvis is fortunate to have remained close to her mother, Mitsuko. Not only has their relationship brought contentment, it has provided her with a deeper understanding of the why and the wherefore.

Mitsuko Yoshida lost her own mother when she was just seven. It was 1931, the middle of the Depression. With four young children on his hands, her father remarried as quickly as possible – to an unhappy woman who proceeded to make the girl's life a misery. Japan was at war by the time the teenager left home and set about supporting herself. 'I worked in a clock shop. I helped out at a sushi shop. I did all sorts of bits and pieces. Of course, I also worked in a military factory.' It was unusual in Kure if you were *not* working for the Imperial Navy or one of its many subcontractors.

When the occupation got underway Mitsuko was sharing lodgings with a girlfriend. Their neighbourhood association received a labour quota from BCOF, and she started a job as a waitress in a sergeants' mess. Cheerful and independent, the 22-year-old eagerly embraced the opportunity. 'I had a fun time working at BCOF. I had lots of friends there. We had Christmas parties. I was able to see a new world.'

The contacts she made helped her trade on the black market. Free of commitments, she spent her profits buying kimonos. At the time, many a family heirloom was being turned into a bag of rice or a pound of sugar. She assembled a wardrobe of splendid garments and loved the feel of fine silk against her skin. Deep down, she was fulfilling a desire to get back at her cruel stepmother and unsympathetic father. She acknowledges this in her old age: 'I was always strongly rebellious. For a young person who wanted to rebel or punish their parents, if you were a boy, you became a gangster; if you were a girl, you had a child outside marriage. I also wanted a child in order to have someone in life who would take my side'.

Having a child with a foreigner was the ultimate defiance. His name was Walder Hansen, an Australian sergeant, in his early forties, 'quiet and reserved'. They tried to keep their relationship quiet, by sneaking away for picnics with a few close friends or going off at night to Mitsuko's rented room. Her uncle, let into the secret, made Walder the present of a Japanese ceremonial sword. The affair lasted a few months. After she became pregnant, Hansen presented her with a pearl necklace and a baby blanket. At her request, he also left his photograph and a note for the child to read some day. She was three months pregnant when he sailed away in June 1947.

Mitsuko makes no claim to have been abandoned.

> Our relationship wasn't deep. It wasn't love. Not love. It came about more out of loneliness. I never thought of marriage, because that wasn't possible. I wasn't even going to ask him to stay. It was just one of those things that happened. It was my choice alone to keep the baby. The only thing I regret is that he was not interested enough to find out whether he had a boy or a girl. I'm sure his friends would have told him about the birth, but he never tried to make contact.

As tongues began to wag, Mitsuko was forced to give up her job at the BCOF camp. The tittle-tattle reached the owners of the house she was renting, who told her to pack her belongings and leave. She moved in with a young married couple; their parents found out, and she was on her way again. Her next move was strategic – to the house of an elderly midwife and her daughter.

She did not tell them she was pregnant by a foreign soldier. When the time came, however, the midwife knew. She probably guessed from the absence of the Mongolian spot, a mark found on the buttocks of most Japanese newborns. Kazumi entered the world in November 1947. As soon as Mitsuko was back on her feet, they were looking for somewhere else to live.

Cheerfulness, tenacity and a capacity for making friends were her survival tools. Everything else in Kure was in short supply. If word came of a better-paying job, people dropped what they were doing and hurried off to sign up. 'One day, I was in an employment queue outside a BCOF camp, and a man who knew me from the time Walter [Walder] was around pulled me aside and gave me a job. I was very lucky. People used to help me out.' One by one, Mitsuko sold her kimonos to pay the rent and put food on the table. The wheel had turned full circle.

The only place where she could get powdered milk for the baby was the Australian residential area. Friends were working there as maids, and a sympathetic family allowed her to help out, in return for meals. While her mother did the ironing, Kazumi would disappear, being passed up and down the street among the expatriate wives. Mitsuko recalls: 'One of them, who had no children, said to me, "Oh, won't you let me keep her? I'll see to it she wants for nothing". I told her, "She's my only treasure. I did not have her just to give her away"'. Most nights, she pushed the baby stroller out the gates of Rainbow Village with gifts of food hidden under the blanket (residents were not supposed to let servants take anything away).

Her next job was house-girl for a BCOF officer. This meant leaving Kazumi at a church crèche during the day. Going back and forth through the streets of Kure, Mitsuko broiled under the eyes of passers-by. A friend, however, encouraged her not to be angry: 'They're just curious about your cute baby'. She came to believe most people felt sorry for them.

The worst seemed to be over. The house they were now renting would remain their home for the next 17 years. A steadily rising pile of silver florins and shilling pieces in Kazumi's keepsake box – tips her mother received – marked off the passage of time.

> I remember starting kindergarten. Maybe I was four and a half. I didn't like to go there. Whether the other children were aware of anything, I don't know. I was a very timid child – introverted. I didn't like to go anywhere in public. But my recollections of being bullied, or anything like that, are very few. Perhaps that was because my mother's friends' children went with me into primary school.

Kazumi knew there was something unusual about her. During visits to relatives, she would hear comments like: 'Because you are different …' or 'Because her father is Australian …'. 'I started to understand through their conversations. I think Mum tried to tell me, but I was in denial. Not exactly in denial, although I remember thinking: "I don't want to hear this".'

Around the time Kazumi started school, Mitsuko took up with another Australian soldier.

> I remember he was of Russian descent. His name was Nick, Nicholas. Nicholas Kapovski – something like that. He became Mum's partner for a short time, about a year. He was a very nice man: divorced, with two boys back in Australia, I remember Mum telling me. He never lived with us but used to come and see Mum. I remember him. He played with me a lot.
>
> After he went back to Australia, he sent money regularly – every month, right on the dot. He felt so bad, I suppose, thinking what his countryman had done to Mum, leaving a child behind. I know Mum used to write to him, because she'd send me down to the post office with the letter. And the money came to the little

bank up the road. They'd call and say, 'Money's in', sort of thing.

The extra income was both a financial and a moral lifeline for Mitsuko, as she struggled to raise a mixed-race child in the face of society's disapproval.

Not until I was around nine or ten did little naughty boys occasionally [Kazumi emphasises the word] say something to me. That was hard to live with, the name-calling. And I was a bit of a crybaby. But, as you know, my mother is a very strong person. She complained to a teacher who told her that all Japanese, originally, were mixed-race. So she went knocking on the door of the boy who'd been taunting me and told his mother to pull him into line.

A day was coming when the lives of both mother and daughter would hang on the courage and resolve of the self-styled 'crybaby'.

After turning up for several years, like clockwork, Nick's monthly remittances suddenly stopped. No more welcome calls from the bank, no more letters in the post.

I came home from school one day and, you know, Mum was sort of quiet. Might have been jobs were scarce, she didn't know how to pay the rent, and all that stuff. So the conversation went: This is not a good life; we are facing so many problems; there must be an easier way …

She promised she would take me to a movie and that I could have anything I wanted to eat, you know. We'd have a really good time – for one day. And, in a roundabout way, she promised, 'It won't, it won't be painful'.

And … I knew that it was very important for me to say 'No'. [She grows emotional.] You know, it's very difficult to say no to your mother, but that was the time … that I … if I … [Crying.]

What it is … if I … did to me … Even at the age of nine, I said: 'No, I'm not going to do that. If you want to do that, do that to yourself'.

I remember I was angry with her, speaking to her in a way I had never spoken to her before. I think I sort of snapped Mum out of it. 'What would I do if you were gone, without a mother?' And she said, 'I'm OK. I'll be all right'. I was so glad the crisis was over. And it was never brought up again.

Other family members must have become aware of the crisis, because Mitsuko's stepmother and sister put in a rare appearance. It was another two years, however, before Kazumi was invited to meet her grandparents. They were living on a vegetable farm in a neighbouring prefecture with her mother's younger brother, Mitsuko's favourite sibling.

Uncle made us very welcome. His wife was lovely too. Having their two children around was especially nice. I had been envious of other children with siblings, with someone to play with, living in a noisy house. Usually I went home to an empty house. My mother was often away working at night, and so I was there by myself, always feeling a bit lonely.

I remember they had chooks running around and lots of food. Fresh eggs. I really enjoyed that time.

It was autumn, a relatively quiet time on the farm: an opportunity for Kazumi to get acquainted with her mother's gentle brother.

He took me for a walk. The wind was blowing. It was cold. The farm covered a huge area and we walked between the vegetable gardens. He said to me … You know … he apologised to me for not being man enough to help us. It was all because of the situation with their father. 'It depresses me to have to confess,

I'm powerless', he said. 'But your mother is a wonderful lady. I'm sorry I can't help you the way I want to …' [Crying.] Then he said … 'Look after your mother …'. And I did [with emphasis] promise him I would look after my mother.

Mitsuko got back on her feet with money borrowed from a cousin. Other relatives stuck by her. It was during a visit to her great-uncle that Kazumi was first shown the photograph of her father. She was 13. 'I immediately saw the resemblance: the dimples, the same high forehead.' She asked if she could keep it. 'No', she was told, 'we'll put it away. We don't want to hurt your mother. But it'll always be here if you want to see it again'. The next time she inquired, it had been burnt. The note Hansen left was lost before she ever saw it.

Her mother moved from job to job, steadily ascending the ladder of social respectability: hostess to laundrywoman to insurance agent. One day, some strangers called at the Yoshida home when Kazumi was there alone. 'They inquired for my mother, but I was their real interest. I just felt that.' Mitsuko was angry when she heard and prepared a hostile reception for their return: 'How dare you. We don't have any *ainoko*!' Then she realised they were offering help. ISS had arrived in town.

Kazumi always preferred to keep out of the public gaze. By taking part in ISS activities, however, she gained a new and reassuring perspective on her situation.

> Even though I didn't want to be there, I felt comfortable. I really
> did. For the first time I saw children who had dark skin. And I
> saw children with blue eyes and very pale skin. And I'm thinking,
> 'Oh, I'm so lucky I'm not them! [Laughs.] I don't stand out'. I felt
> sorry for them, even though I was one of them, if you know what
> I mean.

The Kure Project enabled Kazumi to enter senior high school, by paying her educational expenses and a generous allowance. Her predominantly Japanese features and a genial nature helped her navigate a smoother passage through adolescence than some of the Kure Kids. Even so, she needed to learn how to handle rejection.

> In the last year of junior high school, I was interested in a boy. Then I heard that he had said, because I was different, he didn't want to be seen with me. I remember that was very hurtful.
>
> On another occasion, I went on a trip to Nara with ISS, and our photographs appeared in the newspaper. I had a pen friend from that area. We'd been exchanging letters for two years, though I'd never mentioned I had an Australian father. He wrote to me not long after we got back and said he didn't want to write any more. [Laughs.] I put two and two together and thought, 'Fine'. It hurt a bit, but I was getting used to it by that time. People like that are not worth worrying about.

Mitsuko, however, *was* worried. She doubted that any so-called 'good family' would accept her daughter in marriage. Perhaps she had made a mistake, years ago, by declining her uncle's offer to adopt the child and thereby remove the stigma of illegitimacy. She decided her daughter's best hope of happiness lay outside Japan. She still kept Nick Kapovski's address in Australia and, more out of curiosity than hope, asked Yone Itō to make inquiries. It turned out Nick had been crippled in an industrial accident; there could be no more help from that quarter.

The social worker told her of another possibility. Bill Wiltshire was a BCOF veteran, single, in his mid-forties. He was in the habit of taking his holidays in Japan and always brought gifts for the ISS children. Bill had asked Itō to find him a wife. Within a month of being introduced, he was back in Kure, his mind made up.

No longer in financial need, Mitsuko made it clear to Kazumi that what she was doing was purely for her sake.

I remember feeling very, very nervous about it: having a man in our life. Apart from Nick, there was never a male in the household when I was growing up. Before I met Bill I felt very strange. But I didn't, not in the least bit, reject the idea of having a stepfather. And the prospect of going overseas overrode any uncertainties.

Overseas meant the Australian-administered territory of Papua and New Guinea. Bill was a house painter with the Public Works Department. 'My high school girlfriend and I were so excited I was going to where the head-hunters used to live!' Kazumi laughs, recalling sorties to the library to pour over images of natives with feathered headdress and grisly nose-ornaments.

Bill and Mitsuko were married in Kure in March 1965. A local newspaper hailed the 'love match' as a hopeful sign for the city's fatherless mixed-bloods. 'My 17-year struggle has been rewarded', it quoted Mitsuko as saying.[1] What Kazumi remembers best, however, is city officials urging them to stay: 'Don't go to a strange country; we'll look after you'. This seemed 'weird'.

They set off in high spirits. They had not yet seen the other side of Bill Wiltshire's personality. 'What we didn't know about Bill, and what Itō-san presumably didn't know', says Kazumi, 'was that he was a reformed alcoholic and emotionally unstable'. Trouble began while they were staying in Sydney with Bill's father and stepmother, waiting for their visas to come through. He would frequently disappear, leaving mother and daughter – neither of whom spoke much English – alone with the elderly couple. The house was small and drab. Kazumi remembers being scolded for raising the blinds: 'Don't do that, the sun will fade the furniture'. They fled to the backyard to sew dresses for themselves, cut from unfamiliar patterns.

Six weeks is a long time doing nothing! So, one day, I ventured out on my own and found a milk bar. I took my Australian coins and handed them over to the ladies in the shop and, just using body language, asked what could I buy. They handed me a couple of chocky bars, and this and that. I thought: 'This is great'. And, when I got back, I showed Mum what I had bought.

Next day, Bill must have stopped by the milk bar, and they'd told him about my visit. Well! He came back and accused me of stealing his money. So my mother tried to explain that this was money I brought from Japan. Although he finally accepted it was true, the way he accused me of stealing, I saw the nasty side of him and was so unhappy.

Bill's chronic insecurity went with them to Goroka in the New Guinea highlands. Kazumi did not finish high school; Bill reckoned she was better off going to work to get accustomed to the locals. She wondered whether the real reason was he was jealous of her relationship with her mother. One thing for sure, she did not like having to hand over her salary. 'I'll keep it safe for later', he said.

It dawned on them that, by 'later', he meant the day they would return to Japan to live. Their escape route was leading them right back where they started.

He absolutely loved Japan, everything about Japan. Somehow he lived in a dream world. Bill's idea was that we would eventually all go back to Japan. I'd marry a Japanese. He tried so hard to marry me off to someone in Japan.

Bill arranged for Kazumi to correspond with the son of a war bride – her Japanese child from a previous marriage – who wanted to return to Japan. She found herself being pushed into an arranged marriage. 'I said to Mum, "No, I'm not going to marry someone because someone else wants me to". So I broke it off. But he, Bill, really dreamt of going back.'

Her stepfather grew increasingly nasty – 'not physical but verbal abuse' – particularly after he realised someone else had his eye on Kazumi. Jim Purvis was a young plumber he had employed to fix their roof. 'Bill liked Jim at first, that's why he brought him around. But as soon as he showed interest in me, he turned dead against him.' The resulting arguments only added to the adjustment problems the girl was having in a strange country, struggling with English, with few people her own age for company.

An episode at work brought matters to a head. Kazumi liked her job at the Department of Agriculture: 'I used to straighten up the files or try my best doing whatever they asked me to do'. One lunch hour, she was alone in the office when the telephone rang. 'I picked up and there was something about a sick dog. I couldn't quite understand the story. I never passed on the message.' The dog, left uncollected at the airport, died of heatstroke.

> I felt terribly guilty about that. Not understanding English really started getting to me. I was missing my comfort zone. 'In Japan', I said to Mum, 'with something as simple as catching a bus, I understand the language, I know the money values, I know the customs'. I told her I wanted to go back – and I did.

Kazumi was nearly 19 – not much older than Mitsuko had been when she left an unhappy home.

17

The Kure Project

In April 1964, the various groups campaigning on behalf of the Kure Kids organised the AJ Ferguson Memorial Appeal, with the aim of raising £100 000. The drawcard for the Melbourne launch was to be Yone Itō accompanied by two mixed-race children. As soon as Canberra heard about the publicity plan, pressure was applied to Margaret Kelso to abort it. An Immigration official claimed the children were being 'exploited' and hinted that visas might be denied.[1] Kelso persuaded her Japanese colleagues to leave the children behind.

Dressed in formal kimono for the benefit of press photographers, Itō stepped from the plane at Essendon Airport, alone. Instantly, it went from being an Australian to a Japanese event. The 'Angel of Kure' was 'bereft of firepower', according to journalist Keith Dunstan. 'The children would have been a sensation on every television programme. By herself Miss Ito did not have the personality or the appeal to put it over.'[2] The fundraising target was cut in half.

For Itō, however, the purpose of the trip was not simply to raise money. She wanted to follow up on suggestions some of the children might be invited to Australia to complete their education. Her boss, Kimi Tamura, had raised the possibility, as had the Council of Churches, which thought it could form part of the country's international aid program.[3] The social worker already had her first candidate in mind.

The original *Pix* magazine article that brought the Kure Kids to prominence had profiled a woman with two children by different

Australian fathers. In the seven years since, her son, Suzuo, had grown into a handsome, athletic and exceptionally intelligent youth. If anything, however, his situation had worsened. His mother lived with a day-labourer who violently mistreated the boy, driving him from the house. Suzuo quit school at 15 and went to work in an abattoir, standard employment for someone from a *burakumin* community. Itō believed that, by going abroad to study for a year or two, he could take control of his life.

At the ISS office in Melbourne, she laid out the case and asked for Margaret Kelso's support. We do not know why Kelso declined, but this and other disagreements permanently soured their relationship. The education route to Australia was proving as barren as the adoption route.

The AJ Ferguson Memorial Appeal crawled barely halfway to its reduced target. The response was weakest in New South Wales where a member of the appeal committee, the Liberal politician John Waddy, DFC, OBE, was quoted as saying 'a few waifs [were] a natural corollary of war'.[4]

Getting on with business

Japan celebrated its post-war coming-out in 1964 with bullet trains, transistor radios and the Tokyo Olympics. A year that began in a mood of hope at the Kure Project ended with expectations sharply reduced. Itō realised the children had no choice other than to bear and overcome the difficulties they faced in their local community. They would succeed or fail as Japanese.

The immediate challenge was education: compulsory and free through junior high school, selective and expensive thereafter. The minimum requirement for a skilled job in Japan was a senior high school diploma, a standard being attained by two-thirds of students nationwide. The Kure Kids lagged far behind: more than half were rated 'low' or 'bottom' in academic achievement. The previous year, only four of 16 junior high school graduates entered senior high.[5]

Itō stepped up group activities to build confidence and social skills – and keep the children off the streets. There were club meetings, excursions, English classes and music and typing lessons. Volunteers from Japan's coastguard and Maritime Self-Defense Force helped run sports carnivals, brass band practice and summer camps. ISS penetrated every aspect of its clients' lives, right down to the provision of underwear and toiletries.

Itō was on call, day and night, dealing with problems as they arose: a boy caught stealing, a girl missing from school, a mother needing urgent medical treatment. By 1964, she and three assistants were conducting programs for more than 100 children and their families. That year, six of nine junior high school graduates continued on with their education: a retention rate equal to the national average.

As the Kure Kids began entering their teens, the need for one-to-one counselling increased. The story of two brothers is among the most pathetic on the ISS files.

Their father departed the scene when the elder boy was three. Their mother married another soldier and left for Australia, promising to send for them later. A decade passed before the call came. In anticipation of starting a new life, the brothers quit school. Another letter arrived, cancelling the reunion; she and her husband 'could not afford' to support them (they had four other children). A case report describes what happened next:

> The boys suddenly became destructive. They stole things. They broke windows, chairs, desk and anything they could pick up at the ISS office. They hit staff and quarrelled. Their relatives in Kure were all frightened of their threatening behaviour and refused to let the boys into their homes.[6]

Both went on to lead troubled, peripatetic lives at the lower rungs of Japanese society.

ISS did whatever it could to avoid having a wayward child put under institutional care. Left in the community, some of the Kure Kids turned delinquent: skipping school, engaging in gang fights and dabbling in crime. Physically conspicuous, they quickly caught the eye of the police. (Australian government support for the Kure Project was driven partly by a concern that one of the children might cause the nation embarrassment by committing a serious crime.)[7]

An especially difficult case was a girl called Wendy, the daughter of an Australian soldier. Wendy lived with her mother and Japanese stepfather in Hiroshima. The home life was poor and violent. ISS considered her a strong candidate for overseas adoption, telling the Australian Embassy: '[Wendy] speaks quite good English and is intelligent and personable'. Acquaintances remember her striking beauty and emotional intensity. At 15, she took up with a gangster and drifted around Japan, working as a bar hostess. She returned to Kure an amphetamine user, with tattoos and a police record. Her ultimate fate is unknown.

The American casework methods Itō used – non-judgmental, with an emphasis on self-determination – were not widely approved by Japanese welfare providers. Self-determination tended to be equated with selfishness, and condemned. But if her 'psychiatric method' encouraged behaviour (outspokenness, precociousness) other Japanese found discomforting, it was a necessary trade-off.[8] With no false hope of making the mixed-bloods inconspicuous, the overriding objective was to build self-confidence.

Itō refrained from giving direct advice, allowing her clients to arrive at their own solutions. Occasionally, she lowered her professional reserve, as in this letter to an 18-year-old girl attending college in Tokyo:

My legs are very sore and I cannot concentrate on my work, so I have started to write a letter to fondly-remembered little Mieko. I wish I could forget my pain [neuralgia] … When I arrived at the office this morning, I heard you had rung. It made me feel fit immediately. The soft ice cream we had at Shinjuku was very tasty, wasn't it? I love eating. Let's go again. I am looking forward to your call.[9]

The same month, Itō received a letter from another girl, who was struggling to settle in at boarding school. The social worker encouraged the 15-year-old, by drawing upon her own childhood experiences. When worries about friends and daily life made her reluctant to study,

> I admonished myself and thought, compared to the height and breadth of the sky, what a small view I had, stuck on trivial things. On cloudy or rainy days, I imagined on top of the clouds there was still a wide, blue sky ... No matter the result, if you do your best, and study and live mindfully, you can have nothing to regret.[10]

The teenager replied:

> Recently, I've given up girlish novels and only read philosophers like Nietzsche. I'm also painting with oils and getting involved in stage performances. At last I have grown up. I desperately want to 'live', but I don't want to be part of the current social structure. High schools and universities, after all, are about training people to fit into the social structure. I think it's boring. Even so, I am still here. Impressive.[11]

A few months later, the girl took off without saying a word. Itō tracked her down to an underground theatre company in Tokyo and escorted her back to school. The teenager was eventually reunited with her mother, who had abandoned her as an infant and gone to live in the United States. The reunion was not a success.

In other cases, however, long separations did end happily.

The jeweller

Kanayo Hamashita gave birth to her son, Hideo, in April 1950. The child was baptised in anticipation of going to Australia. By the time this became possible, Kanayo had changed her mind. 'My mother said she didn't go with my dad because she had to look after my sick grandmother. Whether that was just an excuse, I don't know. Because, later on, when we talked about it – usually after a few drinks – all she said was she wanted to tell him she was sorry.'[12]

Kanayo married another soldier, George Gavienas, and departed in 1955, leaving Hideo behind. 'I can remember my mother sent me to the movies with my cousins. I just had the feeling she was going to go. That is, to Australia. She didn't want me to be there, saying goodbye, because she couldn't have taken that. I went to the movies; she caught the train.'

Hideo has fond memories of growing up in Yoshiura. His mother's family welcomed him, and he never felt neglected. 'I'd go to my auntie and say, "I need some pocket money", and she'd give it to me. It wasn't a problem. Sure, I would have loved being with my mother, but I didn't miss out on anything.' School bullies were quickly sorted out: 'I got sent home the first day. Somebody called me a name, and I pushed him over or something'. Teachers encouraged his flair for sport: 'I can remember being a captain when I was in Fifth Grade, because I was so much bigger than the other kids'.

Kanayo and George, meanwhile, settled into a War Service Home in Melbourne. He found a job at a brewery; she went to work at a furniture factory. The factory owner became a close friend and carried gifts to her son on business trips to Japan. He also helped with the paperwork when it was decided to bring Hideo to Australia.

At Sydney Airport, the 11-year-old stared into a sea of faces, trying to recognise his mother from a photograph. On the final leg of the journey, Kanayo prepared him for what lay ahead. 'Once we got on the plane from Sydney to Melbourne she taught me to say "thank you", because a lot of presents would be given me when I arrived. And from then on, bang, no more Japanese. Like, this is where your memory finishes. You arrive in Melbourne. You don't look back.' Hideo Hamashita became John Robert Gavienas.

These early adjustments tested the patience of both mother and son. 'I remember having a fight with her and walking out of the house in my pyjamas. I was going back to Japan. And when I got out into the street, I looked around and thought, which way do I go?' He laughs. 'Then I sat down at the corner, had a cry, and came home. I was missing my friends, family, school friends, so much. That was the hardest part.'

A teacher nicknamed him 'Rooster' because he was getting into fights so often. 'I only reacted when kids got mean. Things like, "We beat you at war" or "Your mother's a Jap". I don't care if I get punched up and finish in hospital, but I won't back down. And I think that's how I made a lot of good friends.' John heeded his mother's advice not to look back. 'I couldn't have made any bigger effort to become Australian than I have.'

Kanayo and George had no children of their own, and John and his stepfather never got on. The defining moment in their relationship came when the boy was 13. 'Him and Mum were having an argument, and he got very agitated. And I know I had him against the wall, and I was going to hit him, until Mum stopped me. And I just said, "If you ever lay one finger on Mum, look out". Never happened after that.'

At 15, John took a holiday job in a jeweller's workshop, liked it, and quit school. He was married and a father by the age of 20. He changed his name by deed poll and went in search of his natural father: Robert James Pate. Dozens of letters to Pates throughout Queensland – where his father came from – reaped no reward. 'I mean if someone said to me, it's not Pate, it's something else, that wouldn't surprise me either.'

His close relationship with his mother put a strain on John's several marriages. She never overcame her guilt for leaving him as a child and was unwilling to let him go again. Third wife, Sharon, explains: 'When I first met John, she was very kind and beautiful to me, but once she thought that I was going to be around, I became a threat. She would not speak to me directly. She would speak through John to me: "Would she like a cup of tea? Would she ..."'.

In 1978, Kanayo went with John to Japan to visit his ailing grandmother. 'We were able to communicate all right. I remember playing cards with her, and she cheated. I said, "No, you can't do that". She just laughed and said, "So, you remember?"' It was one of the few things he did remember. 'Like, the first day, I walked into a house with my shoes on! I was completely different to everybody else. I couldn't even read the signs on railway stations. *Kanji* [ideograms]! I had no hope whatsoever. I spoke Japanese like a kid. Everyone laughed. So Mum interpreted.'

He said his goodbyes and reckons, these days, he could bump into his Japanese relatives in the street and not recognise them.

Claimed for Australia

Visitors to the Kure Project over the years were surprised how 'Australian' the children looked, and spread the word back home. Press coverage of the visit by members of the Australian swimming team in 1964 stressed this theme. A photograph of a mixed-race girl greeting one of the Olympians was carried on the front page of a Melbourne newspaper, under the caption 'Yes, I'm an Australian – like you'. The children deeply impressed reporter Arthur Richards: 'Maybe I'm an old fool, but nothing has ever touched me more'. He described them as 'well-fed, healthy and mostly happy young people', who seemed to be 'over the worst' of their problems and making Japanese friends.[13]

Jillian Robertson of the *Sunday Mirror* took a more sensational approach, portraying them as spiritual exiles from a country they had never seen:

> When I met Yumiko Hori, 16, in the Hiroshima beauty salon where she perms and curls hair all day, she told me: 'I don't want to go to Australia to see its beaches or because you make money there. I want to go because I feel I belong there.'[14]

This story prompted several offers of marriage from Australia. The Melbourne *Truth* shot off a reply-paid cable seeking Yumiko's answer to a proposal from a Box Hill tram conductor twice her age. Margaret Kelso was unimpressed. Itō had no business playing the go-between, she complained, even if the proposal came through 'the Archangel Gabriel'.[15]

The friction between the two social workers was on display again when Kelso wrote to Itō inquiring about the availability of 'adoptable infants of mixed race'. The Immigration Department was considering a request from a couple as a 'special case'. Ignoring the inquiry, Itō surveyed the mixed-bloods she did know and confirmed that seven still wanted to be adopted. Forwarding the results to Melbourne, Kimi Tamura reminded Kelso their role was to find homes for children, not the other way around: 'Perhaps you will agree to accepting the few cases we may have'.[16] Was the issue not dead after all?

That summer, a new volunteer arrived at the Kure Project. DA Calman taught English at a boys' institution in Hiroshima and had experience escorting students on home-stay visits to Australia. Itō thought Calman might be able to provide the same opportunity for her young charges. She soon had reason to regret letting him get involved.

The more Calman saw of the ISS operation, the less he liked it. He claimed Itō's methods were wasteful and inefficient, aid was failing to reach needy cases, and vulnerable children would be better off in institutions. He urged the prefectural government to take over the management and laid his complaints before the Australian Ambassador.[17]

Itō was obliged to provide a detailed rebuttal and attend mediation sessions. Her critic, she said, was 'emotionally unstable' and had accepted the word of 'three twisted children'.[18] Itō and Tamura jettisoned the home-stay idea, disingenuously accusing Calman of plotting to take the children to Australia. It was a sordid end to a bungled episode.

Almost immediately, they were under attack again – from a familiar quarter. Angered by Itō's adoption survey, Margaret Kelso fired off a string of letters questioning the professionalism of ISS Japan. Her outburst prompted this retort from Tamura:

> We have done over seven hundred adoptions in the past ten years in which we think we have pretty closely adhered to the accepted practice of principles of inter-country adoptions. Naturally, we would not ask these children if they want to be adopted – most of them have been from babies up to 10 years old. However, in the cases of the Kure youngsters, it is different, *not because they have Australian fathers* but because the majority of them have already become teenagers and some of them have indicated their wish to be adopted.[19]

It was the last time the two directors would canvass the issue. From now on, if a child, in correspondence with a sponsor, mentioned a desire to visit Australia, the reference was deleted in translation before the letter was sent. Tamura told Kelso: 'We are as aware as you of the danger of over-emphasising their Australian heritage and are always trying to minimize it'.

Calman's complaints about the way Itō managed money do not seem to have been independently investigated. It appears his main objection was that she lavished aid on cases that seemed most prospective while, in his view, neglecting others. The files contain no allegation of misappropriation.

The Kure Project attracted around ¥70 million (approximately ¥700 million, or A$2 million, in current values, ignoring changes in the exchange rate). It was the biggest undertaking by ISS in Japan. The Australian government renewed its commitment in 1968 and provided a total of ¥32 million over ten years. The AJ Ferguson Memorial Appeal was said to have raised almost ¥26 million, although only ¥14 million had been remitted by the end of 1969, and it is unclear how much was ultimately received.[20] Local funding came mainly from expatriates. The Japanese government's subsidy to ISS was not directed to the project, which, however, did benefit from other Japanese public and private contributions in cash and kind.

In a typical year, a third of the budget went on salaries and office administration, and about half on direct assistance, educational expenses and group activities. Given that salaries paid mainly for professional services, the project would rate as an effective charity by today's standards.

It is not possible, however, to fully evaluate the accounts in the absence of a complete breakdown of expenditures. Certain items seem to demand an explanation, such as the ¥360 000 listed as the cost of a high school scholarship and expenses for one girl in 1963–64. This amount exceeded the then average annual starting salary of a university graduate and was three times more than ISS had estimated it would need only a couple of years earlier.

A copy of the audited accounts was supplied to the Australian government each year. It apparently never challenged them. An Embassy official who visited Kure in October 1967 found Itō to be 'an impressive, practical person' who made 'the best possible use' of project funds.[21]

Tracing fathers

A garbled name; a crumpled letter, in a language barely understood; a photograph, since mislaid: from such meagre scraps the Kure Kids conjured up images of missing fathers. BCOF veterans would campaign as a group for sickness benefits, medals and public recognition, without breaking ranks over this other legacy of the occupation.

Up until 1964, Itō knew of just one ex-serviceman who made the journey to Kure to seek out his de facto wife and daughter. They prayed together, she said, but he could not afford to pay maintenance. Media coverage of her Australian fundraising tour pricked other consciences. A man sent photographs of his infant daughter and her mother, in an effort to trace them. They were not known to ISS. Newspapers in Australia and Japan took up another man's search for his child, 'Shirley', also without success.[22]

Inquiries ranged from the fruitless to the frivolous. One veteran wrote to Itō:

> I was in Japan for 5 years and can assure you that there is none of my blood left there. I stayed with one girl during the entire service. I know it is impossible to adopt the children from here but I know also that if I married a girl by proxy from here then the lass can bring the children out as my family with her. I have a car and a very lovely home which I will own shortly.[23]

In another case, a divorcee came straight from a childless marriage in Australia, intending to pick up where he had left off in Kure 13 years earlier. He eventually married the mother of his teenage daughter, and the family settled in Sydney.[24] Three other Kure Kids – two boys and a girl – acquired Australian stepfathers in the 1960s.

Tracing fathers was both difficult and risky. If identification depended solely on the word of the mother, cynics only had to impugn her reputation. Typical was the letter to a Sydney newspaper in 1962: 'Australia can hardly be held responsible for the moral laxity of these women, to whom illegitimate children must surely be just an occupational hazard'.[25] The same glib eye fell on those campaigning for the children: obviously, they needed to make them out to be 'Australian' to gain the public's attention. The merits of individual cases were obscured by a general taint of self-interest.

The price of failure could be high. A feeling of being constantly let down was liable to turn into a personality weakness. Itō used the phrase 'heroes of anguish' about children who nursed disappointment. The most common criticism in case reports was that a child 'lacked guts' or was 'weak-willed'. Group activities set out to overcome this tendency, but nothing could fully make up for the loss of trust resulting from a parent's act of abandonment.

ISS chose not to confront missing fathers or pursue them through the courts. It assumed they were married to someone else, and, as Itō explained when she was in Australia, 'one must also think of the happiness of this family'.[26] Legal remedies, in any case, were probably beyond reach, partly because Australia did not recognise a 1956 United Nations convention on the enforcement of maintenance obligations across national borders.

Only one successful claim was brought on behalf of the Kure Kids.

The officer's daughter

Junko Fukuhara was born in September 1954, and her brother two years later. Their father, Roy Charles Hughes, was a major in the Australian Army. 'He went with the very last of the troops to withdraw from Kure', says Junko. 'He was helping up to the last moment with procedures for those who had married and were going back to Australia with their wives. But his own case was difficult; so he went back alone, saying he would fetch us down. We were waiting for him to come to pick us up.'[27]

Their mother, Toshie, left the house across the river she had shared with Roy and went back to live with her elderly parents. 'My mother once told me she had been going to commit family suicide with us children. At that moment, it seems I said something. I don't know what, but it caused her to stop.'

Toshie kept up the letters to Sydney. 'My mother would tell me to write something [in Japanese]. I wonder how he read that? She said, "Put XXX". She didn't even know what that meant, until later.' Roy sent cards to the children on their birthdays and a regular sum of money to Toshie for the housekeeping. 'Whenever money arrived she would say, "This is from Father", as if it were payday. My mother always bought cakes. So, for me, "cake" equals "father". It was just like that.'

Toshie's health deteriorated after the birth of their son, during Roy's final months in Kure. Junko believes her mother's headaches stemmed from the fear that he would marry someone else. She was forever reminding her daughter of the importance of having wedding photographs taken – as proof. Roy tried to ease her mind by supplying a document that acknowledged her as his de facto wife. It made no mention of the children.

Junko imagined she might become an interpreter when she grew up – a dream that lasted until she began to learn English. She laughs. 'I thought, "No, I can't want that".' Other dreams did not disappear as easily. 'One time, when an Australian Navy ship visited, I was looking at the sailors, and there was one who looked very much like my father – as he was, in his uniform, in a photograph. "My father!" I thought. But that man was young. So, it wasn't. And yet, he really looked like him! I stared so hard, he looked back at me, as if to say, "Who are you?"'

The dreamy girl grew into an attractive young woman. 'When I came of age, some people said, "Because of the colour of your hair, you won't be able to marry". It seemed my friends had a lot of offers of *omiai* [a meeting with a prospective spouse], but I had none. So I felt a little bit lonely.' She eventually did remarry.

Junko was 25 when they received the news that Roy had died. He had kept his word and never married. Who would inherit his estate? Toshie had Roy's testament, and could mount a strong claim, but the case was not straightforward. Before it could be settled, her health failed, and she died without ever knowing. 'Now I have tears. Sorry. It seems, because she was told he was coming back to get us, she was waiting …'

Blood tests were made, and affidavits collected, in an effort to prove the children were Roy's. A lawyer, with links to ISS, met the executor of the estate in Sydney and showed him photographs, pointing out physical resemblances. None of this made much impression. The cause seemed lost, until the lawyer visited Roy's sister and explained the situation. A family council was convened. Her eldest son emerged from the lounge room and announced their decision: 'We're unanimous'.

Using the money they had inherited, Junko and her brother crossed the Pacific to visit their father's grave. They met their cousins and, in the kitchen of the house that formed part of the estate, Junko posed for a photograph in her father's old Army cap. A final, belated, proof.

The reckoning

The Kure Project formally wound up after 17 years (though social activities continued for another three decades). Among the guests at the closing ceremony in 1977 – feeling distinctly uncomfortable – was the Australian Ambassador, John Menadue. In view of his country's 'appalling treatment' of the children, Menadue wondered why he was being thanked: 'That dissonance, I found very difficult to manage. If they'd been forlorn, even hostile, I think I could have understood it'. Yone Itō had similar thoughts, though she directed the blame elsewhere: 'I cannot forget the distress and trials these children have had to bear in Japan's society'.[28]

The Kure Project's greatest achievement was providing access to a level of education unattainable by most other *konketsuji*. It could boast a tally of 14 university graduates (including two with master's degrees), two college graduates and 24 senior high school graduates. The grants and donations that made this possible transformed lives.

In 1985, Yone Itō led a group of Kure Kids on their first trip to Australia – four decades after the war that brought them into existence. The White Australia policy was gone, replaced by multi-culturalism. That year, Asians made up more than one-third of new-settler arrivals. The Hawke government decided it was appropriate to reward Itō for her efforts with an ex-gratia payment of $40 000.

Promoted director of ISS Japan, she was at the peak of her career – a career that ended abruptly in March 1992, when the board stood her down for what were described as 'dishonest, long-term, private accounting practices'.[29] She resigned, and the allegation was never tested in court. The scandal caused a permanent rift between her and most of the Kure Kids. ISS publications no longer mention her name in connection with the project she pioneered. Itō continues to deny any wrongdoing.

18

Half into whole

While they remained at school, the *konketsuji* occupied a place in mainstream Japanese society. Once they stepped out on their own, life's challenges became more daunting.

Major companies tactfully declined job applicants with obscure antecedents. The mixed-bloods were pushed towards small or medium-sized firms offering lower wages and less security. Miki Sawada was so pessimistic about their prospects she bought a farm in Brazil and planned to send most of her boys there. In the end, only a small number went, and the scheme was not a success. The Welfare Ministry stopped another orphanage taking the same route, fearing Japan would be criticised for exporting unwanted citizens.[1] ISS used the Brazilian solution just once.

Two fields of employment positively welcomed mixed-race recruits: fashion and entertainment. So many exotic new faces began appearing in modelling and acting roles, commentators spoke of a '*konketsuji* boom'. The long-legged beauty Bibari Maeda led the way with a hugely popular poster campaign for Shiseido cosmetics.

Recognising the opportunity, Yone Itō arranged for several of her girls to sing on a television variety show and allowed talent scouts to cast an eye over other children. After her overseas study plan for the handsome Suzuo went awry, she placed him with an actors' workshop in Tokyo. He quickly prospered. A successful hair-tonic commercial in the 1970s led to his being offered the starring role in a prime-time television drama. Sadly, with fame beckoning,

Suzuo suffered a breakdown and dropped out of sight.

Another field in which mixed-bloods were expected to excel was sport. Those able to make it to the top became fully fledged Japanese, in the eyes of their fans at least. *What* you were also counted for less in the military. This encouraged several of the ISS boys to join Japan's Self-Defense Forces. A social worker said about one case, 'The reason [he] wants to go into the navy is because there is no bias against mixed-bloods'.[2]

Marriage

'I have this dark shadow in my background. Whenever I think about trying to marry, it makes me shudder.'[3] The girl who made this remark was expressing a common anxiety among *konketsuji*. Japanese private investigators were skilled at digging up the most obscure details about a prospective bride or groom, and a missing foreign father was hardly obscure.

Contrary to expectations, *konketsuji* rarely married other mixed-bloods. Generally, they selected partners from the wider population.[4] When a client started dating, ISS would invite the partner along to a group activity to force any unresolved issues into the open. The first of the Kure Kids to wed, in the summer of 1968, was a 19-year-old girl who had met her spouse at the factory where they worked.

In one instance, a Hiroshima businessman visited the ISS office seeking a bride for his son; he had heard good things about the ISS girls. 'I am happy to report', Itō informed colleagues, 'they were married last summer and are expecting their first child'.[5] (One can only imagine what Margaret Kelso would have thought.) On average, the Kure Kids married later than other Japanese and were more likely not to marry at all. A significantly higher proportion of females than males found marriage partners.

Being mixed-race in Japan did not automatically prevent someone making a socially advantageous marriage. Family background, class and physical appeal were more influential factors. Notable examples include the daughters of an Australian ex-serviceman, Jimmy Beard, who stayed in Japan and went into business after the occupation. Beard's elder daughter (a model) married into the Ishibashi family of Bridgestone Tires fame, while her younger sibling (an actress) became the sister-in-law of a future Prime Minister, Yukio Hatoyama.

Konketsuji revisited

In the 1960s and 1970s, Japanese society reaped what it had sowed during the occupation. The *konketsuji* were growing up, speaking up and acting out. The arrest in 1967 of a 16-year-old black youth for the rape and murder of three women caused much public soul-searching. The words he reportedly screamed as he confessed his crimes – 'I hate my hair and skin' – had a chilling effect.[6] Commentators agreed that society bore much of the blame.

Public interest in the *konketsuji* veered between sympathy and voyeurism. The popularity of mixed-race bar hostesses at Tokyo nightspots could produce this kind of reportage:

> Insulted as '*ainoko*' while growing up, and now the centre
> of a boom, with their mixed blood as a sales point, they have
> advanced into the neon-lit streets in search of the greedy life.
> People say the interesting feature of *konketsuji* hostesses is that
> they express their instincts in a foreigner's way, while thinking
> like Japanese. Hearing them talk, it's hard to believe they are
> Japanese.[7]

A television documentary team found the daughter of a BCOF serviceman working at a seedy bar in Yokosuka. Raised by her grandparents, she had no memory of her father – only a photograph. 'Since everybody hated me, I felt I needn't care what happened to me. Even if I was a good girl, I'd still be bullied.' The 18-year-old was waiting for her GI boyfriend to return from Vietnam. The program moved one critic to comment: 'The way things are going, she will give birth to the child of an American soldier … and her child will murmur the same words as her'.[8]

Not all media coverage was pessimistic. In October 1967, for instance, the respected *Asahi Journal* ran a feature on *konketsuji* success stories. Captions accompanying the wholesome photographs included, 'maintaining a positive attitude', 'lives peacefully as a housewife' and 'cheerful personality'. The publication of a poem by a black mixed-race girl, pleading to be acknowledged as an authentic Japanese, attracted thousands of sympathetic letters. Imao Hirano insisted that 'sad and soapy dramas' of mixed-race misery were out of date: 'They have been patient, honing their skills and cultivating an independent spirit. Encountering these "new people" I am very much encouraged'.[9]

The racial overtones of the Vietnam War stimulated a mood of dissent in Japan, which cast the *konketsuji* in a new light. The black singer Kazuko Kitayama scored a hit with the anti-war ballad '*Ippon no hari*' ('One Needle'). The middleweight boxing champion Cassius Naito was another figure of defiance embraced by the public. Future Nobel laureate Kenzaburō Ōe, writing about a mixed-race boy seen on a train, in earnest conversation with his mother about school entrance exams (a very Japanese topic), commented: 'The most human solution to this new racial issue is evident in the courageous attitude of the mother who dared to give birth to the child of a black soldier, regardless of the circumstances straight after the war'.[10]

If courage were enough to commend the *konketsuji* to their fellow citizens, what if there existed a deeper affinity? To the psychologist Kazuo Seki, all Japanese were marginal people (*shūhenjin*), because they felt inferior to the white world they wished to join and superior to the non-white one they inhabited.[11] Could the public's intense reaction to the *konketsuji* have derived, in part, from a subconscious recognition that, by sharing the same conflicted psychology, they had something fundamental in common?

Various arguments – intellectual, psychological and moral – were advanced for treating *konketsuji* as complete Japanese. After all, non-discrimination suited society's preference for assimilation: the ultimate aim was to conceal differences, not to promote greater tolerance of diversity. As national pride revived, in step with the economy, Japanese were eager to celebrate a homogeneous self-image. Minorities that sat outside this paradigm effectively became invisible.

Cross-currents

A danger lies in corralling the occupation's interracial experience into rigid compartments: birth, either inside or outside marriage; child-rearing, either inside or outside institutions; women, deserted in Japan or taken abroad as war brides; adoption or delinquency; black or white. Individual, three-dimensional lives disclose many themes that traverse these categories.

In the two decades following the war, about 45 000 Japanese women married foreign servicemen and settled abroad, mainly in the United States. The American public at first was wary of the war brides, even hostile. As the women's efforts to assimilate were better appreciated, however, attitudes mellowed. Magazine images of reassuringly Western-looking offspring helped to calm miscegenation fears.[12]

The children were close witnesses to their mothers' adjustment struggles, acting as interpreter and guide to local customs, and comforting them in moments of distress and loneliness. One has described the 'radiant power' she felt from her mother, because of their ties of language and blood, which she never felt with her American father.[13]

At some point in the life of every biracial child, the question would arise: Why am I different? Parents might respond by saying he or she was 'lucky' to be half-Japanese or half-American. Alternatively, they might say the child was 'double', rather than 'half'. The father of author Velina Hasu Houston tackled the identity question by using a food analogy, Neapolitan ice cream:

> I watched as my father took a teaspoonful out of each color of ice cream and stirred it together in a bowl. Soon, the colors melted into a soft, even brown tone. 'You see that?' I nodded. 'That's you,' he said. 'Now, Pumpkin. Think about this. Can you take this blend and separate it back into the three colors?' 'No,' I said, looking at him as if he was being silly. 'You can't take them apart.'[14]

Some children preferred to deny their Japanese heritage altogether. Growing up in southern California in the 1960s, Elena Creef invented an ethnic identity to match her surroundings. One day, pointing to a passing car with a Hispanic-looking woman inside, she told friends, 'That was my mother'.[15]

The dominant theme of commentaries on the brides who went to Australia was their good fortune to be there. As for their offspring, they were something of a mystery. The possibility of 'Jap throwbacks' (with a supposed propensity for cruelty) was canvassed in the press, and bureaucrats exchanged memorandums on the so-called 'genetic' issue.[16]

Miscegenation fears were easily concealed behind an approved anti-Japanese sentiment attributable to the war, but the playground bullying mixed-blood children experienced was as much racial, in origin, as historical. Families were proactive in reducing their visibility, and the war brides shaped their lives in Australia with the aim of reducing shame.[17]

The orphan

My mother was waiting at a bus stop one day to catch the bus into the city. The driver pulled up, opened the doors, saw she was Japanese, shut them again, and drove off, leaving her standing there. People were very bitter about the war. I think she must have had a very, very difficult time.[18]

Barbara Chamberlain (née Evans) was born in 1961, the second child of Eddy and Kazue. She heard the bus-stop story from an aunt, who raised her after her mother died. A terrible, lonely death:

My mother developed cancer of the uterus but, because of the prejudice she met here in Australia, she did not go to a white doctor until it was too late. I remember her being on a La-Z-Boy [lounge] in our sitting room, when she was quite ill, and her standing up, and there was blood on the white cushions. She was obviously bleeding … All I remember was this red on white. It has stuck in my brain.

As the image flashes back, fresh tears scald Barbara's cheeks.

Kazue Taketomo, a war widow, was 31 when she married Sergeant Eddy Evans in 1952. He was 14 years her senior, divorced with three children. They exchanged vows three times: at Kure City Office, before an Army chaplain and at a British consulate. Many couples went through the same routine, like vessels being launched with extra-thick hulls because nobody trusted the design. Barbara believes it was her mother who made the decision that the children should not be taught Japanese: 'She wanted us to be brought up as Australian and not have to be confronted with what she confronted'.

Eddy struggled looking after the two girls on his own. Poor health put him in hospital for long periods.

I have a vision of him coming home after hospital. I was so pleased to see my dad, I ran down the driveway of the family I was staying with and leapt into his arms. But, of course, he was in his early sixties by then, and he just collapsed on the drive. And he said I couldn't do that. As a child, that's all you want to do, isn't it, when you see your dad or your mum?

After their father died, the sisters were separated. Barbara went to live with an aunt, while the elder girl, Mari, moved in with the family of Eddy's best mate from the occupation. Barbara's 'Japanese' appearance ensured she was singled out for attention at the primary school she attended across the road from her aunt's house. Going home for lunch each day, she ran the gauntlet of classmates' jibes about 'heading off to have my rice'. High school was a happier experience, until her aunt fell ill, and Barbara had to move in with her sister's foster-family.

Mari escaped that unhappy household as soon as she could, by marrying. Her parting gift was the chilling advice, 'If he ever hits you, ring me, and I'll come and get you'. Barbara's voice wavers as she repeats the words. She forces herself to go on, 'And he *did* hit me …'. In making her escape, she left behind her mother's kimono and other family heirlooms. Worse than the physical abuse was the theft that followed: 'They had all my mother's things in a trunk. When we went back, he wouldn't let me have anything. He kept them, and we never saw them again'.

She was forced to quit school and look for work. The father of a school friend obtained her a position in the dispensary at an Adelaide hospital. Other people she met also warmed to her, as she made her way in life.

By the age of 20, Barbara had saved enough money for a visit to Japan. She stayed with a friend of her father's, a former BCOF cook. 'Hara-san remembered my father teaching him how to make scones and things like that.' Eddy had paid for a memorial stone for Kazue's parents – victims of the atomic bomb – to be erected at the farm where his wife grew up. Because her mother's ashes were there now, too, Barbara arranged for a Buddhist priest to come, and an aunt and two cousins joined her in offering prayers. She lost her mother when she was six. Her father went two years later. 'I think he died of a broken heart.'

Unhappiness breeds unhappiness. Mari was diagnosed with schizophrenia and attempted suicide several times, before breast cancer claimed her life in her mid-forties. 'I think my sister had it very hard. I was very lucky. My aunt looked after me, and later, when I started work, numerous other people took me under their wing and helped me. And I met Duncan …'

Her husband appears, right on cue, bearing refreshments – time for a break. Barbara says she will take Duncan with her the next time she goes to Japan. On the dining-room table, she lays open Eddy's photo album from the occupation. It is filled with images of Australians and Japanese together, enjoying themselves. Smiling faces, cherry-blossom days.

The professor

Ask Allan Kellehear about being the son of a war bride, and he relates a story from before he was born in 1955: 'Not long after arriving in Sydney – she was pregnant with me at the time – my mother was walking down George Street [in the city centre] when she was king-hit by a woman passer-by'. He bears the emotional wound keenly, as if it had been an attack on him – which, in a sense, it was. 'Because of lifelong experience as a person of mixed race, I do not expect ready acceptance, let alone kindness, from anyone.'[19]

Allan's mother, Tetsuko Kobayashi, was well educated, from a once-prosperous family, and used to the finer things in life. She felt betrayed when her husband, Jack, brought her to Smithfield in the outer suburbs of Sydney. Her son recalls a grim setting: 'The houses were built of fibro-cement and the roads were dirt with no kerbing or guttering. Unemployment was a steady feature of the social landscape, just as violence was part of the domestic one'.

After sticking it out for five years, she returned to Japan, taking Allan with her.

> When my mother and I appeared at my grandma's house [in Tokyo] we were ushered into the eldest brother's room whereupon my mother was lectured. She had been stupid for marrying a foreigner and had brought shame to the house, even now, by bringing a mixed-race child into it … My uncle began physically kicking and beating us. My mother swaddled her body around me to protect me from the blows, and we rolled around the room to his screams and my mother's protesting sobs.

They were driven out into the street.

Tetsuko tried to find work, but the situation was impossible. 'My mother was convinced that the only chance I would have in life – looking as European as I do – was to live in a European country.' They stopped speaking Japanese together. They put away his Japanese name, Sano. They went back to his father.

Things looked up at first. The dusty bleakness of Smithfield gave way to the beachside vistas of Cronulla, in Sydney's south. Jack Kellehear installed the family in a flat with all modern conveniences. The façade collapsed within a year.

> What we didn't know was that everything was rented and, after he took off, the things were progressively repossessed. Right down to the bed. The last time I saw him he put ten bob [ten shillings] into my hand and said, 'This is for you and your mother, to look after her with'. He was a bastard.

Tetsuko found a job as a housekeeper at a Catholic monastery. 'Mum and I lived in two rooms over the old stables. The priests were kind; the money was meagre but steady, and the gardens provided an endless source of contemplation and respite.'

With hazel eyes and fair hair, Allan did not look Japanese. But, from his first day at school, he registered subtle markers of difference, such as his food preferences: rice balls over sandwiches; ramen noodles for breakfast, instead of cereal. 'All of a sudden you live in a parallel universe; the same but not the same.'[20]

This sense of dislocation lasted into adulthood. He tells a story about catching a taxi at the airport: 'I asked the driver how his wing-mirror came to be bingled. "You're the first Australian to mention it", he said, "but every Jap I get in here goes on about it …"'. And again, on a visit to his mother's birthplace, how to explain the mysterious affinity he felt for the windswept Niigata coastline? 'I don't know if it's some kind of symbolic connection.'

The noodle-lover was now Professor Allan Kellehear, a world authority on palliative care. An appointment at Tokyo University in 2003 provided an opportunity for him to explore his *konketsuji* heritage. Seeking out the company of mixed-race Japanese and quizzing his students, he probed whether attitudes had changed since the time of his uncle's tirade. While the country's many *hāfu* actors and fashion models were undoubtedly admired and respected, he detected a more qualified response to *hāfu* of Korean, Chinese or African background: 'In Japan, what you are still counts for more than who you are'.

Allan Sano Kellehear has no wish to exclude race from the statement of 'who' he is. On the contrary, he insists on his mixed-race identity and wants Japanese to confront the source of their anxiety – lodged in the historical turbulence of lost sovereignty, alien romance and war brides.

During her son's teaching stint in Tokyo, Tetsuko came to visit. They went sightseeing and talked about how much the place had changed. 'Her appreciation of the "old Japanese" values and aesthetics gave her conversation an unusually chequered appearance, at once "foreign" yet very "Japanese". I said to Mum that I thought, over the last half-century of her life, she had become "half-Japanese". And we both laughed and laughed about that.'

Half, double, whole

The occupation-era *konketsuji* who remained in Japan were tainted by a presumed illegitimacy and promiscuity. The war brides' children living abroad felt the sting of historical animosity and racial prejudice. Growing up mixed-race, however, was not all trauma and self-doubt. Faced with identity choices from an early age, and learning how to manipulate emotional or psychological separation, some individuals acquired an inner strength. This is better understood today.

One modern approach treats identity formation like a bead moved along an abacus rail. For instance, a biracial man in Japan will choose – through dress, mannerisms and friendships – whether to identify with mainstream Japanese culture or his other, non-mainstream self. The choice may vary over time and from situation to situation. The analogy modifies rather than discards the 'marginal man' dilemma. It still assumes a polarity between mainstream and non-mainstream cultural affiliations: the nearer he approaches one, the farther he departs from the other.[21]

An alternative approach treats racial identity formation as a function of growth, more than choice. Most human beings struggle with identity dilemmas as adolescents; rarely is this assumed to be permanently debilitating. By analogy, a biracial individual may be said to work through an 'adolescence' of conflicting self-images, before being able to arrive at a coherent identity. The mixed-race individual, in other words, most vividly illustrates a universal process of self-realisation.[22]

Recent research among mixed-bloods, in both Japan and the

United States, has tended to confirm that racial marginality is not the social straitjacket it once was. A significant number of interviewees strenuously rejected the notion that they needed to align with just one part of their heritage; they were comfortable managing multiple identities. Others, who deliberately chose a single ethnic identity, could still cope when society perceived them differently. Even Japanese-oriented *konketsuji*, with comparatively low self-esteem, seemed secure in their cultural preference: they valued Japanese ways over any other.[23]

George Tsutsumi's eldest son, Kōji, gives evidence of this new confidence. 'Yes, I was called "*gaijin*" at school – in the same way the fat boy would be called "fatty"', he says. 'Naturally it wasn't pleasant.' When asked how he looks upon his mixed-race heritage, Kōji smiles and replies: 'It is very useful. For instance, if I'm negotiating business, I can say, "Sorry, my Japanese is not so good". It gives me an advantage. Also, my customers find it easy to remember my face'. It is not unusual to observe younger *hāfu* tactically switching between 'foreigner' and 'Japanese'. By deliberately cultivating their marginal status, some enjoy 'the best of both worlds'.[24] The phenomenon intrigues and encourages their parents.

Social marginality is said to be 'easy to acquire and hard to lose in Japan'.[25] It has also been suggested that marginality is easier to cope with in this society than some others. The first proposition is illustrated by the severe adjustment problems experienced by some Japanese children after returning from living abroad. Quirks of behaviour and language set them apart from their peers; as a result, they are likely to be bullied and ostracised. A contrasting case would be the many ethnic Koreans who, despite looking and acting like Japanese, forfeit this alignment if their true heritage is revealed.

The second proposition, about coping better with marginality, recognises that the matrix of 'normal' in Japanese society is complex and dynamic. Imagine a vast pattern of intersecting circles, representing different familial, geographical, occupational or common-interest groups. On this notional map, the irregular, overlapping margins are at least as prominent as the enclosing circles. A proliferation of insider–outsider distinctions increases 'the likelihood of support groups forming, while at the same time allowing those who remain marginal to any group at all to be relatively undisturbed'.[26] This may help explain why most Kure Kids have been able to find a sufficiently comfortable social space in which to lead productive lives.

An excessive emphasis on unresolved identity and discrimination in the *konketsuji* story overlooks the larger pattern of marginality and coexistence in Japanese society. In the end, it is not the fact of difference that counts more, but the explanation one can supply for it.

19

Johnny's story

Life was comfortable for Johnny and his mother, Kazue, while Terry Huxtable was around: money for new clothes, plenty to eat and picnics at the beach from time to time. In the family album, 'Papa' looks proud to be holding his chubby son, and they make a winsome pair sleeping side-by-side on the sand. Johnny learned also to address his mother, in English, as 'Mummy'.

> I remember one night. He called from the army camp to say he had to go to Korea, because the Korean War had started. I remember, because Mummy started crying. So I knew something had happened, something had gone wrong.

Terry Huxtable survived the war, but his return to Kure was only temporary. The soldier departed for Australia in November 1954, when his son was six years old. Mention was made of calling down Johnny and Kazue to join him later, and letters strung out that hope for a few more years.

Johnny was in his mid-teens when his teacher and family helped him set down some early recollections:

> My mother was good at English from her student days (currently she is doing interpreting), and I suppose I have a native-English resource. Unfortunately, I was lazy when I started to learn English in school, and now I'm bad at it.

It seems my father was a very strict person. He used to say it was most important to train children to learn from three or four years of age, and he applied severe discipline. My grandmother told me, 'I often fought with your father about your discipline in those days; now I find he was right'.

My mother was very severe, too. When I was six or seven years old, while visiting a department store, I must have insisted that she buy something, something unimportant. She totally ignored me, as though she hadn't heard my request. I hated her for that, being a child. Now I understand she was thinking of me: not to spoil me, because, by now, my father was no longer with us.[1]

Once it became clear Huxtable was gone for good, memories of their time together were locked up and shut away. Mother and son made an unspoken pact. 'We didn't talk much [about the past]', says the adult Johnny, in long-since-recovered English. 'Tried not to. Trying, you know, to forget about it. Forced to a new life. He did not exist any more for our life. So, just keep going ourselves.'

Little Johnny reverted to being Masaaki Usui. If only he could look the part. A reporter saw him in 1957 at his primary school:

Masaaki is conspicuous among Japanese children. His blue eyes, white skin, brownish hair and large build set him apart. His teacher says he is sympathetic towards others, but apparently doesn't know his own strength because his movements are unrestrained, and he is sometimes rough. 'He has excellent intelligence but is not good at memorising.'[2]

That poor memory was partly an acquired trait: he trained himself to look forward, never back.

His mother supported them by teaching Japanese music, until she fell ill. It was not the kind of profession a single mother, raising a *konketsuji*, was likely to be allowed to succeed in. After she recovered, Kazue moved to Hiroshima and found a job as a maid at a high-class hotel, which also made use of her English language skills.

Masaaki stayed behind with his grandmother, buried away in the Kure hills. The house was small; they had electricity, but water came from a communal tap. His mother visited once a month.

> It seems I was very shy and didn't want to do anything in front of others. My grandmother said I was like my father in this.
>
> Being a *konketsuji*, I was often teased or bullied: 'Hair is red, eyes are blue; you look like a monkey'. I tried to ignore them. My mother and grandmother used to say, as if by rote, 'Never let yourself feel humiliated; inside you runs an Australian's blood'.
>
> Soon after I entered primary school, a kind friend advised me: 'Mā-chan [my nickname], you have red hair. You must eat a lot of seaweed to make it go black'. I was so pleased and told Mummy. She said, 'Mā-kun, no matter how much seaweed you have, your hair will never be black'. I remember feeling so disappointed.[3]

By the time Masaaki was recording these recollections, a great change had overtaken his life. The seaweed story was something the family could laugh about now; the shy, restless child had found a way to conquer society's disdain.

It happened this way. There was to be a running race pitting his high school against another from Hiroshima prefecture to decide which would take on a visiting American team. His athletics coach plucked Masaaki from the 'B' squad ('I thought I'd misheard when my name was read out') to run the third leg. *Ekiden*, a long-distance road relay, is a fiercely competitive, highly prestigious sport in Japan. In high school competitions, teams of seven compete over the marathon distance. Masaaki's school won the race in record time, and his contribution was singled out for praise.

Though he was also a talented volleyball player, he decided to concentrate on a sport in which 'individual effort would be shown'. Sixteen-year-old Masaaki explained his thinking in a magazine article published in 1964:

> After I devoted myself to the track, my view of life changed or, I should say, became clearer ... I don't have any room to think about anything other than the track. I love the track.
>
> Previously, people often described me as facetious. It could be I took an oddly comical attitude to hide my emotions about a faraway father who does not even speak Japanese; the loneliness of not being able to be close to him and hear his voice; or my different skin colour.
>
> But I learned that the running track could never be cheated. And I came to know real pleasure ... Competing counts for more than records. In this way, I believe I can grow up to be a great and useful Japanese, irrespective of the fact I am mixed-blood.[4]

By training his body and devoting himself to athletics, the boy disciplined his mind. Looking back today, he says: 'I tried not to think, you know, to protect myself. Otherwise I become weaker and weaker. As a "Japanese", I don't have to explain everything from the beginning. I'm just sick of it'.

As fate would have it, in proving himself a worthy 'Japanese', Masaaki made a baton change of a different sort. Around this time, another article appeared in a Melbourne newspaper about the mixed-race 'Australian' boy who was burning up the track in Japan. It mentioned his coach was following the training methods of Percy Cerutty, the fitness guru of champions Herb Elliott and John Landy.

Cerutty (who was himself raised without a father) read the story and got in touch with ISS. The Olympics were just around the corner. The day the 69-year-old Cerutty arrived in Tokyo, Yone Itō, Masaaki and his coach were there to greet him. So began an important friendship. Four years later, Johnny interrupted his university studies to attend the famous Cerutty training camp set beside the sand dunes of Portsea, Victoria.[5]

The trip to Australia, financed by ISS, opened up another opportunity. It was just a short hop across Bass Strait to Tasmania, where Terry Huxtable was waiting for his 'Johnny'.

The emotions unleashed in recalling their reunion can still take his breath away. He struggles to explain how he felt: 'Hard to say … Wow … He was getting old … I was 20 …'. Taciturn by nature, he has to be prompted to continue:

> *Were you happy to see him?*
> So, 14 years I didn't see him. So, I was happy to see him.
> *Was he happy to see you?*
> I think so.
> *What did you talk about?*
> What were you doing in Japan, what was your mother doing?
> That sort of thing.
> *Did you ask your father why he returned to Australia without you?*
> No, I didn't ask. I didn't talk about the past.

He stops, gathers himself, and carries on matter-of-factly: 'I have a sister. But I have never met her. She contacted us in Sydney after he passed away –'

'– And I answered the phone.' Johnny's wife, Mamiko, takes up the story. 'I didn't know of the existence of his stepsister, or half-sister, and I didn't quite understand who I was talking to. And she didn't explain, because she hadn't realised that I didn't know of her. I never got the phone number, and I felt really bad afterwards.'

At Portsea, Johnny realised the limits of his athletic ability – not destined to be another Herb Elliott. He went back to Japan to finish his accountancy course at university, with a mind to return to Australia to work. His mother Kazue's death in 1973, at the age of 57, left him with no immediate ties to his birthplace. Around the same time as he was starting his first job, with a plastics firm in Melbourne, Mamiko arrived in rural Victoria as a Rotary exchange student. It was several years, however, before they met.

Mamiko knew her choice of husband was unlikely to appeal to her father. He had spent years in a Siberian labour camp after the war and was a 'traditionalist', as she puts it. 'So I had to tell Johnny, many times, just make sure everything is formally done and do it in the Japanese way. No, it wasn't easy. But the choice for my father was either to lose his daughter or gain an adopted son and daughter.'

Johnny took his wife's family name and became an Akiyama by adoption. The couple went a step further and quietly buried his past. The man Mamiko brought back to Japan was introduced to friends and relations as an Australian, who happened to have a Japanese mother. This was easier to put across than the real tale, with its complicated baton changes. For all his boyhood efforts to prove himself 'a great Japanese', Johnny ended up with the persona of a foreigner.

The Akiyamas make their home in Amakusa, a cluster of islands off the west coast of Kyushu. They run the 'Eucalyptus English School' and maintain close contacts with Australia (their daughter is married to an Australian). Mamiko explains their philosophy:

> Japanese cannot see foreigners as equals; they either look up
> or down at them. We're trying to foster a human-to-human
> relationship, as much as possible, by bringing in teachers from
> various parts of the world and having the children interact
> with them the same as Japanese teachers. Some students ask me
> whether I'm Japanese, and I'm glad, in a way, they can't tell the
> difference.

The Akiyamas have prospered, raised a family and never looked back. Until now, that is. The two of them have decided the time has come to make a journey to the place, tucked beside the Inland Sea, which Mamiko has heard about but never seen.

The Aga district of Kure is so little changed, Johnny is able to guide us directly to the sleepy neighbourhood he left behind 40 years ago. The narrow lane that ascends the last steep hill is navigable only on foot. Mossy tracks and stormwater drains divide the brown rows of weather-stained, wooden houses passed along the way. At a corner, Johnny recognises a thorny shrub poking over a concrete wall – his childhood home lies down this path.

The old house seems to be empty. But, next door, he recognises the name over the entrance and calls out, '*Konnichiwa*'. Eventually, the door slides open, and a tiny white-haired woman peers out, rubbing her eyes. Johnny recognises his friend's mother and greets her. The woman sits on the landing and stares up at him. Deep wrinkles on her uncomprehending face converge at a toothless crater of a mouth. She is 93.

'I used to live below there with my grandmother … You know, Chiyo … My mother's name was Kazue … Your son, Hī-kun, was my friend … I went to Australia and came back … I'm Masaaki, don't you remember?'

Her muddy expression starts to clear as the names retrieve deep memories, like water being drawn from a well.

'I'm Masaaki. I used to play with your son. I sometimes ate dinner at your place.'

Her watery eyes fix on him: 'Mā-kun? You're Mā-kun?'

'That's right!' He turns to me excitedly. 'She remembers my nickname, "Mā-kun".'

'Ah-la!' The old woman leans against the doorjamb, slaps the air, chuckles merrily and repeats his nickname. Then, with a mischievous smile, she says, 'As a child, I think you were different. Now you look like a Japanese'.

In the banquet room of a Hiroshima hotel, the old boys of Johnny Akiyama's high school athletics club are gathering for a reunion. Nobuhisa Mitsuda, his former coach, is waiting for him to arrive. 'I shouldn't say this in front of the others', he confesses, with tears in his eyes, 'but he's the one I've worried about most, how he would turn out. I've wanted to see him especially'.

Once everyone is seated, the special guest is called to the microphone. He explains why, as he puts it, he has been 'missing' for so long: close-knit family, successful business, lifestyle blending the best of Japan and Australia. His version, of course, is a more modest statement of the facts; but, reading the faces in the audience, it is obvious they recognise a winner. Was this the way it was supposed to be? How did this *konketsuji* manage to slip past the pitiful fate prepared for him?

Johnny struggles as he reaches the end of his speech. Long-suppressed emotions well up and demand to be acknowledged. He takes hold with all his might. 'From here on, too, I ask for your support.' Back at his seat, he lifts a handkerchief to his no-longer-blue eyes and acknowledges the applause.

20

Where are they now?

The road travelling away from occupied Japan put out many branches. Along them went newlyweds into an uncertain future; men arrested and forcibly removed from their families; colleagues careless or ignorant of their actions; and others who paved the way with empty promises.

These branches lead on, carrying unacknowledged sons and daughters in search of a name, a connection; ageing war brides resigned to leaving their ashes far from the land of their birth; and new generations of Japanese Australians, Japanese Americans and others moved by a desire to close the circle. Journeys begin to intersect, acquiring a clearer meaning.

We left several individuals at turning points in their lives. Where are they now?

Karumi Inoue – *overseas adoption*

Eleven-year-old Karumi Inoue departed Japan in December 1965. She was bound for the home of her adoptive parents, Ben and Linda Kaesehagen, at Kadena in rural South Australia.[1] More than two years had gone by since the family had met the child at the ISS office in Kure. Arriving at the end of her long journey, Karumi sensed the middle-aged couple were taken aback: 'They expected a skinny, short, nine-year-old. And I was nearly 12 and tall. I had changed'. This sense of unease never left her.

When I came to Australia I was 'damaged goods'. No one ever
stopped and thought about that. I was hurt so badly, I could
never trust anyone. I often questioned why I was adopted. I never
asked them. I just questioned it myself. Adoption was good for
me. I don't think it was good for them.

Her adoption experience is not something she likes to talk about.

At 17, Karumi left home to go nursing. She stepped off the bus
in Adelaide, suitcase in hand, short of cash, knowing nobody. She
found her studies enjoyable, even though the unfamiliar medical ter-
minology challenged her imperfect English. They called her 'Nurse
Smiley' on the wards at Royal Adelaide Hospital.

The year of her graduation, she married George De Mattia, a
clerk at the hospital. Karumi took the opportunity also to change
her given name, which Australians never seemed to be able to pronounce correctly: 'I thought, new life, new beginning, new everything'. She acquired the foolproof name of Kumi.

In 1984, Kumi and George – with two young daughters by now
– visited Kure. ISS organised a party to welcome them. Mayumi
Kosugi was amazed to see the 'cheeky, mischievous' child of former
days transformed into a 'model housewife'. Kumi sent a message to
her mother, Mitsuko, asking whether she would like to meet her
grandchildren.

When my mother saw my younger daughter, she said she
reminded her so much of me as a little one. Then she apologised,
you know, for everything … *Kuro kakete, gomen nasai.* [I'm sorry
I gave you a hard time.] And I said: 'I didn't come here to seek
your apology. I am here to reassure you everything has turned out
OK in my life'. I said all this in Japanese to her. 'Rest your heart.
Don't feel any more guilt. There's no need.'

After she returned to Australia, Kumi kept in touch with Mitsuko by telephone – until she realised the calls were making things awkward for her mother at home. She took the painful decision to break off contact: 'I just … I just … I do love my mother, simple as that. I have special feelings for her'.

Kumi made two discoveries while she was in Kure. One was that her father was English, not Australian. Somehow it hardly seemed to matter. She laughs: 'At least he wasn't American, like kids in Japan used to accuse me'. The more important discovery, for her, was that she had had nothing to do with her grandparents' divorce. 'I blamed myself all those years. I thought, because of me, the family couldn't take it. Right?' It had happened long before she was born.

Guilt and disclosure are recurring themes in Kumi's narrative. When the subject of her youngest child comes up, she relates an episode from a family excursion. The boy needed to relieve him-self; they stopped the car, and he jumped out and stood behind a tree. She could not restrain her laughter at his ineffectual attempt to conceal himself. It brought to mind her own efforts to slip past a world that watched her like a hawk: carrying a stolen watermelon, all-too-obviously hidden under her dress, or hiding behind her great-grandmother as a stranger peered through the window of their lonely house. 'An innocent child thinks it can't be seen – but of course it can!'

One day, her husband, George, was at home by himself, tinker-ing under the family car. He had it propped up on bricks in the yard. Kumi found him. The supports had toppled over, and he lay crushed beneath the vehicle. She was suddenly a widow, in her early forties, with three children to support.

You know what I kept reciting in my head? 'You can get through anything. Remember what you went through as a child, when you had no power to control anything. Just try to think: "This ain't nothing".'

Shortly before she became a grandmother for the first time, Kumi remarried. This change in direction encouraged her to re-establish contact with her mother. She also set out to find her cousin, Jōji, who had been adopted by an American family. She traced him to Kentucky. 'I wanted him to know I had never stopped worrying about him, the delicate one.' She was relieved to learn he had made a family and a successful career.

In her restless search for fulfilment, Kumi continues to acquire new skills as a health professional. The legacy of her traumatic childhood, she knows, is chronic insecurity. But she can also say, with conviction, 'Look at what I have achieved!' As for what might have been had she stayed in Japan?

> I doubt very much I would have gone to university. I probably would have stayed home to look after my grandmother and done menial jobs around the traps. And whether I would have had the opportunity of marrying someone, and how happy I'd be, I don't know. I'm a fairly spirited character – so I think I'd be a bit of a challenge for anyone.

Mitsuyoshi Hanaoka – *the Brazilian solution*

Mitsuyoshi arrived in Brazil with an employment contract to work with cattle on a property outside São Paulo. The job waiting for him was something completely different. He had been deceived.

> Maybe, if I had gone to Australia, everything would have been ready to receive me; I would have been able to work on a farm. But, in South America, people are different: a lackadaisical mob.

After several lean and frustrating years, Mitsuyoshi finally found secure employment with Varig Airlines as a cabin attendant. All his training as a farmer went to waste. 'I didn't go to Brazil to make a fortune. I just wanted a place in which to grow.'

One day, while on stand-by at the airport, he got into conversation with a new stewardess, a third-generation descendant of Japanese immigrants. It seemed like fate was taking a hand when the call came for them both to join the same Tokyo-bound flight. 'I wanted to make a family. Just to get married and have children and own a house, even a small one. That was my dream.'

Mitsuyoshi had not seen his mother, Fujie, since the court hearing, more than 20 years earlier, in which she lost custody of him. Eager to show off his new bride, he tracked her down in Tokyo's Tachikawa district, once home to a big American airbase.

> I recognised her immediately. But she said, 'You must have the wrong person'. Having settled down with my own family, I simply wanted to know what had happened to my mother. That's all. So I told her: 'You don't need to say that sort of thing. I didn't come to complain or be angry with you'.
>
> After separating from me, it seemed she had worked as a domestic servant. I didn't ask a lot of questions. When I tried to ask about my father, she waved me away. I offered to pay her an allowance, but she said she didn't need it.

Fujie insisted, instead, on paying him, and she would also prove a doting grandmother. Encouraged, Mitsuyoshi now went in search of the half-brother he had never seen, his mother's first son.

> It seems he had never been told about me. I visited him at the factory where he worked. He was very happy. We didn't look alike. All we shared was our baldness: the Hanaoka family trait.

Mitsuyoshi was promoted to Varig's catering manager at Narita Airport. The country that, in effect, had exiled him as a young man kept drawing him back.

By this time, Fujie was retired.

> I got a phone call from my big brother, and he told me she was in
> intensive care. When I rang the hospital, the doctor said to come
> immediately. I was able to see her before she died. She opened her
> eyes for me. I came in the evening, and she died at midnight.
>
> They brought her back to Hiroshima, to her grandparents'
> house. She had a little money, and we divided it between us
> brothers. We shared some with my auntie, who would look after
> the grave. So I can visit there now, without feeling hesitant.

Mitsuyoshi and his wife considered resettling in Japan. The past,
however, stood in the way. Visiting the family home in Hiroshima,
he could not help being reminded of the *konketsuji* who had not
been welcome there. The couple stayed in Brazil and concentrated
on giving their daughter and son the best possible education. Both
are now medical professionals in the United States.

> Of course it was better for me that I went to Brazil – a gathering
> place of many races. Even now, when I'm in Japan, people say,
> 'Oh, your Japanese is clever'. I just let it pass.

As he is speaking, he catches sight of Yone Itō in the lobby of the
hotel. They have not seen each other for many years. He creeps up
behind her and, like a naughty child, pretends to snatch her purse.
Laughing, they embrace.

> In a sense I am Japanese; I was educated in Japan. But Brazil
> looked after me. That's why I go about like this, with a Brazilian
> flag [in my lapel]. [Laughs.]
>
> I also thank the Australian people. They helped us; Americans
> didn't. When the Olympics are on, I definitely cheer for

Australians. Talking about America, even now they are doing that. They don't care. Where soldiers go, children will be born.

George Tsutsumi – *Joe Ritchie's boy*

In the mid-1960s, as the Japanese economy was shifting into overdrive, George Tsutsumi found it easy to drift from one job to another. Sometimes he would give up after half a day. 'If you started counting the number of jobs, you'd quickly run out of fingers. It means I didn't have any intention to work.'

George spent his idle time wandering about the country with a couple of disaffected friends from the ISS group. One day, taking in the sights at Hiroshima Castle, he met Hatsue. It was probably the best thing that ever happened to him.

As soon as he came of age, they married and moved to Nagoya. George found employment on the city's busy docks. In the early days, a stevedoring shift lasted for as long as it took to load and clear a vessel. He was constantly on call and once worked 45 days straight.

> When I was a child, I never knew what was happening the next day – much like my work now. Maybe that's why I've lasted so long in this company. I found I could do something. And, if I worked hard, there was a return. Whereas, when I was at school, no matter how hard I worked, nothing could come of it.

This was no saintly conversion. 'The day I was born', says George's first son, Kōji, 'he went out chasing girls. Mum held things together'. Looking back on his early married life, George is hardly less disparaging of his younger self.

> It was often said of me, 'a child produced a child'. I think it was like that. The word 'effort' was not in my vocabulary. I might go

to work – or I might not. I was lazy; I felt that the shirker was the winner in life. It took a long time for me to change my character.

Nobody who knew him back then could have imagined he would stay with the same firm all the way to retirement.

The Tsutsumis raised three sons. The children led George to renew contact with his mother, Sachiko. 'Because she was sick, I took her grandchild to see her. Seeing her grandson for the first time made her look happy – though she didn't look happy to see my face.' Sachiko began visiting them on her annual holidays.

Perhaps it was this contact which encouraged her to pick up other threads from her past. Sachiko made the journey to Canberra, to the Australian War Memorial, to inquire about her husband, Joe Ritchie. On learning that most of the Korean War dead were buried in Pusan, she retraced her steps back up the Pacific. Wandering the neat rows of graves at the United Nations cemetery, she found what she was looking for. A simple bronze plaque, a sunburst crest, a cross and an inscription:

3/1925 Private J. Ritchie
23rd January 1951
Age 23.

On the 33rd anniversary of Joe's death – a date of special significance in Buddhism – she returned to South Korea, taking George with her. Since then he has been back many times.

When I stand in the cemetery something naturally bursts forth.
I buy flowers. Close to his grave there is another victim, just 19 years old.

Each morning, George prays before a small shrine at his Nagoya apartment, in which he displays the photograph he acquired in

Australia of a smiling Joe Ritchie. Robbed of the opportunity as a child to trust in something, in his maturity he draws on an unspent endowment of fidelity.

Keeping faith with Joe's memory redressed part of what had been lost between mother and son. After Sachiko's death, as her body was being prepared for the funeral, Hatsue and George found a small rose tattooed on her thigh. 'It seems a lot of hard things happened to her', he reflects.

These days, the Tsutsumis take their greatest pleasure from their three granddaughters. Hatsue's eyes never tire of consuming their 'rice-cake-white skin', outstanding among the other youngsters at the childcare centre. On a recent trip to Okinawa, George and Hatsue were sightseeing with their second son and his two children when strangers stopped to admire the girls. 'Aren't they cute! Are they foreigners' children?' Calmly, their son explained that his father was *hāfu*, so he was 'a quarter', and they were 'an eighth'. This assured performance made a deep impression on Big George:

> I thought, if I were in my son's position and the same age, definitely hands or legs would have come before words [I would have reacted violently]. Even though I appreciate time has moved along, seeing my son answering them so naturally made me realise how small-minded I was.

Kiyotaka Kawasaki – *moving on*

Kiyotaka was a champion sportsman who had represented his country with distinction. In the eyes of some of his countrymen, however, he could never be the genuine article.

An incident at his health club in Kure brought this realisation crashing down on him. While chatting with a customer, Kiyotaka happened to pass a remark about the Japanese tendency to be over-familiar, quoting an old saying, 'Met once, a friend; met twice, a relation'. The man suddenly erupted. 'What do you know about Japanese? You can't talk like that! You are not Japanese. I don't want to be told such things by you.' Kiyotaka held his temper in check, but something inside him broke.

> I said, I had Japanese nationality; I had competed under the Japanese flag; I had a Japanese passport. I was born here. I grew up here. So I am Japanese. He sneered, 'All right, all right'.

A similar thing happened to his son, Ryo, when he entered senior high school, as the boy explains:

> My new class teacher called me out, together with another mixed-race student. The teacher doesn't know me, so I can't guess whether he's going to punish me or not.
>
> 'All right', he says, 'I'll give you time to speak in front of the class' about such-and-such discrimination in my life. All that kind of stuff: how I'm brought up an Australian, why I look the way I do, the story of my childhood.
>
> 'No', I said, 'I don't want to do that'.
>
> He said, 'Why? You have to tell them. You have to tell the other students that you're mixed-blood'.

Later on, the same teacher asked Kiyotaka whether Ryo had been fingerprinted for his Alien Registration Card.

> So I asked him, 'Do you know what nationality I am? I competed for Japan'. That teacher didn't understand I'm not a foreigner. He thought because my father was a foreigner I was a foreigner, and so was my child. I asked him, 'How many years have you known me?'

Though Ryo went on to complete his education in Kure, Kiyotaka had begun making inquiries about moving to Australia. The family left for Brisbane in 2006.

A few months later, I pay them a visit. Driving up to the house, I catch sight of Kiyotaka and his wife, Ritsuko, sitting on the doorstep waiting. There is something forlorn about their vigil; I wonder what I am about to hear.

Ryo seems to be putting down new roots without much difficulty. He has a job he likes, in a country that asks fewer questions. Ritsuko is studying English and also appears to be adjusting quite well. Kiyotaka, on the other hand, is more like his father, the irascible Charles Nation. He tends to criticise.

First, it was the neighbours, with their all-night parties. That stopped after he confronted them, carrying a wooden sword and bellowing in Japanese ('Kure dialect', he adds – humour never far below the surface). 'The other neighbours thanked us', murmurs Ritsuko. Next, it was the children at the local school he volunteered to coach in athletics. They showed so little interest in improving their skills he quit in disgust.

On the brighter side, Kiyotaka's therapeutic massage business is picking up, after a slow start. Word is spreading about the big man with the healing hands.

> Starting this week, we have bookings for an average of one customer a day, so I think we can make a living. We'll hold a big ceremony tomorrow. Anyway I don't want to work that hard. [Laughs.] My friend in Kure said, 'Don't try to cure them in one go'. I ring him occasionally for advice.

While seemingly reconciled to the fact there can be no going back, Kiyotaka still considers himself 'pure Japanese'. 'My father didn't go back [to Australia] his whole life. So, having his blood, I can understand why not – and the frustration. But, since I'm here now, there's no point making comparisons with Japan …'

Ryo chimes in: 'He's changing while he talks. He'll often say, "If this were Japan …"'.

Ritsuko adds, with a smile: 'Irritating, irritating …'.

Kazumi Yoshida – *on the rebound from New Guinea*

Teenage Kazumi arrived back in Kure in the autumn of 1966. She relished being restored to her comfort zone: 'I could read everything, understand everyone'. She moved in with a relative and found a job at a factory making denim jeans (her job was to sew in the 'Made in USA' tags).

A few months later, her boyfriend, Jim, surprised her with a visit. He was still there when her mother and stepfather turned up, on holiday. Trouble followed immediately.

> Bill didn't want to see me, he said, because I was staying with Jim in Auntie's house. What we were doing was 'all wrong' – not that we were doing anything wrong.
>
> I said to Mum: 'I really don't like him, and he's no good for you either. I'm not sure I want to go back'. Mum said: 'If Jim is a nice man, and that's what you want, I'll do my best to help you get married. But if you're in Japan, and we're in New Guinea, there's not a lot I can do'.
>
> So I decided to give it another go.

Back in Goroka, Bill continued to oppose the romance. If he saw Kazumi and Jim together, he would come banging on her bedroom door later, screaming abuse. He worked himself up into such a state he ended up in hospital.

This was the last straw. Kazumi moved out of the house and took shelter with a girlfriend's family. She and Jim found a magistrate, who witnessed Mitsuko's consent for her under-age daughter to marry. Presented with the fait accompli, Bill turned about-face and asked his stepdaughter if she would let him give her away at the altar. 'He didn't really kick up a fuss anymore after that, though he told anyone who would listen that our marriage would never last.' Fortunately for all concerned, it did.

After the birth of their first child, Kazumi and Jim resettled in Melbourne. Kazumi understood from her mother's letters that she and Bill were managing well enough back in New Guinea. At least they had sufficient money for regular holidays in Japan. It was another coat of veneer.

> Each time they went back to Japan, he would rent a house, buy furniture, invite friends and relatives, and have a big party. Basically, he lived like a king. He never let Mum know what their finances were like: 'Don't worry, everything will be all right'.
>
> Then Bill came back from Japan to attend a wedding in Australia, and I was shocked to find Mum didn't come back with him. He didn't have enough money for her airfare! She had been left behind again! I remember such sadness came over me.
>
> Mum went to live with her brother and her father – and the stepmother whom she loathed. It must have been terrible for her to have to go there. The embarrassment.

Mitsuko earned her keep by working on the vegetable farm. She felt humiliated and trapped.

> One day, Mum heard her stepmother say to her father and brother – she was resting in the next room – 'She's been dumped. She's been dumped by her husband'. Mum knew she had to get out of there. 'My stomach began to boil', she said. 'I knew, if I stayed, there'd be terrible consequences.'

Mitsuko had another reason for wanting to get back to Australia:

Bill had turned up on Jim and Kazumi's doorstep, out of work and with nowhere to live. 'If Bill had been OK, I don't think Mum would have come back. But she had to, for my sake – once again. My mum thought, "I can't let Kazumi look after him for the rest of her life. This is not how it was supposed to be".' Mitsuko borrowed the airfare from her brother.

'Mum's tough life started again.' She and Bill moved from one cheap rental to another. When Bill died, they were living in a tiny Housing Commission flat in Melbourne. Mitsuko was left having to cope, among other things, with the resident ex-soldier who came banging on her door at night, screaming drunken abuse at the 'Jap'.

Kazumi and Jim have rescued her from the ghetto. Keeping faith with the promise she made her uncle, that windswept day long ago, Kazumi has built an annexe onto the family home in Gippsland, country Victoria, where her mother will see out her days.

The journey does not end there. After an exhaustive search, Kazumi has managed to identify her father, Walder Carl Hansen. It turns out, he was born and educated in Copenhagen, and was already a family man when he went to Japan. He died in Sydney in 1988. 'At last, I know', says Kazumi, who suddenly finds she has four half-siblings and a score of other relations. Now begins the delicate task of breaching 60 years of silence.

Mayumi Kosugi – *leader of the Kure Kids*

Mayumi Kosugi immediately gives the impression of someone decisive and resolute. She does not merely cross a hotel lobby, she makes a beeline: striding out, head up, eyes front.

> When I was a young child, I looked Western. Later, when I was an adult, I looked rather Japanese. Now my hair has turned white, I look Western again. It's weird. Foreigners sometimes stop me in the supermarket and ask for my help, in English.

Mayumi became a mother at the age of 36. The happy event turned into another test of character and resolve when her daughter, Ai, was diagnosed with autism.

> This child's human rights are connected to the human rights issues I experienced first hand. I worried at first that she'd be bullied because she was 'quarter', but she didn't suffer because of that. She was bullied because she was slow. Times have changed. Now there are people in Japan from the Philippines, Brazil – new reasons to be picked on.
>
> I thought I shouldn't adopt a negative attitude. I was able to talk openly to my child about these things, drawing on my own experience. I could explain to her. If you look at the results, I think I am right. I may not be a good mother, but I am trying hard.

Ai is listening to the conversation and interjects, 'No, you're a good mother'.

Mayumi and her husband ran a video rental shop in Kure, until changing technology forced them out of business. Her husband took over the household chores, and Mayumi went back to college to train as an aged-care worker. It was a brave step, for a particular reason. Such work would put her in daily contact with older Japanese, who still harboured negative attitudes about *konketsuji*.

> People seeing me for the first time, if they are my mother's generation, with a strong hatred towards Westerners, always look at me with an unkind expression. I feel, 'Oh, it happens again'. I experience this 'being looked at' always.

But Mayumi's fears have not materialised. On the contrary, the old people's home throws up plenty to smile about.

Some clients are still clear in their mind. They greet me in English: 'Nice day'. I say back: 'Hi. Nice day'. They return an embarrassed smile. Other women are suffering from dementia and say to me, 'What a handsome man'. I say back, 'Yes. I'm a *nyū hāfu*' [a transsexual male, from the English 'new half']. Everyone laughs heartily, but I really wonder whether they know what '*nyū hāfu*' means.

Mayumi was a leader and organiser among the Kure Kids. She was also the least equipped to answer questions about absent fathers – not even a name in her case. On her first visit to Australia, in 1985, she went without expectations: 'It was a foreign land, it was beautiful, but I didn't have any familiar feeling directly related to me'. She is left wondering, nevertheless, when Japanese acquaintances describe her way of thinking as 'foreign'.

> For example, even though this child has a bit of a handicap, in junior high I let her go to America for a month. The teacher said it was unbelievable that I let her go: 'You really have the blood of "over there"'. So, while I'm not conscious of having a different way of thinking, others have commented. Perhaps, without being aware of it, I am partly influenced by my father's genes.

The trip to Australia was a disappointment for Mayumi and the other Kure Kids, in one important respect: they were unable to meet Alex Ferguson's descendants or visit his grave. Twenty-one years would pass before another opportunity arose to honour their benefactor's memory. As usual, Mayumi was the driving force.

In October 2006, 14 ISS members gathered at Melbourne's Springvale Cemetery to lay a wreath and offer prayers for 'AJ': the man of action they revered like a father – or, as Mayumi once wrote, 'better than a father'. The perfume of spring roses filled the air, and bright sunshine bathed the solemn gathering. Mayumi's customary composure gave way. She looked painfully alone and lost for words. The unbearable wistfulness of the moment was unrelieved by any applause.

21

A mixed future

War not only destroys. It may clear the ground for new and sounder ideas to take root. Less than a year after Pearl Harbor, when President Roosevelt predicted that nations in the future would be more racially mixed, could he have guessed where the process was already under way?

Japanese formed the largest non-white minority in Hawaii. Before the sirens went, a public display of affection between a Japanese woman and a white man would have caused a 'mild sensation'.[1] Afterwards, it became an everyday occurrence. In the cauldron of war, 600 ethnic Japanese women married white servicemen or civilians, and others embraced freedom of expression by 'shacking up' with white boyfriends, in defiance of their elders. Illegitimate births doubled.

Fast-forward to President-elect Barack Obama's first news conference in 2008. He is in a light-hearted mood, fielding a question about the pet dog he has promised to buy his daughters. What kind will it be, a reporter asks. 'Our preference would be to get a shelter dog', replies Obama. 'But, obviously, a lot of shelter dogs are mutts like me.'[2] Amid the laughter, none can fail to recognise a serendipitous act of consolation for all the despised 'mutts' of history.

Between Roosevelt and Obama, what direction has Japan taken?

Internationalisation

The sceptics were wrong about Japan rearming for war. They were wrong to believe democracy could not take root. But the occupation did fall short in one important respect: it left intact the Japanese wartime presumption to a unique and homogeneous ethnicity.

In the succeeding decades, this self-image was reinforced by various socio-economic trends: diminishing regional diversity; narrowing income disparities; increasing social mobility; and greater lifestyle conformity from the effects of consumerism and urbanisation. Japanese moving from the countryside to the cities felt nostalgia for a lost communal solidarity and eagerly embraced parables of cultural exclusivity.

As integrated as Japan became with the rest of the world, economically, it remained an insular society. Even the 1980s fashion for internationalisation (*kokusai-ka*) was not what it seemed. People felt more comfortable interacting with foreigners because they felt surer about themselves; by perceiving the heterogeneity of others, they reaffirmed their own homogeneity. Few embraced *kokusai-ka* with the thought of diversifying the nation's ethnic identity.

Prime Minister Yasuhiro Nakasone, an outspoken, English-speaking politician, who could command a presence on the world stage, became *kokusai-ka*'s headline act. Nakasone articulated views that gave the lie to internationalisation as a force for social change. He once declared: 'Japanese-like Japanese are respected [in other countries]. People of unknown nationality, like *omajiri*, are not respected'. (*Omajiri* is a thin rice gruel given to infants or sick people.)[3] Asked whether he meant mixed-race Japanese, he said he was referring to anyone lacking a clear identity.

Political and civic responses to multiculturalism have been slow to emerge in Japan. As recently as 1980, the government stated that 'minorities of the kind mentioned in [the United Nations] Covenant [on Civil and Political Rights] do not exist in Japan'.[4] The Ainu were not formally recognised as an indigenous people until 1997. Critics have cited the tiny number of asylum seekers granted refugee status as further proof of Japan's desire to hold itself aloof from a too-promiscuous engagement with the outside world.

In hindsight, *kokusai-ka* can appear a missed opportunity – when the country's star was still in the ascendant. In certain ways, however, the economic boom and bust of the 1980s and 1990s *did* force Japanese to look at themselves differently.

During the bubble economy, many foreign workers entered the country to fill a demand for semi-skilled labour. Non-permanent residents overstaying their visas formed an exploited underclass that swelled to well over half a million. Recession and mass lay-offs led many of these, mainly Asian, workers to depart, though not all.

Economic opportunity attracted members of the Japanese diaspora back to the motherland. More than 300 000 mainly Brazilian-born *nikkeijin* (émigrés and their descendants) entered under special visa arrangements.[5] The public's perception of them was complicated by the fact they spoke Portuguese and behaved like foreigners. *Nikkeijin* simultaneously evoked sympathy (because of their shared ancestry) and disfavour (because of their perceived lower-class status). Sensing their marginal position, some chose to assert their alternative cultural affiliation (for example, by performing the samba in public for the first time in their lives).

Another episode that challenged assumptions underlying the national self-image was the return of many of the estimated 5000 Japanese who were left behind in China, as children, after the war. Highly publicised family reunions thrust before the public a group of people who, though ethnically the same as them, spoke a foreign language, behaved differently and often showed the physical signs of their alien upbringing (weathered by life in a Chinese peasant village). Changes in government policy made it easier for these *zanryū koji* ('orphans left behind') to visit or settle in Japan.

Around the same time, tens of thousands of Chinese, Filipina and Korean women began entering the country to marry farmers who were no longer able to persuade Japanese women to share their demanding lifestyle. In rural areas – where traditional values remained strong – strange blood joined the body politic.

About 4.5 million permanent residents of Japan could be regarded as having minority status, or nearly 4 per cent of the population. The number of foreign residents doubled between 1990 and 2009, from 1.1 million to 2.2 million. In a few industrial towns expatriates made up 10–20 per cent of the population. While the nation, as a whole, grappled with the problems of an ageing population and falling birth rate, interracial unions and mixed-race births were on the rise. Marriages in which at least one partner was a foreigner increased from 0.5 per cent of the total in 1970 to 5.8 per cent in 2005 (but declined to 4.8 per cent in 2009). The proportion of international births nearly doubled over the same period.[6]

A UN report made headlines by estimating that Japan would need to admit 600 000 migrants a year through until 2050, if it were to stabilise its working-age population.[7] While this obviously exceeded any tolerable or practical scale of immigration, some observers felt the nation was inexorably heading towards a multicultural future or, at least, a more vibrant ethnic diversity.

A Japanese quilt

The conditions that allowed Japanese to complacently equate ethnicity with nationality were breaking down. Changes to the law, and precedents set by the courts, made it easier for children with a foreign parent to acquire Japanese nationality, regardless of the parent's gender or marital status. Access to social security was no longer dependent upon citizenship, and local governments and NGOs were more responsive to the needs of non-Japanese long-term residents.

Relaxed entry requirements enabled about 70 000 foreign-born children to be enrolled in the public school system.[8] For thousands of non-Japanese-speaking *nikkeijin*, however, language remained a serious educational barrier. Rates of confinement in juvenile detention centres for this minority were up to five times higher than the national average.

Another contentious issue was the nationality claims of mixed-race children, mainly born to Filipinas on temporary entertainment visas, whose Japanese fathers refused to acknowledge them. Their indeterminate status exposed gaps in the law and challenged the cultural assumption that nationality and ethnicity must follow the male line. It was the occupation scenario given a contemporary twist.

With catchphrases like 'turning difference into richness', government officials were encouraged to consider ways in which foreign residents could 'revitalize and reenergize Japan'. At the same time, nevertheless, anyone who looked Japanese felt strong pressure to assimilate, especially those living outside urban centres. A study of the mixed-race offspring of Asian farm-wives found a pronounced conformity with mainstream culture.[9]

No single phrase or word can adequately describe these contending forces. The sense of a nation in flux, or at a crossroads, and seeking a new vocabulary for itself comes across in the comments of a leading adviser on integration policy. 'Support in government circles for ethnic groups retaining their own language and culture does not yet coincide with Australian or Canadian multiculturalism', says Keizo Yamawaki. '[Separate] community building is not encouraged.'[10] And yet, by identifying this deficiency, Yamawaki hints at a desire for change that would have enormous implications for the state.

While today's Japan still contains many voices pushing claims of a homogeneous ethnicity, the increasingly visible presence and activism of mixed-race Japanese constitutes a strong counterpoint. Numerous websites cater to this diverse minority, providing a forum in which individuals, including those living outside Japan, can share experiences and insights. Not only do they enjoy an expanded range of opportunities to interact with other *hāfu*, but also they can express their differences in a climate of increased social acceptance. In the popular imagination, being *hāfu* is 'cool and cute'.[11]

These trends have been confirmed in a series of interviews conducted by Marcia Yumi Lise for the Hafu Project.[12] A Swedish-Japanese woman, living in Tokyo, felt people gave her leeway 'to be a little bit different'. For a German-Japanese woman, being *hāfu* was a vital part of her public persona: 'People find an interest in me'. A Japanese-British woman, born and raised in London, described her mixed ethnicity this way: 'My Japanese-ness is as large as my British-ness, although in a way it's the secret part of myself because I'm not recognised as Japanese. It's like a secret dream, a secret fantasy that I have'.

These observations stand in sharp contrast to the comments of many occupation-era *konketsuji*. The stigma has gone, leaving only the comparatively mild irritation of being perceived as a 'foreigner's child' rather than a Japanese. A Japanese-British man, raised in London and Tokyo, told the Hafu Project: 'I've had people say, "Oh my god you speak Japanese, *kimochiwarui* (creepy)"'. But this did not make him wish to escape his indeterminate identity. 'I feel like I fit in different places. I can blend.'

The old foreigner–Japanese, insider–outsider distinction is blurred by the presence of ethnic Japanese with different cultural orientations and of *hāfu* in any number of multiracial forms, and by the altered mentality and behaviour of citizens returning from time spent living abroad. Being 'Japanese' has come to mean an infinite number of possibilities.

It is worth reiterating that this is not entirely new. The 'mixed nation' discourse of the Meiji era explicitly acknowledged the human variety underlying Japanese ethnicity. And, before then, Tokugawa society, with its complex sumptuary laws, divided the population according to social function. Gender differentiation was – and remains – another dividing line. Mainstream society's interaction with long-established minority groups has always troubled the homogeneity myth.

What seems new today is that physical and behavioural differences are borne more lightly and the concept of ethnicity itself is more diffuse – in much the same way as markers of class, regional origin, education and lineage have lost clarity over the past half-century.

Moving on

This book set out to reclaim 'sad, unspoken stories' of the past. Searching behind the reticence of history, it has found nations paying homage to race mythologies – willing to use military dictate, political deception and public scaremongering to break up families and deny individual rights.

The modern idea of race served not only to codify and entrench human differences; it was *felt* to be necessary, because differences could attract as well as repel. The mixed-race child subverted power structures, defied class barriers and altered nations from within. Colonisers planted this assumption wherever they planted their flags, not least in Australia and the Americas. The Japanese did so, too, in their empire. The image of the 'miserable half-caste' has been emblazoned on the masthead of every modern form of race-inspired nationalism.

Japan's *konketsuji* seemed to conform perfectly to the stereotype of mixed-race misery entrenched in the minds of Australians, Americans and Japanese. *Life* magazine in 1969 found a glue-sniffing and promiscuous tribe of 'true outcasts' in the mean streets of Tokyo's Shinjuku district. The African-American magazine *Ebony* reported on 'Japan's Rejected', who 'must choose between a life of drudgery and a career of crime'.[13] These and other one-dimensional portrayals condemned Japanese 'race and class superiority', while largely ignoring the effects of war, occupation and the American bases. The partial and misleading historical perspective that coalesced between the 1950s and 1970s has held sway ever since.

Academic studies, in turn, placed excessive reliance on media accounts and research findings derived from a tiny number of highly disturbed clinical cases. The most influential researcher, the American-based sociologist Hiroshi Wagatsuma, spread the notion that 'most of these children are emotionally insecure, immature, dependent, passive or even apathetic, and often harbouring hatred'. Wagatsuma claimed, incorrectly, that 'only a few successful fashion models and movie stars have been able to marry Japanese men'.[14]

Many observers assumed the children were rejected primarily because of their skin colour and other physical differences, whereas society's attitude was influenced more by the perceived low socio-economic status of the mothers and lingering bitterness over the war defeat. Politicians and journalists portrayed them as unwanted waifs, even though the great majority were raised by relatives and acculturated as Japanese. Academics claimed they could not obtain a proper education, marry or find a decent job, and yet, with guidance and financial help, all these outcomes were possible. They could and did pursue productive lives.

In the context of a savage century, the mixed-race legacy of occupied Japan may seem a small episode (though what military history would rate a battle with 10 000 casualties 'small'?) Depth of prejudice and scale of inequality count for more, in this instance, than numbers. A David and Goliath contest pitted powerless women and children against military and government establishments. A sledgehammer immigration policy crushed the fortunes of a few needy boys and girls. Mass hysteria twisted public and official responses to the *konketsuji*. It is a story with contemporary resonance, too, wherever an unwanted minority is suffering under society's intolerance.

Any attempt to chart historical attitudes to race mixing inevitably records a depressing amount of cruelty and unhappiness. In describing lives dogged by shame and ridicule, we confront humanity's dark side. If there is a saving grace, it is to be found in the individual narratives of this book. Mingled with the bitter memories are many moments of laughter – as personal dreams and foibles, fate's accidents and ironies and the ignorance of others are seen through hindsight's wry, restorative eye. Each smile, in a way, marks a small victory over inhumanity. Kazumi Purvis speaks for others, as well as herself, when she says: 'The impact on my life as I was growing up, and the shame I have felt all these years, is almost cleansed'.

The Kure Kids are now reaching retirement age. Their children live, beyond the shadow of war, in a country somewhat more tolerant of racial diversity. As different demographic, social and economic forces bear down, the answer to the question 'Who is a Japanese?' is understood to be more complex than the narrow formulae once trotted out. Guest-worker schemes, immigration and interracial marriage are recognised to be among the few available means for Japan to counter the effects of an ageing population, diminished economic vigour and increased global competition for creative skills. Whether the Japanese are prepared to surrender something as familiar and comfortable as a homogeneous ethnic identity – even one more imagined than real – remains to be seen. It may represent the best hope for a nation in decline.

Notes

Introduction

1 That part of the building containing the auditorium used for the trials has been reconstructed at another site.
2 Dower (1999), p. 211.
3 Porter (1958), p. 155.
4 Takemae (2002), pp. 80–81.
5 *SMH*, 21 August 1908. San Francisco *Examiner*, 6 May 1908.
6 NAA: A446, 1966/45427.
7 Radio address, 8 December 1941. *SMH*, 27 March 1942. Thorne (1978), p. 259.
8 Rivett (1946), p. 334. MacArthur (2005), p. 177. *SMH*, 7 February 1945.
9 On Wewak: The commanding officer was General Robertson, who later headed BCOF. Johnston (2000), p. 122.
10 Janssens (1995), pp. 51–55. Thorne (1978), pp. 158–59, 167–68n. Ibid., p. 158.
11 *Argus*, 12 August 1945. *Argus*, 4 September 1945 (also for editorial). *SMH*, 11 September 1945.
12 'Do we want the Jap as an ally?' *Sunday Telegraph*, 12 October 1947. Ball (1948), p. 200.
13 Clune (1950), pp. 145, 37–38. On the other hand, Clune considered the atomic attack on Hiroshima 'an atrocity' (p. 128).
14 *Age*, 23 February 1946. The ship's rated capacity was 200 passengers.
15 NAA: A4940, C4046.
16 6 October 1948, *CPD*, vol. 198, p. 1283.
17 *Mirror*, 12 October 1962.

1 Karumi's story

1 ISSJ: Case report.
2 ISSJ.
3 Dunstan (1966), p. 134.

2 Butterfly and child

1 Baelz (1974), p. 196.
2 Erwin Baelz, *Dainihon shiritsu eiseikai zasshi* 43 (December 1886), p. 16.
3 Baelz (1974), pp. 104–109.
4 Quoted in Mulder (1985), p. 149n (punctuation amended).
5 A larger number of Chinese traders were also allowed to stay in Nagasaki in their own enclave.

6   Screech (2005), p. 109.
7   Andō (1966–67), vol. 2, p. 56.
8   Dower (1975), p. 339.
9   Miyoshi (1994), pp. 71–72.
10 Griffis (1913), p. 721. Knapp (1897), vol. 1, p. 5. Keane (1896), pp. 316–17.
11 Oguma (2002), p. xxi, passim.
12 Whitney (1979), pp. 38, 54, 141.
13 Koyama (2002), pp. 16–21.
14 Takahashi (1883), p. 10.
15 Inoue (1894–95), vol. 1, p. 100. Katō (1990), vol. 3, p. 44.
16 Duncan (1908), pp. 322–23 (emphasis in original).
17 Nitobe (1909), pp. 68, 287.
18 Cooper (1981), p. 40. Arnold (1891), p. 325.
19 Keyserling (1925), vol. 2, p. 206.
20 Lawton (1912), vol. 1, p. 720; vol. 2, pp. 742, 750, 759. Levenson et al. (1982),
    p. 15. 'Japanese "Curios"', *Illustrated London News*, 3 June 1893. Bousquet
    (1877), vol. 1, p. 349.
21 Watanna (2003), p. 10.
22 Yayoi Aoki, in De Bary et al. (2005), p. 1208.

3   War of purification

1   Quoted in Rosenfeld (1999), p. 121.
2   Keene (2010), pp. 16–17.
3   Yamashita (2005), pp. 205, 305. Tamayama (2005), p. 259.
4   Tsurumi (1986), p. 31.
5   Guillain (1981), p. 103. Toland (1970), vol. 2, p. 639. Miyake (1991), p. 282.
6   Baelz (1974), p. 275. Yamashita (2005), pp. 119, 112. Kawai (1950), p. 57.
7   Kiyosawa (1999), pp. 110, 313.
8   Katō (1999), p. 201.
9   Kato (1946), p. 253.
10 George E Jones, 'Writer over Tokyo says ruin is real', *NYT*, 29 August 1945.
11 Frank L Kluckhohn, 'Japan's war scars are dim at Atsugi', *NYT*, 31 August 1945.
12 Maj Faubion Bowers, quoted in Cohen (1987), p. 123.
13 'Japanese bitter in defeat', *NYT*, 1 September 1945. 'First impressions of
    conquered Japan', *NYT Magazine*, 9 September 1945.
14 Tanaka (2002), pp. 116–27. *Seikatsu*, August–September 1945, quoted in
    Nishimura (1989), pp. 14–15.
15 Bungo Ōtake, ('Flesh seawall'), *Diamond* (special issue), 15 May 1952, p. 68.
16 Kaburagi (1974), p. 142.
17 Shukan Bunshun, 16 August 1965, p. 38.
18 Deverall (1953), p. 95. Lark (1999), p. 140.
19 PSS, 6 November 1945.
20 Goodman (2005), p. 57.
21 Weldon and Austin (2005), p. 59.
22 Hilgard (1946), pp. 343–48.
23 'Guide to Japan', CINCPAC-CINCPOA Bulletin No. 209–45, 1 September
    1945, p. 55.

24 Itagaki (1953), p. 163. Maruyama (1965), p. 144. Sodei (2001), pp. 120–21.
25 William L Worden, 'The GI is civilizing the Jap', *Saturday Evening Post*, 15 December 1945, p. 104. 'GI's in Japan obey fraternizing ban', *NYT*, 21 September 1945. Some individual units took a hard line on fraternisation, but it was never made SCAP policy.
26 Brines (1948), p. 27. Kelley and Ryan (1947), p. 145.
27 McDonald (1998), p. 294.
28 Cary (1984), pp. 121, 123.
29 Gayn (1981 [1948]), p. 51. Quoted in Kanō (2007), p. 217. Gayn (1981 [1948]), p. 179.
30 Darrell Berrigan, 'Japan's occupation babies', *Saturday Evening Post*, 19 June 1948, pp. 117–18.
31 Takasaki (1952), pp. 19, 14.
32 *PSS*, 10 March 1946. *PSS*, 16 March 1946.

4   Mitsuyoshi's story

1 Kang (2004).
2 *Mombu-shō* (1957).
3 ISSJ: Case report.
4 Hemphill (1969), pp. 115, 174–76.
5 *Chu S*, 23 August 1967.

5   Conquering Kure

1 Seaman (1905), p. 74.
2 Quoted in Maruyama (1965), p. 508n.
3 Quoted in Drea (1992), p. 48.
4 Memo of conversation with Secretary of War Stimson, 29 May 1945, US National Archives, College Park, Record Group 107. Drea (1992), p. 223.
5 Kanzaki (1953), pp. 199–200.
6 Archer (2009), p. 125. Bates (1993), p. 105. 'The Ashes' is a cricket trophy contested between England and Australia.
7 Harrison (1966), p. 16.
8 *Chu S*, 18 February 1946.
9 Extraordinarily, there is no official figure for the number of Australians who participated in BCOF. An unofficial nominal roll, for Army personnel only, stands at 20 000 (personal communication with Lt Col Neil Smith).
10 Kay (1982), p. 1475. Rice diverted from BCOF stores helped avert a food crisis in Japan in July–August 1946, soon after Robertson's appointment. See *The Yoshida Memoirs: The Story of Japan in Crisis* (London: Heinemann, 1961), p. 205.
11 Kay (1982), pp. 1366–67. *Kure-shi Shi*, vol. 8, p. 653. *The Forgotten Force*, Film Australia, 1994.
12 *Age*, 16 March 1946. Moore (1997), p. 6. War bride and soldier's daughter: Personal communications.
13 *Sun-P*, 22 November 1946. See also McDonald (1998), p. 275. For invaliding: NAA: A5954, 1886/2.
14 For VD cases and Robertson's reaction: NAA: A5954, 1886/2. For 'morally

rotting': *SMH*, 13 January and 14 May 1948.

15 Elliott (1995), p. 68.
16 Author's interview.
17 Tanaka (2002), p. 126.
18 Rupert Ryan (Member for Flinders), 17 September 1948, *CPD*, vol. 198, p. 567. 'Women in Japan are sold for less than stock', *Argus Week-End Magazine*, 5 January 1946. 'The Japan our occupation troops will enter', *SMH*, 10 January 1946.
19 *Australian Women's Weekly*, 11 May 1946, p. 11.
20 *PSS*, 22 July 1946.
21 Wood (1998), p. 98.
22 C-in-C to JCOSA, 27 June 1947, NAA: A816, 52/301/295. C-in-C to JCOSA, 2 October 1947, NAA: A5954, 1883/6.
23 *Sun-P*, 16 July 1948.
24 *BCOF Bound*, n.p., 1947, pp. 1, 10.
25 NAA: AWM114, 130/1/23 Part 1; *Sun*, 10 September 1947.
26 Cunneen (2003), p. 143.
27 Harrison (1966), p. 14.
28 *The 7.30 Report*, ABC-TV, broadcast 19 April 2005.
29 Author's interview.

6   Remaking Japanese women

1 'The menacing shadow', *NYT Magazine* 16 September 1945. 'We bring a revolution to the Japanese', *NYT Magazine* 14 October 1945. 'Now a Japanese woman can be a cop', *NYT Magazine*, 2 June 1946.
2 *Fujin Koron*, July 1948, p. 37.
3 Fujita (1956), pp. 487–88. *PSS*, 23 March 1946.
4 Cohen (1987), pp. 134, 131.
5 *Tokyo Shimbun*, 9 August 1946. A small tin of condensed milk, for example, cost about ¥60 on the black market. See Clifton (1950), p. 52 for black-market prices.
6 Cary (1984), p. 303.
7 *New York Times*, 11 January 1947. For killings: Matsuzawa (2006), p. 67.
8 Takami (1965), vol. 6, p. 265.
9 Sōichi Ōya, ('It was women who profited most'), *Bungei Shunjū* (special issue), 5 June 1952, p. 194. 'Roundtable', *Fujin Koron*, September 1953, p. 48. Ōya, op. cit.
10 Ishikawa (1998), pp. 56–57.
11 Ayako Koyanagi, ('This child is pitiable'), *Fujin Koron*, May 1952, pp. 112–13.
12 Kawai (1950), p. 89. See also Richie (2001), pp. 113–14.
13 Mizuno (1953), pp. 283–84. Keiō Gijyuku Daigaku (1953), pp. 20–23. Mizuno, op. cit., p. 286.
14 Kanzaki (1953), pp. 226–27.
15 '*Hoshi no Nagare ni*' ('In the Flow of the Stars'). Tanaka (1957), p. 66.
16 Inoue (1991), pp. 221–65.
17 Sakanishi (1956), p. 134.
18 Lark (1999), pp. 204–205.

19 *PSS*, 24 June 1947.
20 On infanticide: Coleman (1983), pp. 18–19. The comparison is between 1940 and 1950. For Germany: Hertog (2009), p. 3.
21 Williams (1958), p. 135. Williams's outlook was that of the expatriate for whom the blundering or lascivious new arrival was a constant source of embarrassment.
22 Johnson (1984), p. 84. For Pia Kurusu: *PSS*, 14 August 1947.
23 Perry (1980), pp. 185–86.
24 For marriage numbers: *PSS*, 22 August 1947. Associated Press reported the number as 823. For Montana case: *PSS*, 7 August 1947.
25 Ochimi Kubushiro, ('Various new issues of mixed-blood children'), *New Age* (March 1953), p. 28. See also Graham and Giga (1953), p. 51.
26 Hungerford (1954), pp. 159, 200, 277.
27 Porter (1968), p. 162. Porter taught school for children of BCOF families.
28 Haigh (1995), p. 27 (typographical errors corrected). She probably visited the 'Garden of Light' orphanage (*Sei Yozefu Shūdōin*).
29 BCOF Administrative Instruction 39: 'Marriages in Japan', 28 September 1946, NAA: AWM114, 130/3/16 Part 1. Stephen Kelen, 'Brides in a foreign land', *Sunday Mail* (Qld), 21 April 1996. On suicides: Mancktelow (1991), pp. 20, 24, 43.
30 *SMH*, 25 March 1946. *SMH*, 4 April 1946.
31 *Argus*, 12 March 1948.
32 A Japanese academic, Yuki Tanaka, who raised the issue of rapes by BCOF servicemen in 1993, met a hostile response from the RSL. Several veterans questioned by the author declined to discuss the subject.

7   Mayumi's story

1 ISSJ: Case report.
2 Arthur Richards, 'The "waifs" are growing up …', *Sun-P*, 23 December 1964.
3 ISSJ: Letter, 10 June 1967.
4 ISSJ: Letter, 16 June 1970.

8   Mixed-blood mythologies

1 Padover (1943), p. 503.
2 Quoted in Frederickson (2002), p. 56. Snyder (1962), p. 103.
3 Knox (1850), p. 52. Nott and Gliddon (1855), p. 398.
4 Quatrefages (1879), p. 282.
5 Quoted in Gould (1981), p. 48.
6 Quoted in Menand (2001), p. 115.
7 Herder (1800), p. 249.
8 Annesley (1809), vol. 1, p. 241.
9 Quoted in Ballhatchet (1979), p. 100.
10 'Henry Lawson & I', Dame Mary Gilmore Papers, vol. 41, Mitchell Library.
11 'The why and the wherefore', *New Australia*, 28 January 1893.
12 Pearson (1894), p. 90.
13 *SMH*, 17 May 1888.
14 6 September 1901, *CPD*, vol. 4, p. 4633. 26 September 1901, *CPD*, vol. 4, p. 5233.

15 *The Worker*, 16 April 1908. 'The Port O' Call' (1908).
16 *Bulletin*, 16 November 1895, p. 6. Henry Lawson, 'To Be Amused' (1906).
17 *The Worker*, op. cit.
18 Rowell (1909), pp. 3–4. Daniels (1977), pp. 20, 47.
19 Hichborn (1913), p. 230.
20 Kawakami (1914), p. 73. Kawakami's views were close to those of the Japanese Foreign Ministry, which quietly subsidised his journalism.
21 Gulick (1937), p. 4.
22 Quoted in Okihiro (1991), p. 118.
23 *The Melting-Pot* was first staged in 1908.
24 Galton (1892), p. 1.
25 Pearson (1900), p. 368.
26 Davenport (1912), pp. 286, 300, 309.
27 Davenport (c. 1920), n.p. DW Griffith's 1915 film *The Birth of a Nation* contains a vicious portrayal of 'mulatto treachery'.
28 Pascoe (2009), pp. 124–30.
29 Grant (1916), pp. 92, 60, 49.
30 Spengler (1961 [1918]), vol. 1, p. 126.
31 Quoted in Keane (1896), p. 155.
32 Finch (1911), p. 108. Gulick (1937), pp. 212, 48. Keane (1896), p. 155.
33 Hearn (2009), p. 451. Contained in *Two Years in the French West Indies* (1890).
34 Lacerda (1911), p. 380.
35 Park (1931), p. 547; Park (1928), p. 893.
36 Reuter (1925) p. 64. Park (1928), p. 893 (emphasis in original).
37 Reuter (1928), p. 59. Thomas Mann, *The Magic Mountain* (1924): 'disease was life's lascivious form'.

9 The Eurasian malaise

1 Watanna (2003), p. 152.
2 Tamagawa (1932), pp. 24, 34, 46–56, 70–71.
3 Geoffrey (1926), pp. 41, 188. Tamura (2007), p. 35. Smith and Wiswell (1982), p. xxii.
4 Ridley (1913), p. 54.
5 Hedin (1934), p. 168.
6 Williams (1928), p. 167.
7 Blackford (2000), p. 41.
8 Lee (2004), p. 25. Quoted in Sweeting (1990), p. 395.
9 Butcher (1979), p. 186.
10 Clune (1939), pp. 148, 347.
11 See Nakashima (1992), pp. 168–69.
12 Shiel (1929), pp. 17, 30, 64.
13 Shiraishi (2001), p. 9.
14 Tanizaki (1985 [1924]), pp. 10, 207.
15 Silverberg (2006), pp. 51–72. Kiyosawa (1985), pp. 145, 156–58.
16 Tamaki Uemura, *Fujin Koron*, April 1953, p. 44 ('ticks'); Tatsuki Taniuchi, ('Study of panpan outbreak'), *Diamond*, op. cit., p. 64 ('weeds'). Hitoyoshi Tazaki, quoted in Szpilman (2004), p. 89. Silverberg (1991), p. 264.

17 Hara (1921), pp. 139–40.
18 Tsurumi (1937), vol. 2, pp. 25–26.
19 Mizushima and Miyake (1942), p. 21. *Minzoku* (ethnic group) and *jinshu* (race) were often used synonymously.
20 Quoted in Tamanoi (2000), p. 258.
21 (Kōsei-shō Kenkyūjo …) *Minzoku Jinkō Seisaku Kenkyū Shiryō*, vol. 3, pp. 303–308.
22 Oguma (2002), pp. 210–11. Reid (1986), pp. 35–36, 54.
23 Kon (1942), pp. 49–50.
24 Kratoska (1997), p. 114.
25 Morris (1944), pp. 16–17.
26 Imao Hirano, ('Fatherless Remi and their mothers'), *Fujin Koron*, August 1963, pp. 222–28.
27 Burke-Gaffney (1995), pp. 51–74.

10 George's story

1 ISSJ: Case report.
2 'Shame on you, Australia', *Australasian Post*, 18 October 1962.
3 'Service Record' of VX97087 Pte Joseph Ritchie, NAA (Melbourne): B2458, 31925.

11 Occupational hazards

1 Author's interview.
2 Handwritten inscription on memo, 5 March 1948, NAA: A446, 1966/45427197 (emphasis in original). 6 October 1948, *CPD*, vol. 198, pp. 1271, 1281–82; 7 April 1948, *CPD*, vol. 196, p. 595.
3 Letter of Lt Col Gordon King, 8 September 1987, in John (1992), Appendix. In King's recollection, Henderson was sent to Japan as a POW and put to work on the Kure docks, where he became acquainted with Mary Abe through her brother, a kind guard. Henderson's service record, however, indicates he was repatriated from Singapore in September 1945, and contemporary newspaper accounts make no reference to his being held in Japan. On Mary Abe: Gerster (2008), pp. 225–26.
4 *Sun-P*, 9 March 1949.
5 *Herald*, 5 March 1949.
6 *Telegraph*, 9 May 1951. See also *SMH*, 22 January 1951.
7 Letter, 20 April 1949 (author's copy).
8 NAA: A471, 80197. *People* magazine of 1 August 1951 gives a detailed account of Weaver's exploits up until then. For Hodgson: Weatherstone interview.
9 NAA: A816, 52/301/295.
10 Defence Committee minute, 6 October 1949, NAA: A816, 52/301/295. John (1992), p. 83.
11 *Sunday Sun*, 18 June 1950.
12 Note to Minister, 12 September 1950, NAA: A446, 1966/45427.
13 Author's interview.
14 ISSJ: Case report. Few *konketsuji* actually had blue eyes; the description applied to anything lighter than dark brown.

15 Author's interview.
16 NAA: A466, 1966/45427. Drover and his wife, Fumiko, eventually settled in Canberra.
17 Heyes to Holt, 3 December 1951, NAA: A446, 1966/45427.
18 Diary entry, 11 August 1951, Casey Papers, vol. 13, NLA: MS6150/4/26. For poll: *Sun-P*, 26 September 1952.
19 21 February 1952, *CPD*, vol. 216, p. 243. 22 February 1952, *CPD*, vol. 216, p. 290.
20 Press Release, 30 March 1952, NAA: A446, 1966/45427.
21 Nutt to Beale, 22 September 1952, ibid.
22 Memorandum, 31 October 1950, ibid.
23 Carter (1965), p. 131.
24 Ibid., p. 62
25 NAA: A446, 1966/45427.
26 Author's interview.
27 NAA: A1838, 3103/10/12/1 Part 1.
28 NAA: A816, 19/323/189.
29 *Chu S*, 23 November 1956.
30 *Chu S*, 9 and 25 December 1954.
31 NAA: A816, 19/323/189; *Age*, 19 November 1956.
32 NAA: A1838, 3103/10/12/1 Part 1.

12 Enemies in miniature

1 Sawada (1953), pp. 6–8.
2 Hemphill (1980), pp. 15–16, 82–88, passim. The name sometimes appears as 'Sanders', from the Japanese mispronunciation.
3 Quoted in Fish (2002), p. 166.
4 Takasaki (1952), p. 53.
5 Coaldrake (2003), p. 219. For his low opinion of Sawada, see p. 488.
6 Sawada (1953), p. 131.
7 Iglehart (1952), p. 303.
8 The pregnant friend's nickname is 'Kuro', which can also mean 'black', and she has a '*taijin ponpon*' (extra large tummy), which sounds like '*gaijin panpan*' (foreigner's prostitute).
9 Peter Kalischer, 'Madame Butterfly's Children', *Collier's*, 20 September 1952, p. 15. Braw (1991), p. 121.
10 Berrigan, op. cit., pp. 24–25, 117–18.
11 Sams (1998), p. 62.
12 On hospital scandal: Seidensticker (1990), p. 209. On LARA: Rhoads (1952), p. 322.
13 Tatara (1975), pp. 431–32.
14 *Tokyo S*, 4 May 1952.
15 Ogawa (1960), p. 140; Graham and Giga (1953), pp. 53–55.
16 Kubota et al. (1953), p. 83; Yamauchi (1960), pp. 81–85. The question arises: Did any of the abandoned mixed-race children have non-Japanese mothers? The answer can be no more than a tentative 'maybe'. Thousands of foreign women came to Japan during the occupation, mainly wives of servicemen. There is

anecdotal evidence of sexual contact with Japanese men, and a small number of marriages occurred (involving *Nisei* servicewomen). Only about 100 Australian women (apart from wives) were attached to BCOF, nearly all nurses, who were placed under 'extraordinarily stringent restrictions' on their movement and activities (Wood, p. 109). The subject is among the least explored aspects of occupation historiography.

17 *New York Herald-Tribune,* 21 April 1952. The Japanese text is in *Fujin Koron,* May 1952, pp. 36–40. There are different versions of where the figure originated – the Welfare Ministry, a newspaper office or Miki Sawada – which indicates how widely it was believed.

18 *Kōsei-shō* (1953); Graham and Giga (1953), pp. 51–53.

19 For estimate: Kiyoshi Kanzaki, ('White and black') *Fujin Koron,* March 1953, p. 130. Compare the 37 000 children reportedly fathered out of wedlock by American soldiers in Germany and Austria in the decade from 1945. See Biddiscombe (2001), pp. 611–47. On deaths: It has been claimed more than 800 *konketsuji* are buried at Negishi Foreigners' Cemetery in Yokohama (*Japan Times,* 25 August 1999).

20 Suda (1952), pp. 31–32.

21 *Yomiuri,* 2 November 1952; *Nikkei,* 2 February 1953; *Asahi* (am), 10 July 1952; Yoshio Koya, ('*Konketsuji* story'), *Fujin Koron,* April 1953, pp. 164–69.

22 Kubota et al. (1953), p. 93, passim. For a more careful approach, see Furushō (1960).

23 *Mainichi* (am), 20 March 1952.

24 On special schools: *Mainichi* (pm), 28 November 1952; ibid., 28 February 1953 (editorial); *Shukan Asahi,* March 1953. For 'Children's Charter': *Kōsei-shō* (1959), p. 75; Tatara (1975), p. 438. For Education Ministry: *Asahi,* 27 November 1952.

25 On *koseki* registration: Kanzaki, op. cit., *Fujin Koron,* March 1953, p. 134. On Hirano offer: *Asahi,* 3 August 1965.

26 Mombu-shō Shotō Chūtō Kyōiku-kyoku, ('Points requiring attention in guidance for school entrance of *konketsuji*'), in *Kyōiku Geppo* (Tochigi Education Board), April 1953, pp. 51–55.

27 *Asahi,* 30 April 1960.

28 Takeda (1957), p. 140; Takasaki (1952), p. 51; *Shukan Asahi,* March 1953, pp. 6, 8.

29 *Enka* singer, Jero (Jerome Charles White), NHK-TV documentary, broadcast 20 March 2009. For girl's comment: Don Moser, 'Japan's GI babies: A hard coming-of-age', *Life,* 5 September 1969, p. 43.

30 Ōya, ('It was women …'), *Bungei Shunjū,* op. cit., p. 199. Sōichi Ōya, ('The issue of "blood" from the "Pacific War"'), as told to Shigeo Sakaguchi, *Shōsetsu Shinchō,* June 1952, p. 71.

31 Kanzaki, op. cit., *Fujin Koron,* March 1953, pp. 134, 132.

32 Katsuo Takenaka, ('Itami base'), *Fujin Koron,* December 1953, p. 181.

33 Takasaki (1952), pp. 27–28, 16.

34 *Shukan Asahi,* March 1953, p. 11. Kataoka (1985), pp. 127–28.

35 Keiichi Aoki ('Are *konketsuji* Japanese?'), *Ushio,* October 1952, p. 37.

36 *Yomiuri,* 19 February 1953.

37 Yamauchi (1960), p. 17. He applied theories developed by the American social psychologist Kurt Lewin.

38 Deverall (1953), p. 95.

39 Florence Boester, 'Background information', January 1954, ISSAm: box 34, folder 1; Eveland (1956), pp. 112–25.

40 Iglehart (1952), p. 304.

41 Laurin Hyde and Virginia P Hyde, 'A study of proxy adoptions', Child Welfare League of America/ISS America, June 1958, ISSAm: b11, f14. Graham (1958), ISSAm: b17, f4.

42 'Surveying the International Social Service after 25 years', ISSAm: b16, f7; 'Summary report, May–August 1955', ISSAm: b34, f7. For ISS in Australia: NAA: A10651, ICR5/1 Part 2 and A440, 1952/12/1513. In the decade to 1955, a related body, the Australian Council for International Social Service, conducted or attempted similar activities. It had a vexed relationship with both Immigration and External Affairs. See Pertzel (2010), pp. 12–27.

43 Boester, Report to ISS Geneva, 9 June 1958, NAA: A1838, 3103/10/12/1 Part 1. Letter, Boester to Moffit, May or June 1958, NAA: A10651, ICR5/1 Part 2.

13 Kiyotaka's story

1 *The Forgotten Force*, Film Australia, 1994.

14 Plausible deniability

1 *Chu N*, 5 May 1952. *Chu N*, 5 June 1952.

2 *Chu N*, 7 May 1953. *Chu N*, 20 June 1953.

3 *Chu S*, 13 May 1955.

4 Niwa (1957), p. 119. Miyano (1960), p. 106. Yamauchi (1960), p. 23.

5 *Argus*, 12 March 1948. For editorial: *Sun-P*, 28 April 1948. *Gen* 8, no. 9, September 1950, pp. 19, 23–24.

6 Woods (1995), p. 220.

7 Letter, 15 July 1955, NAA: A1838, 3103/10/12/1 Part 1. Letter, 11 January 1956, ibid.

8 22 February 1956, *CPD* (*New Series*), HoR, vol. 9, p. 101. *Herald*, 20 February 1956; *Sunday Telegraph*, 19 February 1956. For charge: Memo, 10 February 1956, NAA: A1838, 3103/10/12/1 Part 1.

9 Heyes memo, 5 October 1961, NAA: A1838, 3103/10/12/1 Part 2. 'My Japanese Shiralee …', *Weekend*, 10 and 17 January 1959. Author's interview.

10 Draft memo, 25 July 1955, NAA: A1838, 3103/10/12/1 Part 1. Memo, c. 21 July 1955, ibid.

11 *Sun-P*, 27 February 1956. See also Cairns (1975), pp. 87–88.

12 A person seeking to enter the country needed to pass a dictation test, if required by a Customs Officer. The test was administered to anyone considered racially unsuitable and always in a language they were not expected to know.

13 Separately, a doctor from Newcastle wrote to Prime Minister Menzies in April 1956 pleading to be allowed to adopt one of the 'little orphans' from Japan. She enclosed a newspaper photograph of an American mother playing with her newly adopted Korean girl. See NAA: A463, 1957/1908.

14 Immigration Department briefing note, NAA: A446, 1962/67628. The then

minister was Harold Holt. See also NAA: A2169, 1956.

15 *Pix*, 17 August 1957, pp. 6–10. The article was published without a byline.

16 Personal communication.

17 Memo, 19 September 1957, NAA: A1838, 3103/10/12/1 Part 1.

18 Letter, 13 September 1957 and report by Kure City Social Relief Centre, 20 October 1957, ibid.

19 Memo, 26 September 1957, ibid.

20 Nobusuke Kishi made the first visit by a Japanese Prime Minister to Australia in late 1957. The Kure Kids were not discussed. See NAA: A10302, 1957/1171.

21 Letter, 7 November 1957, NAA: A1838, 3103/10/12/1 Part 1.

22 Memo, 17 September 1957, ibid.

23 *Chu N*, 3 October 1957.

24 *Sun*, 5 and 8 May 1958.

25 Statement for *Sun* newspaper, 6 May 1958, NAA: op. cit.

26 Letter, c. 30 November 1959, NAA: A1838, 3103/10/12/1 Part 2. 29 March 1960, *CPD (New Series)*, HoR, vol. 26, p. 701. Handwritten inscription on memo, 9 January 1962, NAA: A463, 1963/2728.

27 The Australian states brought their adoption laws into closer conformity during the 1960s. A national policy on inter-country adoption was framed in 1975. Already, by then, couples could obtain approval to adopt from overseas prior to nominating a specific child.

28 At various times, the Northern Territory, Queensland and Western Australia prohibited marriages between Aborigines and white Australians or aliens. They could not agree, however, on whether racial homogeneity was better served by encouraging or preventing female half-castes marrying white males. See NAA: A659, 1940/1/408. On 'fifth column': Col Charles Spry, ASIO director-general, July 1958, NAA: A452, 1970/4424.

29 Kure official, quoted in memo of 18 August 1958, NAA: A1838, 3103/10/12/1 Part 1.

30 Same official, quoted in memo, 11 September 1958, ibid.

31 Memo, 27 January 1959, ibid.

32 29 August 1957, *CPD (New Series)*, HoR, vol. 16, p. 173. 29 March 1960, *CPD (New Series)*, HoR, vol. 26, p. 701.

33 Letter, 20 November 1959, NAA: A1838, 3103/10/12/1 Part 2.

34 RSL Records, NLA: MS6609, Series 1, 3007c, boxes 612, 613. On Legacy: *Sun-P*, 4 October 1962 (the approach was made in 1957). For Vasey: *Japan Times*, 2 October 1959.

35 Brookes to Menzies, 30 December 1959, and reply, NAA: A463, 1957/1908. Cabinet Submission No. 570, 7 March 1960, NAA: A4940, C3054 (it was discussed on 15 March). For 'hypothetical question': Cabinet Secretary's note, ibid.

36 ACC Papers, NLA: MS7645, boxes 26, 27.

15 Our mixed-bloods

1 *Kent Record*, May 2001, <www.louisville.edu/kent> (accessed 20 January 2011). Author's interview. ISSJ: 'Report of ISS Kure Project', October 1977.

2 *Chu N*, 25 November 1952.

3   ISSJ: 'Actual situation of mixed blood children in Kure and surrounding area', Spring 1960. For an alternative ISS view, see Miyano (1960).
4   ISSJ: 'Report of ISS Kure Project', op. cit.
5   'Interim Report on Kure Project', November 1960, NAA: A1838, 3103/10/12/1 Part 2.
6   'Sky in Hiroshima', Radio Chugoku, broadcast 15 March 1961.
7   Itō (1976), p. 113.
8   Pearl S Buck, 'The children waiting', *Woman's Home Companion*, September 1955, pp. 33, 129–32. UN Department of Social Affairs, 'Study on adoption of children' (New York: United Nations, 1953), p. 77. Efforts to regulate inter-country adoption, which began in 1956, led to the Hague Adoption Convention, in effect from May 1995.
9   For Boester: Letter, May or June 1958, NAA: A10651, ICR5/1 Part 2. For 'difficulties': H Marshall, record of conversation, 20 January 1958, NAA: A1838, 3103/10/12/1 Part 1.
10 Letter, 27 February 1960, NAA: A1838, 3103/10/12/1 Part 2. Commonwealth Police visited the home of another man who had deserted his Japanese wife, but the strategy does not seem to have been repeated.
11 *SMH*, 28 March 1960. Segal's reply is in *SMH* of 29 March.
12 'The children of Japanese unmarried mothers and of non-Japanese paternity, living in Kure, Japan', NAA: op. cit. For instance, it changed the views of journalist Denis Warner. Compare his *Herald* articles of 23 January and 18 May 1960.
13 Rivett (1962), p. 40.
14 'Special report on Australian-Japanese children in Japan', July 1960 and 'Special report no. 3', December 1962.
15 *Asahi*, 11 July 1960.
16 *Mainichi Daily News* (English), 4 January 1963.
17 *Mainichi Daily News*, 3 April 1960.
18 Protection Section, Children's Bureau, 19 May 1960, NAA: op. cit.
19 *Herald*, 17 October 1960. Letter, 18 November 1960, NAA: op. cit.
20 *Chu N*, 25 December 1960. *Chu S*, 6 January 1961. *Chu S*, 18 August 1962.
21 Letter, 16 June 1962, author's copy.
22 Quoted in *M Truth*, 6 October 1962. *Sunday Mirror*, 14 October 1962.
23 *Sun-Herald*, 23 September 1962. *M Truth*, 29 September 1962. See also *Herald*, 24 September; *Sun-P*, 24 and 25 September; *M Truth*, 6 October; *Australasian Post*, 18 October. On Japanese diplomats: Memo, 29 January 1960, NAA: A463, 1963/2728.
24 *M Truth*, 29 September 1962. *Mirror*, 4 October 1962. What readers could not know was that she had been happily feeding chooks in her backyard when the image was captured.
25 *Sunday Mirror*, 7 October 1962.
26 *SMH*, 4 October 1962.
27 *Sunday Mirror*, 14 October 1962. See editorials in *Herald*, *Mirror*, *Adelaide News* and *Advertiser*, 4 October; *SMH*, 5 October; *West Australian*, 6 October 1962.
28 ISSJ: Kelso to Tamura, 28 August 1964.
29 Editorial, *Herald*, 8 October 1962.

30   Ferguson family papers.
31   *Chu S*, 9 October 1962. For letters: Ferguson family papers.
32   Letter, West to Glynn, 8 January 1963, author's copy.
33   Diary entry, 31 October 1961, Heydon Papers, NLA: MS3155, b22, f184.
34   Memo, 5 November 1959, NAA: A463, 1963/2728.
35   Dynon, 'Progress report no. 3', December 1962, ibid.
36   Cabinet Submission No. 469, 8 November; Cabinet Decision No. 548, 28 November 1962, NAA: A1838, 3103/10/12/1 Part 3. For views on Japanese racism, see Cabinet Submission No. 414, 28 November 1968, NAA: A5619, C421.
37   Press statement: 1 December 1962, NAA: A1838, 3103/10/12/1 Part 3. For Dynon's anger: *Herald*, 3 December 1962. On one or two ex-servicemen: *Canberra Times*, 28 March 1963; Letter, 11 January 1963, NAA: op. cit.
38   Memo, 12 October 1962, ibid.
39   Personal communication.
40   Treasury memo 16 March 1967, NAA: A1209, 1968/10193. During the Vietnam War, officials identified a moral obligation to assist foreign orphans fathered by Australian servicemen. Entry of adopted children was underway as early as 1968. See correspondence between DoEA and the Saigon Embassy, August–December 1974, in NAA: A1838, 1490/5/74 Part 3.
41   On 15 September 1964, Cabinet set aside the 75 per cent European-origin rule ('without public announcement'). Approval for the entry of persons of mixed race for permanent residence was placed at the discretion of the Immigration Minister. The Commonwealth awarded its first annual grant to ISS Australia the following month.

16 Kazumi's story

1   *Chu S*, 15 March 1965.

17 The Kure Project

1   *Herald*, 25 September 1962; *Sun-P*, 18 December 1963; *Asahi* (pm), 14 January 1964; ACC Records, NLA: MS7645, box 70. On being 'exploited': Note of conversation, NAA: A1838, 3103/10/12/1 Part 3.
2   Dunstan (1966), p. 135.
3   ACC Records, NLA: MS7645, box 27.
4   *Herald*, 12 January 1966; ISSJ: Activities reports. For Waddy: *Telegraph*, 9 October 1962.
5   The Welfare Ministry estimated that less than 10 per cent of *konketsuji* reached senior high school (*Asahi*, 9 May 1962).
6   ISSJ: Case report.
7   Tokyo Embassy report, 25 October 1967, NAA: A1209, 1968/10193.
8   Itō et al. (1984), pp. 18–21.
9   ISSJ: Letter, 25 June 1969.
10 ISSJ: Letter, 8 July 1969.
11 ISSJ: Undated letter (1969).
12 Author's interview.
13 *Sun-P*, 23 October 1964.

14 *Sunday Mirror*, 19 July 1964.

15 For *Truth* telegram: ISSJ. See also *Mirror*, 29 July and 30 August 1964. For 'Archangel Gabriel': ISSJ: Letter, 27 August 1964.

16 ISSJ: Kelso letter, 8 September 1964, quoted in correspondence. Tamura letter, c. November 1964, ibid.

17 Memos, 7 December 1964, NAA: A1838, 3103/10/12/1 Part 4. Calman's views are as reported by Itō, the Embassy and Japanese officials.

18 ISSJ: Undated note and other documents, December 1964.

19 ISSJ: Letter, 8 January 1965. Emphasis in original. The five Kelso letters that prompted this response appear to be missing from the files.

20 A sum of ¥66.17 million, identifiable from ISSJ accounts, excludes small and/or local contributions in cash and kind. For Memorial Appeal: ISSJ: 'History of A.J. Ferguson Memorial Fund', 12 May 1969 (with additional data added later).

21 Tokyo Embassy report, NAA: A1209, 1968/10193. See also Cabinet Submission No. 414, 28 November 1968, NAA: A5619, C421.

22 ISSJ: Letters, 1 June and 2 October 1964. On 'Shirley': *Sunday Mirror*, 2 and 16 August 1964; *Yomiuri*, n.d.

23 ISSJ: Letter, 25 August 1964.

24 *Sun-P*, 7 March 1967.

25 *Mirror*, 9 October 1962.

26 ISSJ: 'Report of ISS Kure Project', October 1977; *Advertiser*, Letters, 12 and 13 May, 1964.

27 Author's interview.

28 Author's interview. 'Report of ISS Kure Project', op. cit.

29 International Social Service Japan, *Kokkyō o koete ai no te o* (Extending a hand of love beyond borders) *45-Year History* (Tokyo: ISSJ, 1998), p. 90.

18 Half into whole

1 On Sawada and Brazil: Hemphill (1980), pp. 140–43; Fish (2002), p. 163. On ministry intervention: *Tokyo S*, 22 April 1960.

2 ISSJ: Case report.

3 Don Moser, 'Japan's GI babies: a hard coming-of-age', *Life*, 5 September 1969, p. 42.

4 Robert Trumbull, 'Amerasians', *NYT Magazine*, 30 April 1967, p. 114.

5 ISSJ Newsletter, 16 January 1973, ISSAm: b34, f9.

6 Quoted in Susumu Sawakai, *Kōmei*, March 1967, pp. 54–55.

7 'Konketsuji hostesses' extravagant night life', *Asahi Geinō*, 17 September 1967, p. 108.

8 'Girlfriend in Yokosuka', *Kamera wa Mita!* Tokyo Channel 12, broadcast 19 April 1967. Mitsuharu Inoue, *Asahi Graph*, 12 May 1967, p. 68.

9 'We are Japanese', *Asahi Journal*, 22 October 1967, pp. 82–91.

10 ('Clean hands'), *Shukan Asahi*, 18 January 1959, p. 27.

11 Seki (1964), p. 30.

12 For war bride numbers: Annual Reports, 1947–75, Table 6, US Commissioner of Immigration and Naturalization, Washington, DC. On American reaction: Strauss (1954), p. 99; Simpson (1998), pp. 48–49, 65–67; Shukert and Scibetta (1988), p. 217; Janet Wentworth Smith and William L Worden, 'They're

bringing home Japanese wives', *Saturday Evening Post*, 19 January 1952, pp. 26–27, 79–81.

13 Waters (2003), p. 132. See also Murphy-Shigematsu (1986), p. 71.
14 'On being mixed Japanese in modern times', *Pacific Citizen*, Holiday Issue: 20–27 December 1985, B-3.
15 Quoted in Shukert and Scibetta (1988), p. 256.
16 *Sunday Times* (Perth) Magazine, 13 April 1952. For 'genetic' issue: Memo, 14 January 1960, NAA: A463, 1963/2728.
17 On miscegenation fears: Tamura (2001), pp. 43–45; Carter (1965), p. 149. On reducing visibility: Tamura (1997), p. 46.
18 Author's interview.
19 *Fireflies in the Snow* (2004), p. 23. Unless otherwise noted, quotes are from either this unpublished Kellehear memoir or the author's interview.
20 'Start spreading the new', *Age Education Supplement*, 7 February 2001.
21 Nakashima (1992), pp. 173–77; Motoyoshi (1990), pp. 84–89; Williams (1992), pp. 280–83.
22 Kich et al., *Pacific Citizen*, op. cit., A-9; Kich (1982), pp. 235–36; Williams and Thornton (1998), pp. 255–67.
23 Spickard (1989), pp. 114–15; Hall (1980), pp. 74, 125–26; Christine C Iijima Hall, 'Denial of dual ethnicity unwarranted', *Pacific Citizen*, op. cit., B-9, B-65; Strong (1978), pp. 49–51, passim; Williams (1992).
24 Author's interview. Williams and Thornton (1998), pp. 255–67; Valentine (1990), p. 48.
25 Merry White, quoted in Gaynor (1995), p. 298.
26 Valentine (1990), p. 47. See also Gaynor and Kowatari (1995), p. 265.

19 Johnny's story

1 Masaaki Usui, ('The *konketsu* long-distance runner'), undated (1964) and unidentified Japanese magazine article in Akiyama family collection.
2 *Pix*, 17 August 1957, p. 10.
3 Masaaki article, op. cit. On living conditions: Keith Dunstan, 'The children on our conscience', *Sun-P*, 18 December 1963.
4 Masaaki article, op. cit.
5 *Chu S*, n.d. March and 6 October 1964; *Mainichi*, 16 August 1968. ISSJ: Case report and letters.

20 Where are they now?

1 ISSJ: Activities report, 29 January 1964.

21 A mixed future

1 Lind (1946), pp. 20, 97, passim.
2 Reuters, 7 November 2008.
3 William Wetherall, 'Nakasone promotes pride and prejudice', *Far Eastern Economic Review*, 19 February 1987, pp. 86–87.
4 *Gaimu-shō*, <www.mofa.go.jp/policy/human/civil_rep8011.pdf> (accessed December 2011).
5 Debito (2007); Tsuda (1998), pp. 319–23.

6 On permanent residents: The figure includes those living in areas traditionally associated with *burakumin*; Okinawans; non-naturalised Korean and Taiwanese descendants of colonial-era migrants; *nikkei* Brazilians; *hibakusha* A-bomb victims; Ainu; and *konketsuji*. For mixed-race births: Ministry of Health, Labour and Welfare statistics at <www.mhlw.go.jp/english/database/db-hw/report/1.html> (accessed December 2011).

7 'Replacement migration: Is it a solution to declining and aging populations?' (New York: UN Secretariat, 2001); Tsuda (2001).

8 Keizo Yamawaki, 'Too many foreign kids falling through the cracks', *International Herald Tribune-Asahi*, 17 December 2002.

9 Debito (2007); Yamawaki (2008), p. 43. For farm-wives study: Burgess (2004).

10 Keizo Yamawaki, presentation at Japan Foundation, Sydney, 4 March 2009.

11 Sekiguchi (2002), pp, 204–205, 209.

12 Marcia Yumi Lise, 'The interviews', '*Hafu/Half Japanese*', exhibition and online resource, <www.hafujapanese.org>.

13 Moser, op. cit., p. 40. Era Bell Thompson, *Ebony*, September 1967, pp. 42–54.

14 Wagatsuma (1973a), pp. 261–62. Writing in Japanese, and in later English-language studies, Wagatsuma was more guarded: 'Of course, we don't have figures showing the crime rate among *konketsuji* boys is especially high, nor do I mean to claim most *konketsuji* boys have distorted personalities' (Wagatsuma, 1973b, p. 222). His views are not always quoted with such qualifications. Another researcher has described 3 per cent in his sample group as 'seriously self-destructive' (Strong, 1978, pp. 222, 194). See also Burkhardt (1983), p. 538. There is no empirical evidence of abnormal rates of delinquency or suicide among *konketsuji*.

Select bibliography

(See other sources cited in the notes.)

Annesley, George, Viscount Valentia. *Voyages and Travels*. 3 vols. London: William Miller, 1809.

Archer, Basil. *Interpreting Occupied Japan: The Diary of an Australian Soldier 1945–1946*. Ed. Sandra Wilson. Perth: Hesperian Press, 2009.

Arnold, Sir Edwin. 'Japonica – fourth paper – Japanese ways and thoughts.' *Scribner's Magazine* 9, no. 3 (March 1891), pp. 321–41.

Baelz, Erwin. *Awakening Japan: The Diary of a German Doctor*. Ed. Toku Baelz, 1932. Reprod. with introd. George Macklin Wilson. Bloomington: Indiana University Press, 1974.

Ball, W Macmahon. *Japan: Enemy or Ally?* Melbourne: Cassell, 1948.

Ballhatchet, Kenneth. *Race, Sex and Class under the Raj*. New Delhi: Vikas, 1979.

Bates, Peter. *Japan and the British Commonwealth Occupation Force 1946–52*. London: Brassey's, 1993.

Biddiscombe, Perry. 'Dangerous liaisons: The anti-fraternization movement in the U.S. occupation zones of Germany and Austria, 1945–1948.' *Journal of Social History*, 34, no. 3 (2001), pp. 611–47.

Blackford, Stan. *One Hell of a Life: An Anglo-Indian Wallah's Memoir from the Last Decades of the Raj*. Adelaide, South Australia: n.p., 2000.

Bousquet, Georges. *Le Japon De Nos Jours: Et Les Échelles De L'Extrême Orient*. 2 vols. Paris: Librairie Hachette, 1877.

Braw, Monica. *The Atomic Bomb Suppressed: American Censorship in Occupied Japan*. Armonk, New York: M.E. Sharpe, 1991.

Brines, Russell. *MacArthur's Japan*. Philadelphia: J.B. Lippincott, 1948.

Burgess, Chris. 'Multicultural Japan? Discourse and the "myth" of homogeneity.' www.japanfocus.org, 2004.

Burke-Gaffney, Brian. 'The man who could not take sides: A sketch of the life of Kuraba Tomisaburo.' *Crossroads*, no. 3 (summer 1995), pp. 51–74.

Burkhardt, William R. 'Institutional barriers, marginality, and adaptation among the American-Japanese mixed bloods in Japan.' *Journal of Asian Studies* 42, no. 3 (May 1983), pp. 519–44.

Butcher, John G. *The British in Malaya 1880–1941: The Social History of a European Community in Colonial South-East Asia*. Kuala Lumpur: Oxford University Press, 1979.

Cairns, William. *Padre Jock O.F.* ACT: Fortress Press, 1975.

Carter, IR. *Alien Blossom: A Japanese-Australian Love Story*. Melbourne: Lansdowne Press, 1965.

Cary, Otis, ed. *From a Ruined Empire: Letters – Japan, China, Korea 1945–46*. Tokyo:

Kodansha International, 1984.

Clifton, Allan S. *Time of Fallen Blossoms*. London: Cassell, 1950.

Clune, Frank. *Sky High to Shanghai*. Sydney: Angus & Robertson, 1939.

—— *Ashes of Hiroshima: A Post-War Trip to Japan and China*. Sydney: Angus & Robertson, 1950.

Coaldrake, William H, ed. *Japan from War to Peace: The Coaldrake Records 1939– 1956*. London: RoutledgeCurzon, 2003.

Cohen, Theodore. *Remaking Japan: The American Occupation as New Deal*. Ed. Herbert Passin. New York: Free Press, 1987.

Coleman, Samuel. *Family Planning in Japanese Society: Traditional Birth Control in a Modern Urban Culture*. Princeton, New Jersey: Princeton University Press, 1983.

Cooper, Michael, comp. *They Came to Japan: An Anthology of European Reports on Japan, 1543–1640*. Berkeley: University of California Press, 1981.

Cunneen, Tony. *Suburban Boys at War: Past Students of St Pius X College (previously Christian Brothers Chatswood) in World War II, the Occupation of Japan and the Korean War*. Sydney: n.p., 2003.

Daniels, Roger. *The Politics of Prejudice: The Anti-Japanese Movement in California and the Struggle for Japanese Exclusion*. Berkeley: University of California Press, 1977.

Davenport, Charles B. 'Inheritance of physical and mental traits' and 'The geography of man in relation to eugenics.' In *Heredity and Eugenics*, ed. William Ernest Castle et al. Chicago: University of Chicago Press, 1912.

—— 'Race crossing in man' (draft, c. 1920), Charles B. Davenport Papers, American Philosophical Society.

De Bary, Wm Theodore, Carol Gluck and Arthur E Tiedemann, comps. *Sources of Japanese Tradition*. 2nd edn. Vol. 2. New York: Columbia University Press, 2005.

Debito, Arudou. 'Japan's future as an international, multicultural society: From migrants to immigrants.' www.japanfocus.org, 2007.

Deverall, Richard L-G. *The Great Seduction: Red China's Drive to Bring Free Japan behind the Iron Curtain*. Tokyo: Richard Deverall, 1953.

Dower, John W. *Embracing Defeat: Japan in the Wake of World War II*. New York: W.W. Norton/New Press, 1999.

Dower, John W, ed. *Origins of the Modern Japanese State: Selected Writings of E.H. Norman*. New York: Pantheon Books, 1975.

Drea, Edward J. *MacArthur's ULTRA: Codebreaking and the War against Japan, 1942–1945*. Lawrence, Kansas: University Press of Kansas, 1992.

Duncan, David, ed. *The Life and Letters of Herbert Spencer*. London: Methuen, 1908.

Dunstan, Keith. *Supporting a Column*. Melbourne: Cassell, 1966.

Elliott, Murray. 'Occupational hazards: A doctor in Japan and elsewhere.' *Australians in Asia*, no. 14 (September, 1995).

Eveland, Virginia Dudley. 'A welfare program for children of mixed parentage.' *Contemporary Japan* 24, nos 1–3 (1956), pp. 112–25.

Finch, Earl. 'The effects of racial miscegenation.' In *Papers on Inter-Racial Problems*, ed. G Spiller. London: P.S. King & Son, 1911.

Fish, Robert A. 'The Heiress and the Love Children: Sawada Miki and the Elizabeth Saunders Home for Mixed-Blood Orphans in Postwar Japan.' PhD diss., University of Hawai'i, 2002.

Fredrickson, George M. *Racism: A Short History*. Princeton, New Jersey: Princeton University Press, 2002.

Fujita, Taki. 'Prostitution Prevention Law.' *Contemporary Japan* 24, nos 7–9 (July–September 1956), pp. 484–97.

Galton, Francis. *Hereditary Genius: An Inquiry into its Laws and Consequences.* London: Macmillan, 1892.

Gayn, Mark. *Japan Diary.* Tokyo: Tuttle, 1981. First published in 1948.

Gaynor, Macdonald. 'The politics of diversity in the nation-state.' In Maher, op. cit.

Gaynor, Macdonald and Akiko Kowatari. 'A non-Japanese Japanese: On being a returnee.' In Maher, op. cit.

Geoffrey, Theodate. *An Immigrant in Japan.* Boston: Houghton Mifflin, 1926.

Gerster, Robin. *Travels in Atomic Sunshine: Australia and the Occupation of Japan.* Melbourne: Scribe, 2008.

Glynn, Paul. *'Like a Samurai': The Tony Glynn Story.* Sydney: Marist Fathers Books, 2008.

Goodman, Grant K. *America's Japan: The First Year, 1945–1946.* Trans. Barry D Steben. New York: Fordham University Press, 2005.

Gould, Stephen Jay. *The Mismeasure of Man.* New York: W.W. Norton, 1981.

Graham, Lloyd B. 'Those G.I.'s in Japan.' *Christian Century* 71, no. 11 (17 March 1954), pp. 330–32.

—— 'The Adoption of Children from Japan by American Families, 1952–1955.' Abst. doctoral thesis, University of Toronto, 1958.

Graham, Lloyd B and Seiji Giga. 'More information on "occupation" children.' *Japan Christian Quarterly* 19, no. 1 (winter 1953), pp. 51–57.

Grant, Madison. *The Passing of the Great Race: Or, The Racial Basis of European History.* New York: Scribner's, 1916.

Griffis, William Elliot. 'Are the Japanese Mongolian?' *North American Review* 197, no. 691 (June 1913), pp. 721–33.

Guillain, Robert. *I Saw Tokyo Burning.* Trans. William Byron. Garden City, New York: Doubleday, 1981.

Gulick, Sidney L. *Mixing the Races in Hawaii: A Study of the Coming Neo-Hawaiian American Race.* Honolulu: Hawaiian Board Book Rooms, 1937.

Haigh, Joan. *With the 'Y' and B.C.O.F. in Japan and Germany.* n.p., c. 1995.

Hall, Christine Catherine Iijima. 'The Ethnic Identity of Racially Mixed People: A Study of Black-Japanese.' PhD diss., University of California, Los Angeles, 1980.

Hara, Takashi. 'Harmony between East and West.' In *What Japan Thinks*, ed. KK Kawakami. New York: Macmillan, 1921.

Harrison, Kenneth. *The Brave Japanese.* Adelaide: Rigby, 1966.

Hearn, Lafcadio. *Lafcadio Hearn: American Writings.* New York: Library of America, 2009.

Hedin, Elmer L. 'The Anglo-Indian community.' *American Journal of Sociology* 40, no. 2 (September 1934), pp. 165–79.

Hemphill, Elizabeth Anne. *The Road to KEEP: The Story of Paul Rusch in Japan.* New York and Tokyo: Walker/Weatherhill, 1969.

—— *The Least of These: Miki Sawada and Her Children.* New York: Weatherhill, 1980.

Herder, Johann Gottfried von. *Outlines of a Philosophy of the History of Man.* Trans. T Churchill. New York: Bergman, 1800. Originally published in German in 1784–91.

Hertog, Ekaterina. *Tough Choices: Bearing an Illegitimate Child in Contemporary*

Japan. Stanford, California: Stanford University Press, 2009.

Hichborn, Franklin. *Story of the Session of the California Legislature of 1913*. San Francisco: James H. Barry, 1913.

Hilgard, Ernest R. 'The enigma of Japanese friendliness.' *Public Opinion Quarterly* 10 (fall, 1946), pp. 343–48.

Hungerford, TAG. *Sowers of the Wind: A Novel of the Occupation of Japan*. Sydney: Angus & Robertson, 1954.

—— *Straightshooter: A Knockabout with a Slouch Hat*. Fremantle: Fremantle Arts Centre Press, 2003.

Iglehart, Charles W. 'The problem of G.I. children in Japan.' *Japan Christian Quarterly* 18, no. 4 (autumn 1952), pp. 300–305.

Inoue, Kyoko. *MacArthur's Japanese Constitution: A Linguistic and Cultural Study of its Making*. Chicago: University of Chicago Press, 1991.

Ishikawa, Jun. 'The Legend of Gold.' In *The Legend of Gold and Other Stories*, trans. William J Tyler. Honolulu: University of Hawai'i Press, 1998. Originally published in Japanese in 1946.

Janssens, Rudolf VA. *'What Future for Japan?': U.S. Wartime Planning for the Postwar Era, 1942–1945*. Amsterdam: Editions Rudolph, 1995.

John, Arthur W. *Uneasy Lies the Head that Wears a Crown*. 3rd edn. Melbourne: Gen Publishers, 1992.

Johnson, U Alexis, with Jef Olivarious McAllister. *The Right Hand of Power*. Englewood Cliffs, New Jersey: Prentice-Hall, 1984.

Johnston, Mark. *Fighting the Enemy: Australian Soldiers and their Adversaries in World War II*. Cambridge: Cambridge University Press, 2000.

Kang, Sangjung. 'Memories of a Zainichi Korean childhood.' Trans. Robin Fletcher (from *Zainichi*. Tokyo: Kodansha, 2004). www.japanfocus.org.

Kato, Masuo. *The Lost War: A Japanese Reporter's Inside Story*. New York: Knopf, 1946.

Katō, Shuichi. *A Sheep's Song: A Writer's Reminiscences of Japan and the World*. Trans. Chia-ning Chang. Berkeley: University of California Press, 1999.

Kawai, Michi. *Sliding Doors*. Tokyo: Keisen-Jo-Gaku-En, 1950.

Kawakami, Kiyoshi K. *Asia at the Door: A Study of the Japanese Question in Continental United States, Hawaii and Canada*. New York: Fleming H. Revell, 1914.

Kay, Robin, ed. *The Surrender and Occupation of Japan*. Vol. 2 of *Documents on New Zealand External Relations*. Wellington: Historical Publications Branch, Dept. of Internal Affairs, 1982.

Keane, AH. *Ethnology*. Cambridge: University Press, 1896.

Keene, Donald. *So Lovely a Country Will Never Perish: Wartime Diaries of Japanese Writers*. New York: Columbia University Press, 2010.

Kelley, Frank and Cornelius Ryan. *Star-Spangled Mikado*. New York: Robert M. McBride, 1947.

Keyserling, Hermann. *The Travel Diary of a Philosopher*. Trans. J Holroyd Reece. 2 vols. London: Jonathan Cape, 1925.

Kich, George Kitahara. 'Eurasians: Ethnic/Racial Identity Development of Biracial Japanese/White Adults.' PhD diss., Wright Institute Graduate School of Psychology, 1982.

Kiyosawa, Kiyoshi. *A Diary of Darkness: The Wartime Diary of Kiyosawa Kiyoshi*. Ed. Eugene Soviak. Trans. Eugene Soviak and Kamiyama Tamie. Princeton, New

Jersey: Princeton University Press, 1999.

Knapp, Arthur May. *Feudal and Modern Japan*. 2 vols. Boston: Joseph Knight, 1897.

Knox, Robert. *The Races of Men: A Fragment*. Philadelphia: Lea & Blanchard, 1850.

Koshiro, Yukiko. *Trans-Pacific Racisms and the U.S. Occupation of Japan*. New York: Columbia University Press, 1999.

Koyama, Noboru. 'Three Meiji marriages between Japanese men and English women.' In *Britain & Japan: Biographical Portraits*, ed. Hugh Cortazzi. Vol. 4. London: Japan Library, 2002.

Kratoska, Paul H. *The Japanese Occupation of Malaya: A Social and Economic History*. Honolulu: University of Hawai'i Press, 1997.

Lacerda, Jean [João Batista] de Baptiste. 'The *metis*, or half-breeds, of Brazil.' In *Papers on Inter-Racial Problems*, ed. G Spiller. London: P.S. King & Son, 1911.

Lark, Regina F. 'They Challenged Two Nations: Marriages between Japanese Women and American GIs, 1945 to the Present.' PhD diss., University of Southern California, 1999.

Lawton, Lancelot. *Empires of the Far East: A Study of Japan and of Her Colonial Possessions, of China and Manchuria and of the Political Questions of Eastern Asia and the Pacific*. 2 vols. London: Grant Richards, 1912.

Lee, Vicky. *Being Eurasian: Memories across Racial Divides*. Hong Kong: Hong Kong University Press, 2004.

Leupp, Gary P. *Interracial Intimacy in Japan: Western Men and Japanese Women 1543–1900*. London and New York: Continuum, 2003.

Levenson, JC et al. *The Letters of Henry Adams*. Vol. 3: 1886–1892. Cambridge, Massachusetts: The Belnap Press of Harvard University Press, 1982.

Lind, Andrew W. *Hawaii's Japanese: An Experiment in Democracy*. Princeton, New Jersey: Princeton University Press, 1946.

MacArthur, Brian. *Surviving the Sword: Prisoners of the Japanese in the Far East, 1942–45*. New York: Random House, 2005.

McDonald, Lachie. *Bylines: Memoirs of a War Correspondent*. Sydney: Kangaroo Press, 1998.

Maher, John C and Gaynor Macdonald, eds. *Diversity in Japanese Culture and Language*. London and New York: Kegan Paul International, 1995.

Mancktelow, Douglas H. *Atsuko and the Aussie*. Canada: DMA Press, 1991.

Maruyama, Masao. 'Patterns of individuation and the case of Japan: A conceptual scheme.' In *Changing Japanese Attitudes toward Modernization*, ed. Marius B Jansen. Princeton, New Jersey: Princeton University Press, 1965.

Menand, Louis. *The Metaphysical Club*. New York: Farrar, Straus & Giroux, 2001.

Miyake, Yoshiko. 'Doubling expectations: Motherhood and women's factory work under state management in Japan in the 1930s and 1940s.' In *Recreating Japanese Women, 1600–1945*, ed. Gail Lee Bernstein. Berkeley: University of California Press, 1991.

Miyoshi, Masao. *As We Saw Them: The First Japanese Embassy to the United States*. New York: Kodansha International, 1994.

Molasky, Michael S. *The American Occupation and Okinawa: Literature and Memory*. London and New York: Routledge, 2001.

Moore, WS. *Occupation of Japan, 1947 to 1949*. n.p., 1997.

Morris, John. *Traveller from Tokyo*. London: Readers Union/Cresset, 1944.

Motoyoshi, Michelle M. 'The experience of mixed-race people: Some thoughts and theories.' *Journal of Ethnic Studies* 18, no. 2 (summer 1990), pp. 77–93.

Mulder, WZ. *Hollanders in Hirado 1597–1641*. Haarlem: Fibula-Van Dishoeck, 1985.

Murphy-Shigematsu, Stephen LH. 'The Voices of Amerasians: Ethnicity, Identity, and Empowerment in Interracial Japanese Americans.' PhD diss., Harvard University Graduate School of Education, 1986.

Nakashima, Cynthia L. 'An invisible monster: The creation and denial of mixed-race people in America.' In Root, op. cit.

Nishimura, Sey. 'Medical censorship in occupied Japan, 1945–1948.' *Pacific Historical Review* 58, No. 1 (February 1989), pp. 1–21.

Nitobe, Inazō. *Thoughts and Essays*. Tokyo: Teibi, 1909.

Nott, JC and Geo. R Gliddon. *Types of Mankind*. 7th edn. Philadelphia: Lippincott, Grambo, 1855.

Oguma, Eiji. *A Genealogy of 'Japanese' Self-images*. Trans. David Askew. Melbourne: Trans Pacific Press, 2002.

Okihiro, Gary Y. *Cane Fires: The Anti-Japanese Movement in Hawaii, 1865–1945*. Philadelphia: Temple University Press, 1991.

Padover, Saul K, ed. *The Complete Jefferson: Containing His Major Writings, Published and Unpublished, Except His Letters*. New York: Duell, Sloan & Pearce, 1943.

Park, Robert E. 'Human migration and the marginal man.' *American Journal of Sociology* 33, no. 6 (May 1928), pp. 881–93.

—— 'Mentality of racial hybrids.' *American Journal of Sociology* 36, no. 4 (January 1931), pp. 534–51.

Pascoe, Peggy. *What Comes Naturally: Miscegenation Law and the Making of Race in America*. Oxford: Oxford University Press, 2009.

Pearson, Charles H. *National Life and Character: A Forecast*. London: Macmillan, 1894.

Pearson, Karl. *The Grammar of Science*. London: Adam and Charles Black, 1900.

Perry, John Curtis. *Beneath the Eagle's Wings: Americans in Occupied Japan*. New York: Dodd, Mead, 1980.

Pertzel, Barbara. *A Very Personal Service: A History of International Social Service Australian Branch 1955–2005*. Melbourne: Urber & Patullo, 2010.

Porter, Hal. *A Handful of Pennies*. Sydney: Angus & Robertson, 1958.

—— *The Actors: An Image of the New Japan*. Sydney: Angus & Robertson, 1968.

—— *Mr Butterfry and Other Tales of New Japan*. Sydney: Angus & Robertson, 1970.

Quatrefages, Armand de. *The Human Species*. London: C. Kegan Paul, 1879.

Reid, Anthony and Oki Akira, eds. *The Japanese Experience in Indonesia: Selected Memoirs of 1942–1945*. Athens, Ohio: Ohio Center for International Studies, Ohio University, 1986.

Reuter, EB. 'The hybrid as a sociological type.' *Publications of the American Sociological Society* 19, (1925), pp. 59–68.

—— 'The personality of mixed bloods.' *Publications of the American Sociological Society* 22 (1928), pp. 52–59.

Rhoads, Esther B. 'LARA (Licensed Agencies for Relief in Asia).' *Japan Christian Quarterly* 18, no. 4 (autumn 1952), pp. 322–24.

Richie, Donald. 'from *Japan Journals*.' In *Silence to Light: Japan and the Shadows of War*, ed. Frank Stewart. *Mānoa* 13, no. 1. Honolulu: University of Hawai'i Press, 2001.

Ridley, HN. 'The Eurasian problem.' In *Noctes Orientales: Being a Selection of Essays Read before the Straits Philosophical Society between the Years 1893 and 1910.* Singapore: Kelly & Walsh, 1913.

Rivett, Kenneth, ed. *Immigration: Control or Colour Bar? – The Background to 'White Australia' and a Proposal for Change.* Melbourne: Melbourne University Press, 1962.

Rivett, Rohan D. *Behind Bamboo: An Inside Story of the Japanese Prison Camps.* London: Angus & Robertson, 1946.

Root, Maria P. ed. *Racially Mixed People in America.* Newbury Park, California: Sage, 1992.

Rosenfeld, David Martin. '"Unhappy Soldier": Hino Ashihei and Japanese World War Two Literature.' PhD diss., University of Michigan, 1999.

Rowell, Chester H. 'Chinese and Japanese immigrants – A comparison.' *Annals of the American Academy of Political and Social Science* 34, no. 2. (September 1909), pp. 3–10.

Sakanishi, Shio. 'Women's position and the family system.' *Annals of the American Academy of Political and Social Science,* 308 (November 1956), pp. 130–39.

Sams, Crawford F. *'Medic': The Mission of an American Military Doctor in Occupied Japan and Wartorn Korea.* Ed. Zabelle Zakarian. Armonk, New York: M. E. Sharpe, 1998.

Schnepp, Gerald J and Agnes Masako Yui. 'Cultural and marital adjustment of Japanese war brides.' *American Journal of Sociology* 61, no. 1 (July 1955), pp. 48–50.

Screech, Timon, ed. *Japan Extolled and Decried: Carl Peter Thunberg and the Shogun's Realm, 1775–1796.* London: Routledge, 2005.

Seaman, Louis Livingston. *From Tokio through Manchuria with the Japanese.* New York: D. Appleton, 1905.

Seidensticker, Edward. *Tokyo Rising: The City since the Great Earthquake.* Tokyo: Tuttle, 1990.

Sekiguchi, Tomoko. '*Nikkei* Brazilians in Japan: The ideology and symbolic context faced by children of this new ethnic minority.' In *Exploring Japaneseness: On Japanese Enactments of Culture and Consciousness,* ed. Ray T Donahue. Westport Connecticut: Ablex, 2002.

Shiel, MP. *The Yellow Peril.* London: Victor Gollancz, 1929. Originally published in 1913 as *The Dragon.*

Shukert, Elfrieda Berthiaume and Barbara Smith Scibetta. *War Brides of World War II.* Novato, California: Presidio, 1988.

Silverberg, Miriam. 'The modern girl as militant.' In *Recreating Japanese Women, 1600–1945,* ed. Gail Lee Bernstein. Berkeley: University of California Press, 1991.

—— *Erotic Grotesque Nonsense: The Mass Culture of Japanese Modern Times.* Berkeley: University of California Press, 2006.

Simpson, Caroline Chung. 'Out of an obscure place: Japanese war brides and cultural pluralism in the 1950s.' *Differences* 10 (1998), pp. 47–81.

Smith, Robert J and Ella Lury Wiswell. *The Women of Suye Mura.* Chicago and London: University of Chicago Press, 1982.

Snyder, Louis L. *The Idea of Racialism: Its Meaning and History.* Princeton, New Jersey: D. Van Nostrand, 1962.

Sodei, Rinjirō. *Dear General MacArthur: Letters from the Japanese during the American Occupation*. Ed. John Junkerman. Trans. Shizue Matsuda. Lanham, Maryland: Rowman & Littlefield, 2001.

Spengler, Oswald. *The Decline of the West*. Trans. Charles Francis Atkinson. 2 vols. New York: Knopf, 1961. Originally published in German in 1918–23.

Spickard, Paul R. *Mixed Blood: Intermarriage and Ethnic Identity in Twentieth-Century America*. Madison: University of Wisconsin Press, 1989.

Strauss, Anselm L. 'Strain and harmony in American-Japanese war-bride marriages.' *Marriage and Family Life* 16, no. 1, (February 1954), pp. 99–106.

Strong, Nathan Oba. 'Patterns of Social Interaction and Psychological Accommodation among Japan's Konketsuji Population.' PhD diss., University of California, Berkeley, 1978.

Sweeting, Anthony. *Education in Hong Kong Pre-1841 to 1941: Fact & Opinion*. Hong Kong: Hong Kong University Press, 1990.

Szpilman, Christopher WA. 'Fascist and quasi-fascist ideas in interwar Japan, 1918–1941.' In *Japan in the Fascist Era*, ed. E Bruce Reynolds. New York: Palgrave Macmillan, 2004.

Takemae, Eiji. *Inside GHQ: The Allied Occupation of Japan and its Legacy*. Trans. and adapted from the Japanese by Robert Ricketts and Sebastian Swann. New York: Continuum, 2002.

Tamagawa, Kathleen. *Holy Prayers in a Horse's Ear*. New York: Ray Long and Richard R. Smith, 1932.

Tamanoi, Mariko Asano. 'Knowledge, power, and racial classifications: The "Japanese" in "Manchuria".' *Journal of Asian Studies* 59, no. 2 (May 2000), pp. 248–76.

Tamayama, Kazuo. *Railwaymen in the War: Tales by Japanese Railway Soldiers in Burma and Thailand, 1941–47*. Basingstoke: Palgrave Macmillan, 2005.

Tamura, Keiko. 'Border crossings: Changing identities of Japanese war brides.' *Asia-Pacific Magazine* 8 (1997), pp. 43–47.

—— *Michi's Memories: The Story of a Japanese War Bride*. Canberra: Pandanus Books, 2001.

—— 'Harold S Williams and his Japan.' In *Unexpected Encounters*, ed. Michael Ackland and Pam Oliver. Melbourne: Monash Asia Institute, 2007.

Tanaka, Yuki. *Japan's Comfort Women: Sexual Slavery and Prostitution during World War II and the US Occupation*. London: Routledge, 2002.

Tanizaki, Jun'ichirō. *Naomi*. Trans. Anthony H Chambers. New York: North Point Press, 1985. Originally published in Japanese in 1924.

Tatara, Toshio. '1400 Years of Japanese Social Work from Its Origins through the Allied Occupation 552–1952.' PhD diss., Bryn Mawr, Pennsylvania, 1975.

Thorne, Christopher. *Allies of a Kind: The United States, Britain and the War against Japan, 1941–1945*. London: Hamish Hamilton, 1978.

Toland, John. *The Rising Sun: The Decline and Fall of the Japanese Empire 1936–1945*. 2 vols. New York: Random House, 1970.

Tsuda, Takeyuki. 'The stigma of ethnic difference: The structure of prejudice and "discrimination" toward Japan's new immigrant minority.' *Journal of Japanese Studies* 24, no. 2 (summer 1998), pp. 317–59.

—— 'Reluctant hosts: The future of Japan as a country of immigration.' *Research & Seminars* 7, no. 4 (February 2001), www.ucdavis.edu/rs/ (accessed February 2011).

Tsurumi, Shunsuke. *An Intellectual History of Wartime Japan 1931–1945*. London: KPI, 1986.

United Nations Department of Social Affairs, 'Study on adoption of children: A study on the practice and procedures related to the adoption of children.' New York: United Nations, 1953.

Valentine, James. 'On the borderlines: The significance of marginality in Japanese society.' In *Unwrapping Japan: Society and Culture in Anthropological Perspective*, ed. Eyal Ben-Ari, Brian Moeran and James Valentine. Honolulu: University of Hawai'i Press, 1990.

Wagatsuma, Hiroshi. 'Some problems of interracial marriage for the Japanese.' In *Interracial Marriage: Expectations and Realities*, ed. Irving R Stuart and Lawrence Edwin Abt. New York: Grossman Publishers, 1973a.

—— 'Mixed-blood children in Japan: An exploratory study.' *Journal of Asian Affairs* 2, no. 1 (1977), pp. 9–17.

Watanna, Onoto [Winnifred Eaton]. *'A Half Caste' and other Writings*. Ed. Linda Trinh Moser and Elizabeth Rooney. Urbana and Chicago: University of Illinois Press, 2003.

Waters, Mary Yukari. *The Laws of Evening*. New York: Scribner, 2003.

Weldon, Yaeko Sugama and Linda E Austin. *Cherry Blossoms in Twilight*. St Louis: Moonbridge, 2005.

Whitney, Clara AN. *Clara's Diary: An American Girl in Meiji Japan*. Ed. M William Steele and Tamiko Ichimata. Tokyo: Kodansha International, 1979.

Williams, Gertrude Marvin. *Understanding India*. New York: Coward-McCann, 1928.

Williams, Harold S. *Tales of the Foreign Settlements in Japan*. Tokyo: Tuttle, 1958.

Williams, Teresa Kay. 'Prism lives: Identity of binational Amerasians.' In Root, op. cit.

Williams, Teresa Kay and Michael C Thornton. 'Social construction of ethnicity versus personal experience: The case of Afro-Amerasians.' *Journal of Comparative Family Studies* 29, no. 2 (22 June 1998), pp. 255–67.

Wood, James. *The Forgotten Force: The Australian Military Contribution to the Occupation of Japan 1945–1952*. Sydney: Allen & Unwin, 1998.

Woods, Jennie. *Which Way Will the Wind Blow*. Sydney: n.p., 1995.

Yamashita, Samuel Hideo. *Leaves from an Autumn of Emergencies: Selections from the Wartime Diaries of Ordinary Japanese*. Honolulu: University of Hawai'i Press, 2005.

Yamawaki, Keizo. 'The challenges for Japanese immigrant integration policy.' *Around the Globe* 4, no. 2 (summer 2008), Monash University Institute for the Study of Global Movements, pp. 41–44.

Japanese language publications

Andō Shōeki. *Tōdōshinden* (Thoughts). Ed. Tatsuya Naramoto. 2 vols. Tokyo: Iwanami, 1966–67.

Furushō Toshiyuki. 'Nipponjin to hakujin oyobi kokujin tono konketsuji no chōsa seiseki hōkoku' (Report on achievement survey of mixed-blood children between Japanese and white or black men). In *Konketsuji Shidō Shiryō*. Tokyo: Mombu-shō Shotō Chūtō Kyōiku-kyoku, 1960.

Inoue Tetsujirō. *Inoue-hakase Kōron-shū* (Collected Lectures of Dr Inoue). 2 vols. Tokyo: Keigyōsha, 1894–95.

Itagaki Naoko. 'Konketsuji no ryōshin' (Parents of mixed-blood children). *Kaizō*

(March 1953), pp. 162–64.

Itō Yone. 'Sengo Nippon no konketsuji mondai to gaikokujin katei eno yōshi engumi ni tsuite' (On post-war Japan's mixed-blood children issue and adoption to foreign families). In *Yōgo Shisetsu 30-nen*. Tokyo: Zenshakyō Yōgoshisetsu Kyōgikai, 1976.

Itō Yone et al., eds. *Shakaifukushi Jissen no Hōhō* (Practical Methods of Social Welfare). Tokyo: Kawashima Shoten, 1984.

Kaburagi Seiichi. 'Shinchūgun ian sakusen' (Comfort operation for occupation army). In *Sesō o Otte*. Vol. 4 of *Shinpen Watashi no Showa Shi*, ed. Tokyo Channel 12 Shakai Kyōyō-bu. Tokyo: Gakugei Shorin, 1974.

Kanō Mikiyo. '"Konketsuji" mondai to tanitsu minzoku shinwa no seisei' ('Mixed-blood children' issue and the formation of the myth of racial homogeneity). In *Senryō to Sei: Seisaku, Jittai, Hyōshō*, ed. Keisen Jogakuen Daigaku Heiwa Bunka Kenkyūjo. Tokyo: Impact, 2007.

Kanzaki Kiyoshi. *Yoru no Kichi* (Bases at Night). Tokyo: Kawade Shobō, 1953.

Kataoka Kaoru. 'Konketsuji.' In *Kataoka Kaoru Shinario Bungaku Senshū* (Kataoka Kaoru Selected Scenarios). Vol. 3. Tokyo: Ryūkei Shosha, 1985.

Katō Hiroyuki. *Katō Hiroyuki Bunsho* (Katō Hiroyuki Collected Writings). 3 vols. Tokyo: Dōhōsha Shuppan, 1990.

Keiō Gijyuku Daigaku Shakaijigyō Kenkyūkai, ed. *Gaishō to Kodomotachi* (Streetwalkers and Children). Tokyo: Keiō Gijyuku Daigaku, 1953.

Kiyosawa Kiyoshi. 'Modan gāru no kenkyū' (A study of the modern girl). In *Kindai Shomin Seikatsu Shi*, ed. Hiroshi Minami. Vol. 1. Tokyo: Sanichi Shobō, 1985.

Kon Hidemi. 'Bunka sensen nite' (At the cultural battleline). *Bungei* 10, no. 10 (October 1942), pp. 46–51.

Kōsei-shō. '"Iwayuru konketsujidō" jittai chōsa hōkokusho' (Report on 'so-called mixed-blood children' actual situation). Kōsei-shō Jidō-kyoku, February 1953.

—— *Jidō Fukushi 10-nen no Ayumi* (10-year History of Child Welfare). Ed. Hidesaburō Kurushima. Tokyo: Nihon Jidō Mondai Chōsakai, Kōsei-shō Jidō-kyoku, 1959.

Kōsei-shō Kenkyūjo Jinkō Minzoku-bu, ed. *Minzoku Jinkō Seisaku Kenkyū Shiryō* (Papers on Nationality and Demographics). 8 vols. Tokyo: Bunsei Shoin, 1981.

Kubota Yoshinobu et al. 'Nipponjin to hakujin oyobi kokujin tono konketsuji no chōsa' (Anthropometric study of mixed-blood children between Japanese and white or black races). *Minzoku Eisei* 19, nos 5, 6 (April 1953), pp. 93–140.

Kure-shi Shi Henshū Iinkai, ed. *Kure-shi Shi* (Kure City History). 8 vols. Kure: Kure-shiyakusho, 1956–95.

Matsuzawa Kureichi. '"Nikutai no bōhatei" baishunfutachi no shirarezaru shin no sugata' ('Flesh seawall': The unknown true identity of prostitutes). *Tokyojin*, no. 231 (September 2006), pp. 62–67.

Miyano Seiho. 'Konketsuji shidō no yōten ni tsuite' (Main points of mixed-blood children guidance.' In Mombu-shō (1960), op. cit.

Mizuno Hiroshi, ed. *Nihon no Teisō: gaikokuhei ni okasareta joseitachi no shuki* (Chastity of Japan: Journals of Women Raped by Foreign Troops). Tokyo: Sōjusha, 1953.

Mizushima Haruo and Miyake Katsuo. '1941-nen jūichi-gatsu jūyon, jūgo-nichi ni kaisaishita dai 5-kai jinkō mondai zenkoku kyōgikai ni okeru hōkoku' (Report on the 5th Population Problem National Council, 14–15 November, 1941). *Jinkō*

Seisaku to Kokudo Keikaku (November 1942).

Mombu-shō. *Konketsuji Shidō Kiroku No. 4* (Records on Guidance for Mixed-Blood Children No. 4). Tokyo: Mombu-shō Shotō Chūtō Kyōiku-kyoku, 1957.

—— *Konketsuji Shidō Shiryō* (Documents on Guidance for Mixed-Blood Children). Tokyo: Mombu-shō Shotō Chūtō Kyōiku-kyoku, 1960.

Murakami Kimiko. *Senryōki no Fukushi Seisaku* (Welfare Policy under the Occupation). Tokyo: Keisō Shobō, 1987.

Nakamura Saburō. *Nippon Baishun Shi* (History of Japanese Prostitution). Vol. 3. Tokyo: Nippon Fūzoku Kenkyūkai, 1954.

Niwa Yoshiko. 'Konketsuji no chōsa – Sono shakaiteki tekiōsei no mondai' (Survey of mixed-blood children – Problem of social adaptability). In Mombu-shō (1957), op. cit.

Okazaki Ayanori. 'Sensō hanayome to konketsuji' (War brides and mixed-blood children). Kōsei-shō Jinkō Mondai Kenkyūsho, 1 July 1958.

Ogawa Masahiro. 'Konketsuji fukushi' (Welfare for mixed-blood children). In Mombu-shō (1960), op. cit.

Ozawa Nobuo. 'Panpan.' In *Onna no Sengo Shi* (The Post-War History of Women). Vol. 1. Tokyo: Asahi Shimbunsha, 1984.

Sawada Miki. *Konketsuji no Haha* (Mother to Mixed-Blood Children). Tokyo: Mainichi Shimbunsha, 1953.

Seki Kazuo. 'Konketsuji no mondai' (The issue of mixed-blood children). *Kyōiku to Igaku* (March 1964), pp. 29–32.

Shiraishi Hiroko. *Jagatara Oharu no Shōsoku* (News on Jagatara Oharu). Tokyo: Bensei Shuppan, 2001.

Suda Masaaki. 'Konketsuji mondai no shōten' (The focus of the mixed-blood children issue). *Ibaragi Kyōiku Jihō* (September 1952), pp. 31–32.

Takahashi Yoshio. 'Dō kotae' (In answer to the question). *Kōjun Zasshi*, no. 112 (5 March 1883), pp. 8–14.

Takami Jun. *Takami Jun Nikki* (Takami Jun Diaries). 8 vols. Tokyo: Keiso Shobō, 1965–77.

Takasaki Setsuko. *Konketsuji*. Tokyo: Dōkōsha Isobe Shobō, 1952.

Takeda Toshio. 'Konketsuji no shidō ni kansuru ichi kōsatsu' (One view on mixed-blood children guidance). In Mombu-shō (1957), op. cit.

Tanaka Kimiko. *Onna no Bōhatei* (Female Firewall). Tokyo: Dai-ni Shobō, 1957.

Tsurumi Yūsuke, ed. *Gotō Shimpei*. 4 vols. Tokyo: Gotō Shimpei-haku Denki Hensankai, 1937–38.

Wagatsuma Hiroshi, ed. 'Eiga o ji de ikōtoshita konketsu shōnen (gōkan satsujin misui) no jirei' (Case of a mixed-blood boy (attempted rape-murder) who sought to imitate a film character), *Hikō Shōnen no Jirei Kenkyū: Rinshō-Shindan no Riron to Jissai*. Tokyo: Seishin Shobō, 1973b, pp. 221–50.

Yamauchi Mitsuya. '"Konketsuji" no kyōiku shinriteki mondai' (Educational psychology issues with 'mixed-blood children'). In Mombu-shō (1960), op. cit.

Index

About the Author

WALTER HAMILTON is a journalist with close to four decades of experience working for Australian Associated Press and the Australian Broadcasting Corporation in Sydney, Canberra, London, Singapore and Tokyo. He was Northeast Asia Correspondent for the ABC for a total of 11 years between 1979 and 1996. He covered civil strife and democratic change in South Korea, Taiwan, China and the Philippines; economic boom and bust in Japan; natural disasters, including the Kobe Earthquake; and man-made terrors, such as the Aum Shinrikyo sarin nerve gas attacks. He has published two books, *Serendipity City: Australia, Japan and the Multifunction Polis* (ABC Books) and *Koala No Hon* (with Hamish McDonald, for Simul Press).

CPSIA information can be obtained at www.ICGtesting.com
Printed in the USA
BVOW010428220113

310998BV00002B/6/P